WAR ON TERROR, INC.

WAR ON TERROR, INC.

Corporate Profiteering from the Politics of Fear

SOLOMON HUGHES

VERSO

London • New York

First published by Verso 2007
© Solomon Hughes 2007

1 3 5 7 9 10 8 6 4 2

Verso
UK: 6 Meard Street, London W1F 0EG
USA: 180 Varick Street, New York, NY 10014-4606
www.versobooks.com

Verso is the imprint of New Left Books

ISBN-13: 978-1-84467-123-6

British Library Cataloguing in Publication Data
A catalogue record for this book is available from the British Library

Library of Congress Cataloging-in-Publication Data
A catalog record for this book is available from the Library of Congress

Typeset in Bembo by Hewer Text UK Ltd, Edinburgh
Printed in the USA by Maple Vail

For Kate

Contents

Acknowledgements

I rehearsed some of the stories and arguments in this book working as a journalist, and would like to thank the people who helped me then. I owe a debt to Ian Hislop for being a sympathetic and perceptive editor for my work at *Private Eye*, and especially to the late Paul Foot of the same magazine for his encouragement and guidance, and the other *Eye* staff who helped me on my way. Thanks also to Antony Barnett for his help when he was investigations editor at the *Observer*. Hilary Wainwright and all at *Red Pepper* also gave me an opportunity to work on some of these issues in print. I would like to thank those who assisted with improving the writing, especially Moira Paterson and David Turley. Thanks to James Heartfield for introducing me to one of the important reference points in the book. Thanks also to Sean and Rory Hughes for putting up with those difficult days when their father was more interested in his computer than in them.

Thanks also to my agent Robert Dudley, and to Giles O'Bryen at Verso for guiding me on the journey from half-baked idea to fully formed book. Special thanks to Charles Peyton for polishing the text – all remaining rough edges are my responsibility. While all these people contributed to this book, the opinions and the mistakes are all my own.

Introduction: 1984 plc

In January 2003 investors were invited to give their cash to men who promised they could make big profits from the aftermath of the terrorist attacks of 11 September, 2001. Potential shareholders were told that the war on terror 'offer[s] substantial promise for homeland security investment'. Investors were invited to put money into a high-powered fund called Paladin Capital. The firm would use the funds they raised 'to invest in companies with immediate solutions designed to prevent harmful attacks, defend against attacks, cope with the aftermath of attack or disaster and recover from terrorist attacks and other threats to homeland security'. Paladin's managers hoped to raise $300 million in a year, a modest sum given that they estimated the US government would spend an extra $60 billion on anti-terrorism, thanks to the hijackers' murderously effective use of civilian aeroplanes as weapons.[1]

The US has never been short of entrepreneurs ready to make a dollar from a disaster. But this particular investment opportunity was the work of some very important men close to the centres of power, not of marginal characters looking for the 'main chance'. Former CIA Director James Woolsey was one of the firm's managing directors. Woolsey held an official post as an adviser to the serving US defence secretary, Donald Rumsfeld, through his membership of the Defence Policy Board. He also held an unofficial position as purveyor of some of the most alarmist and least true tales about al-Qaeda in the wake of the destruction of the Twin Towers. Woolsey peddled complex tales that were too unconvincing even for a Bush or Blair dossier. Instead, Woolsey spread his claims through the newspapers. Woolsey's stories included the suggestion that Saddam Hussein was linked to the New York attacks by a meeting in Prague between one of the hijackers, Mohammed Atta, and Iraqi secret agents. He also suggested Saddam was supplying anthrax to al-Qaeda, who then sent the poisonous powder in a series of mysterious letters, which created panic but caused no injury in the wake of 9/11. His theories appeared in the media in the run-up to the attack on Iraq, helping to create the unfounded scare about Saddam's WMD and Iraqi support for al-Qaeda. In fact there was no such Prague meeting, and the anthrax letters seem to have been unconnected to al-Qaeda or Iraq, and eventually stopped.

However, the stories did their work in building political support for the launch of a war on Iraq. By the time they were exposed as inaccurate gossip the damage was done. Instead of defeating terrorism, the war on Iraq created the conditions for more terror, which in turn boosted military and homeland defence spending to even greater heights. Woolsey was not the only member of the company's board connected to the US political and military elites: Paladin's advisers also included a former director of the National Security Agency, a former deputy director of the Defense Advance Research Agency – the organization running the United States military weapons laboratories – and a former Secretary of the Army.[2]

Mixing business and politics in the war on terror was not just an American sport. From 1998 Britain's Labour government faced repeated accusations that it had allowed favoured lobbying companies to sell access to ministers.[3] These 'cash for access' claims surfaced yet again in 2007, when the *Sunday Times* sent one of its reporters to work for a lobbying firm called 'Golden Arrow Communications'. This lobbying company hired one former Labour minister, Derek Jamieson, and another former Labour member of parliament, Ivan Henderson. Golden Arrow promised to help companies relate to the government because, according to their publicity, 'We know how best to influence policy development and the thinking of decision-takers.'

The undercover reporter found that the former members of parliament kept up good relations with a current Home Office minister called Gerry Sutcliffe. At this time his boss, the home secretary, was trying to remodel the Home Office along the lines of the US Department of Homeland Security, creating a ministry that focused all its activities on the fight against terrorism. The lobbyists said the minister was begging them to approach him with businessmen interested in making money out of the new security agenda. The lobbyists said Sutcliffe told them there was 'lots in the Home Office. Security, border controls and security in ports. He said there's going to be big issues around that'. In one of the more sickly expressions of Labour's urge to prostrate itself before big business, the lobbyists said minister Sutcliffe had told them, 'Come on, you use me . . . I am there to be used. I want to help you. Use me.'[4]

The British lobbyists' claim that ministers were begging to be 'used' by the security business, and the US advisers' decision to set up a security investment company, underlined the fact that the war on terror relied to an unprecedented degree on private enterprise. Roman orator Cicero said that endless money formed the sinews of war. After 9/11, it seemed that the new, endless war on terror provided a sure route to money. From 'homeland security' to the new international interventions, every element of the war on terror relied on private contractors. This was more than just war profiteering: the private sector was so integrated into the new campaigns that it influenced the direction and continuation of the central policies of the US and British governments, in what they called the 'long war'.

When Tony Blair and George Bush launched their new military and security initiatives after 9/11, they relied heavily on private enterprise to deliver their aims. This went beyond a few insiders trying to capitalise on politics: the whole direction of transatlantic responses to the terrorist attacks relied on profit-making companies. This shaped the nature of the new political, military and security strategies gathered under the umbrella of the 'war on terror'.

The war on terror began with the murderous hijack attacks of 9/11; but it was far more than simply a response to these terrible events. It is important not to underestimate the shock of thousands of US citizens being murdered on the United States mainland, but the political and military reaction to these events went way beyond finding the terrorist culprits. Within a couple of hours of the fall of the Twin Towers, Donald Rumsfeld's assistant's notes recorded the US defence secretary's response: 'Near term target needs – go massive – sweep it all up, things related and not.' Rumsfeld saw the attack as an opportunity to strike back on all his perceived enemies, whether or not they were related to the hijackers. The top US military official didn't just want to pursue the murderers and their accomplices: he saw the burning American landmarks as a sign of national weakness, and wanted to respond with a new assertion of military and political strength.

The most obvious expression of Rumsfeld's doctrine was the linking of Saddam to al-Qaeda, and the shoe-horning of the invasion and occupation of Iraq into the war against terror. In fact the strategy went much further.

The US Joint Chiefs of Staff made clear that for them the lessons of 9/11 went way beyond how to deal with bin Laden and his acolytes. In their 2004 National Military Strategy, the leaders of the US armed forces announced, unsurprisingly: 'We must win the War on Terrorism.' They explained that this would mean that the US public, its political system and its international allies must all pull behind the military leadership to achieve this victory, because 'This mission requires the full integration of all instruments of national power, the cooperation and participation of friends and allies and the support of the American people.' The military leadership thought the New York attacks exposed US weakness, and responded by stating that 'The goal is full spectrum dominance (FSD) – the ability to control any situation or defeat any adversary across the range of military operations.'[5] The US military was arguing that the response of the US to the killing of 3,000 people by hijacked aeroplanes should be the establishment of complete military and political dominance throughout the entire world, and across all areas of conflict. In this formulation the 'war on terror' is not aimed precisely at terrorists; rather it is a grand strategic scheme to ensure US military dominance across the board. The aims of this project, inspired by an enemy far smaller and weaker than the Soviet Union, seemed more ambitious than the Cold War 'balance of power'. The 'war on terror', in this formulation, meant that national and international affairs would be forced to follow the lead of the US military and political elites in the name of a battle against an idea. National politics would be dominated by 'homeland security', with the struggle against an invisible fifth column and its supporting ideas fought by ever larger and more expensive systems of control. International politics would be shaped by demands that other nations subordinate themselves to a wide range of military interventions. In this programme the particular dynamics of any situation were less important than the need to establish US leadership and dominance.

British Prime Minister Tony Blair decided to lock the United Kingdom into the strategy of the war on terror as firmly as his predecessors had sought to join their US allies in the Cold War. Blair's chief of staff, Jonathan Powell, told Britain's ambassador to Washington to 'get up the arse of the White House and stay there', and British policy on the war on terror maintained this level of closeness in an attempt to build British influence on the back of US power. Britain both supported the international military actions of the US, and aped its 'homeland security' responses. The two leaderships announced that traditional civil liberties must be sacrificed in the new, unending battle. The 9/11 attacks prompted US Vice President Dick Cheney to say his country must 'work . . . sort of . . . the dark side'. Reacting to the July 2005 suicide-bombing attacks on London's public transport system, Tony Blair declared, 'Let no one be in any doubt: the rules of the game are changing.'

President Bush and Prime Minister Blair set the US and Britain upon interlocking paths in response to the terrorist attacks in New York and London. In the name of the war against extremism, they committed their nations to military adventures abroad and new security measures at home. Other nations experienced terrorism and felt the injuries of bombs exploded in the name of Islam, but they did not sign up to the same package of responses.

Under the new rules, both leaders set out to institute authoritarian solutions in the West and military solutions in the East, tearing up accepted legal and diplomatic protections and procedures in favour of force. In the process, ideas that had been floating around on the political agenda for years were dusted off and rebranded as part of the new war on terror. Old enemies were roped into the new war; previously rejected laws were relaunched as new tools for a new conflict. The war on terror became a way of trying to rally home and international opinion behind an Anglo-US leadership. Uniquely, this new application of force depended heavily on private companies: from the wars in the Middle East to the databases and systems of detention at home, the new weapons in the 'war on terror' were both supplied and operated by corporations.

In his novel *1984*, George Orwell described a country where the constant threat of external enemies was used to justify internal surveillance and repression. Oceania, home of Winston Smith, is alternately at war with Eastasia or Eurasia, and under constant threat of subversion by the sabotage movement of Emmanuel Goldstein. While we find ourselves a very long way from Orwell's dystopia, the discovery of new external and internal threats has increased a tendency to control and surveillance in our own societies: were Orwell alive now, it is hard to imagine that he would be surprised by a government introducing identity cards for its own citizens while fighting wars in other countries. But Orwell described a new governing class growing out of the 'barren world of monopoly industry and centralised government'. He might have been surprised to find that many of the soldiers in the 'war on terror' are actually employees of competing private companies; that the people fitting electronic tags, preparing the databases for the new identity card or imprisoning unwanted foreigners are all working not for an authoritarian Party, but for multinational corporations. It seems that some of Big Brother's methods have indeed arrived – but they are being operated by holding companies.

The discovery of new enemies leads traditionally to a strengthening of the state. Attacks by the Irish nationalist Fenian Brotherhood led to the creation in 1883 of Special Branch – the closest thing Britain has had to a secret police force. The Cold War saw an expansion of every part of the state. In a familiar pattern, the Russian threat provided the stimulus for the construction of massively expensive weapons aimed at the foreign enemy, and powerful secret services to monitor internal 'subversion'. But the new political landscape led to the growth of the new security state. The Thatcher era inaugurated a wave of privatizations that spread to the US and beyond. By the time Blair's Labour administration replaced the Conservatives, this privatization drive had become a new orthodoxy. The British and US states had been handing over responsibilities for welfare and basic services to the private sector for two decades.

The war on terror was a strange new hybrid, fusing an increase in state power to meet a new threat with the shrinking state of the privatizers: the British and US governments seized new powers, and then promptly delegated them to private companies, giving rise to the new security industries. While in the past security companies might have had responsibility for *things*, the new security companies had authority over *people*. Security firms could lock people up in private detention centres at home and shoot at them abroad. This fundamental shift between the powers of the state and those of the private sector took place with little debate. A whole new security-industrial complex sprang into life, ready to sell commercial solutions to the government. From private asylum detention centres to private soldiers fighting alongside the army in Iraq and Afghanistan; from military adventures to identity cards, the war on terror became 'War on Terror, Inc.'.

In 1961 President Eisenhower made his farewell address to US voters. Eisenhower was alarmed enough by the peacetime growth of the arms industry to use this keynote speech to warn that a lobby made up of arms manufacturers and Pentagon officials could distort US politics. He feared that the combined pressure from industrialists and bureaucrats seeking profit and influence might tip the US into unwanted conflicts. Eisenhower warned his fellow citizens that 'in the councils of government, we must guard against the acquisition of unwarranted influence, whether sought or unsought, by the military-industrial complex. The potential for the disastrous rise of misplaced power exists and will persist.' Since the war on terror is so often fought by private companies, we face the development of a new security-industrial complex. Like Eisenhower's military-industrial complex, this business lobby has a vested interest in maintaining and extending the military and security aspects of the 'war on terror'; and it has money, power and influence to lobby politicians to continue down this road. The influence of the military lobby on US politics is widely recognised. The influence of the traditional arms makers on British ministers is also increasingly understood, particularly in relation to the ongoing scandals surrounding BAE Systems. However, it is less well understood but equally true to say that the new security industries also enjoy political access at the highest levels in Britain and the US.

Britain and the US responded to the 9/11 attacks with a cocktail of more wars and stricter laws: they became more ready to use both military force internationally and more authoritarian police methods domestically. These measures, collectively known as the war on terror, were set in motion by the terrorist outrages, but they were not the only possible response to them. Nor were they only a response to the attacks: the 'war on terror' became a scheme to increase the power of the British and US states – both internationally in relation to other countries, and nationally in relation to their own citizens. In the process, this warlike and repressive cocktail of policies actually increased the danger of terrorism, with the Iraq intervention creating a training ground for terrorists and an inspiration to their supporters. The Bush and Blair governments were perfectly capable of going down this road of their own accord; but because they used private companies so extensively to carry out the war on terror, governments on both sides of the Atlantic created a well funded and well connected industrial lobby with a financial interest in extending and prolonging the war on terror. It was in the business interests of the security companies to offer to operate new surveillance methods and forms of imprisonment, and to participate in new armed interventions. Security firms could encourage the government to take military action simply by being there: the existence of companies who could help extend military action or increase 'homeland security' could seduce the British and US governments into more militaristic and authoritarian policies simply by presenting them as options. In addition, the security firms used their lobbying contacts, their employment of former ministers and officials, and their funding of bodies linked to the political parties to encourage governments to intensify the war on terror. Many of the Anglo-US policies in the war on terror faced resistance and protest. Senior figures in the establishment and demonstrators on the streets objected to attacks on civil liberties and the use of military force. Lobbying by the new security industries pushed in the opposite direction, making new extensions of the security state and more far-reaching military interventions look like workable, businesslike objectives. The voice of the new security industry helped counterbalance any political misgivings about the aggressive policies of the war on terror.

This book tells the story of that new security-industrial complex. It is a transatlantic story, because the business and political elites in Britain and the US have worked closely together on the development of the new security state and the new international interventions. It is a story of how a new industry grew slowly in the 1980s and 1990s, taking work that had formerly been carried out by public servants in blue and khaki uniforms into the private sector. This market expanded massively after 9/11, and encouraged the British and US governments to take ever more militaristic and authoritarian steps in the war on terror. The private companies encouraged ministers who were already convinced of the superiority of business methods to buy their security wares, and influenced national policy – but they often delivered disasters. There have been many well reported protests against the excesses in the war on terror. This book is an attempt to tell the story of the companies who helped to encourage and deliver the new disasters of war.

1

Economic Migrants

Some of the leading security companies who would later make money from the war on terror cut their teeth in the war on crime. After 9/11 the British and US governments gave contracts to firms whose staff wore khaki uniforms and carried guns. Long before the 2001 terror attacks, those governments had given contracts to firms whose staff wore blue uniforms and carried batons. Privatization of prisons, prison transport, probation services, and of youth and immigration detention allowed governments to experiment with the transfer of power over people to private firms. This experiment was carried out on marginal groups in society – prisoners and refugees. The political shift that allowed governments to subcontract the fighting of wars first took place on the home front. The security industry won control over people when prisons and asylum detention centres fell into commercial hands. The new security industries made a qualitative leap from holding property to holding people: where nightwatchmen once guarded empty factories, the new security industries would guard whole prisons. Companies that had only transported money or bullion in armoured vans now drove buses full of restrained men.

If prison and asylum privatization had not already established the principle that the state's monopoly of force could be subcontracted to profit-making firms, the British and US governments would have found it much harder to make the international and 'homeland security' elements of the war on terror so reliant on private contractors. The prison and asylum privatizations also showed all the dangers that would later be magnified in the war on terror: the creation of a political–industrial coalition driving new authoritarian measures, the botched contracts, and the loss of social control over security matters had all appeared in the privatized war on crime before they became features of the privatized war on terror.

In 1981, two years after Mrs Thatcher's first election victory, her home secretary, Willie Whitelaw, was under intense pressure. Fears of lawlessness and a perceived crime wave encouraged the right wing of the Conservative party to make ever more shrill demands on Whitelaw, with calls for the return of corporal and capital punishment, advocacy of which moved from the fringes towards the mainstream. In the summer of 1981, urban riots in London's Brixton and Liverpool's Toxteth added substantially to fears of a breakdown in social discipline. The steep rise in unemployment spurred by the new government's monetarist policies fuelled the riots and a general rise in crime; but, as Hugo Young noted,[1] the Tory failures on crime were accompanied by success at the ballot box: while the government presided over an increase in lawbreaking, polls showed that 45 per cent of the population trusted the Conservatives to take on the criminals, whereas only 19 per cent felt the same way about the Labour Party. The more crimes committed on the Tory government's watch, the more people clamoured for the Conservative cocktail of policing policies: an increasing crime rate made the Conservative promise to crack down on criminals ever more popular. Any company that could buy into this self-perpetuating market would certainly be onto a good thing.

Britain's first private prison, the Wolds Remand Centre, opened in April 1992, but the debate that had paved the way for the jail's foundation began long before then. In 1984 the US opened its first new commercial jails since the turn of the century. Nashville money man Jack Massey, whose financial experience included funding the Kentucky Fried Chicken company, and former Tennessee Republican Party Chairman Tom Beasley put together a bid to run private prisons in their home state. The experiment was encouraged by the Reagan White House, and the new Corrections Corporation of America opened its first facility – an 'alien detention centre' for would-be immigrants housed in a former motel.[2] While Britain generally led the world in privatization, the US pioneered private prisons. The country's federal structure meant this novel concept could be introduced gradually, state by state. Private prisons proliferated regionally, and did not need any national politician to sponsor the controversial programme overtly. This made the commercialization of incarceration more quickly achievable than in the UK, where central government would need to take a positive, high-profile role in order to take the same steps.

Eager Thatcherites, uncomfortable about losing their first place in the privatization race to their American friends, urged that the UK should hand over its prisons to the profit-making sector. In 1984 the Adam Smith Institute – one of the intellectual driving forces behind the Thatcher government – recommended privatization, arguing: 'Both security firms and hotel operations are commonplace in the private sector: it may be an over-simplification but a prison, borstal, or detention centre involves little more than a combination of these two talents.'[3] The same report recommended the use of electronic tags and curfews, and so the ultra-free-market Adam Smith Institute wrote the policy that Labour would put in place in the next decade. But the journey from the 1984 paper to a full private prison sector was slow. The Adam Smith Institute's use of the word 'hotel' was probably to blame: the demand for new prisons, new offences, and new policemen was driven by a desire for toughness. Cracking down on crime; short, sharp shocks; an end to leniency; no soft sentences: all the anti-crime slogans ran against the perceived 'softness' of the private sector's approach to its 'customers'. Denouncing prisons for being as soft as hotels was a standard rhetorical device of the authoritarian right – the suggestion that firms that actually ran hotels might also run prisons was enough to set the possibility of commercial jails back by a decade.

The private prison operators needed wholehearted Conservative backing to overcome the initial hostility of the official opposition; Labour politicians and trade unionists denounced the concept as soon at it was mooted. But Conservative ministers were initially also suspicious of corporate incarceration. When Peter Young, of the Adam Smith Institute, visited then Home Office Minister David Mellor in 1985 to promote the idea, the minister, he said, 'basically rubbished it. He laughed at us.'[4] Douglas Hurd was equally frosty about the proposal, telling the Commons in 1987 that 'I do not think there is a case, and I do not think the House would accept a case, for auctioning or privatising the prisons or handing over the business of keeping prisoners safe to anyone other than Government servants.'

The private prisons industry therefore needed to work hard to get the government to respond with legislation, rather than dismissiveness. Careful and persistent lobbying was necessary. Most importantly, the new incarceration industry had to integrate its business into an already business-friendly Conservative culture in order to turn private prisons into a reality. One property developer hired a lobbying company, GJW – a firm that would later become central to the 'cash for access' allegations that dogged Labour's new government. But in the 1980s the company had strong Conservative connections: GJW put gave the task to Ann Strutt, a one-time Tory parliamentary candidate for Glasgow, who later married Conservative defence minister Bernard Jenkin.[5] Another former employee of Conservative Central Office now at GJW, Tony Hutt, joined Strutt's campaign for private jails.[6]

To be persuasive the private prisons lobby needed more than just hired help: the Conservative party machine is a coalition between powerful business interests and an active middle-class base. The private prisons industry made its voice heard when it started to become part of that coalition. The Home Affairs Select Committee backed the idea of private prisons, making them a real possibility. It probably helped that John Wheeler, a member and ultimately Chairman of the Committee, was also paid to represent the British Security Industry Association, whose members included firms, like Securicor, that would later join private jail consortia. In 1986, Wheeler and Sir Edward Gardiner, who was then Chairman of the Committee, inspected private prisons in Tennessee and Florida. They returned to say that these jails were 'stunning', and beyond criticism. Within three years, Gardiner became the Chairman of Contract Prisons plc, a new firm bidding to run British jails.[7]

The Corrections Corporation of America (CCA) jails in Tennessee that had so impressed Tory MPs were indeed 'stunning' – but not in a good way. Nearby Wisconsin exported many of its prisoners to the private Tennessee jails run by CCA. In 1998, Wisconsin prisons boss Michael Sullivan admitted that several of his state prisoners in the Tennessee jails had been abused with stun-guns: guards had attacked prisoners after one of their own was severely assaulted by an inmate. CCA, who faced other scandals over prison conditions at the same time, denied any assaults – but the Wisconsin official revealed that the firm had not told the truth. The jail's security chief and other employees were sacked.[8]

By the time the real state of America's private jails began to filter through to British politicians, however, the UK was already committed to the new private prisons policy. The links between the establishment and the new industry were thoroughly cemented by the early 1990s. In 1990 Norman Fowler, former chair of the Conservative Party, joined the board of Group 4. In 1993, former Metropolitan Police Commissioner Peter Imbert joined the board of Securicor. Former deputy chief of the defence staff, Lieutenant General Sir Maurice Johnstone, headed up an unsuccessful private prisons bidder called the Detention Corporation. A more successful firm – UK Detention Services – offered a particularly clear example of the international coalition behind the new incarceration industry: the British partners in this consortium were Mowlem PLC and Sir Robert McAlpine – two building firms with a long history of making donations to the Conservative Party. Lord McAlpine had been the party's treasurer for many years. The American partner was CCA, which ran the 'stunning' US jails. CCA was in fact part-owned by a French catering and hotel firm, Sodexho. This association between private prisons and the hotel industry prevented the project from getting off the ground for a decade; but now that the new punishment firms were thoroughly intertwined with the British elite, this no longer mattered. CCA also made an effort to hire prison governors, as did Group 4, who had bagged fourteen of them by 1997, selling back to the public sector expertise it already had.[9]

Britain's other leading jail company, Premier Prisons, also made efforts to hire former prison governors. Premier also had many other impressive qualifications for the job. The new security industries had two central business strategies: the first was the exploitation of fear to build their business; the second was the use of this fear to take functions formerly operated by the state into private hands. Premier Prisons was a joint venture between British company Serco and a US company called Wackenhut, a family firm with a long history of this kind of commercial vigilantism. Wackenhut had been exploiting political fears for private profit since the 1950s, most notably by means of a political blacklist of supposedly dangerous individuals. Wackenhut started running Doncaster Prison in 1995. As fear of crime and disorder among the under-16s grew, Wackenhut was hired in 1998 to build and run a borstal for 12–14-year-olds in County Durham and a £32 million Young Offenders Institute at Pucklehurst, near Bristol.

Wackenhut certainly knew how to make money out of the fear of crime. The firm was founded in 1954 by an ex-FBI man called George Wackenhut. He built his business on the fear of communist subversion in Cold War America. Using the resources of a number of far-right organizations and individuals, Wackenhut built up an impressive database of alleged communists, subversives, agitators, union militants, and other dissidents. In its 1965 prospectus, Wackenhut claimed to have files on 2.5 million Americans, against which it could – for a charge – check prospective employees. The company then acquired the files of House Un-American Activities Committee staff member Karl Barslaag. In addition to Wackenhut's own snooping, these expanded its private files to cover over 4 million 'subversives'. Wackenhut boasted of having 'more dossiers than any other organization in the country outside the FBI'. In 1975, when the post-Watergate Congress began to investigate black-listing and invasions of privacy, Wackenhut claimed to have ditched its files. The records were not destroyed, however, but instead donated to the Church League of America. The Church League was a Christian far-right organization that also offered 'name checks' against 7 million index card records of supposed subversives. Wackenhut had friendly relations with the Church League, and admitted to a Congressional Investigation in 1977 that it continued to use the old files it had donated to them.[10]

As well as running prisons, consortia including Wackenhut won contracts to electronically 'tag' prisoners for community-based sentences. Reassuringly, Wackenhut had plenty of experience of electronic and other types of surveillance. When the menace of communist subversion had evaporated, Wackenhut had found a new subversive group to chase for corporate America: it had built new snooping business based on the fear of growing 'green' activism. Wackenhut demonstrated its high-tech snooping skills when it was hired by an Exxon-led oil consortium to hound Charles Hamel, an American environmentalist. Hamel had information from whistleblowers inside the industry, in particular relating to problems at the Valdez terminal. His knowledge of company mal-practice could have averted the Exxon Valdez disaster – the 1989 oil spill that caused enormous damage off the Alaskan coast, and became a byword for environmental pollution by big business. The consortium was more interested in leaks by employees than in leaks from its pipelines, so it hired Wackenhut agents to watch Hamel's home, steal his garbage, and set up a phoney environmental campaign called 'Ecolit' to entrap him. This tactic came unstuck when two of Wackenhut's agents could stomach the deceit no longer, and exposed the operation. The former agents testified about Wackenhut's deceit at the US House of Repre-sentatives and in the press.

American lawmakers criticized Wackenhut's operation severely, especially because the firm had widened its surveillance net to include spying on a member of Congress called George Millar, who was in touch with the oil industry whistleblower. A Senate committee concluded that 'Wackenhut agents engaged in a pattern of deceitful, grossly offensive and potentially, if not blatantly illegal conduct.' Wackenhut was fined $10,000 by the state of Virginia,[11] and Hamel settled a lawsuit against the consortium, reportedly for $5 million.

But Wackenhut was soon embroiled in another spy scandal. Florida saw intense competition between telephone and cable TV companies over who would control the valuable cables that could be used not only for television and telephone systems, but also for the new, booming internet market. The Florida Cable Television Association hired private detectives to snoop on the local Public Service Commission, the body that would decide who controlled the cables. They turned to Richard Lund, the undercover agent who had run Wackenhut's Alaska operation. Lund had left the firm to go independent, but he hired other Wackenhut agents to help him, acquiring records of telephone calls made by the government Commissioners. Lund and the Wackenhut agents mounted surveillance of the Commissioners' homes and cars – investigating their sex lives in particular – until their cover was blown.

Wackenhut's dubious history did not discourage the Conservatives from hiring the firm. The signs were that Labour would take a different attitude, but such signs were misleading. In 1994, shadow Home Secretary Tony Blair wrote to the Prison Officers Association, promising: 'All private prisons will be returned to the public sector.'[12] In 1995, shadow Home Secretary Jack Straw made what was described as 'Labour's only firm commitment to renationalize a sector privatized by the Conservatives', when he told a meeting of a prison welfare organization, the Bourne Trust, that all the Tories' private jails would be taken back into public hands. He said the business was 'morally repugnant', arguing, 'It is not appropriate for people to profit out of incarceration. This is surely one area where a "free market" certainly does not exist.'[13] He restated his belief that the private prisons were 'morally repugnant' in 1996. With the motley crew of Cold War witch-hunters, Franco-US businesses with a record of abuse, and companies employing top Tories queuing up to take over British jails, Straw's opposition to prison privatization seemed uncontroversial – uncontroversial to everyone, at least, except Jack Straw, who, upon becoming home secretary, immediately began authorizing new private prisons.

To a government committed to being business-friendly and to cracking down on crime, the new formula of paying businesses to do the cracking down was clearly irresistible. Straw claimed that accepting private prisons was the only way to deal with increased prison populations. In fact, the new private prisons were apparently less effective than their public predecessors. In October 1999, Jack Straw announced that Wackenhut had won a tender, and would stay in charge of the 1,000 prisoners in Doncaster prison, which the firm had run since 1994. But a leaked Home Office report revealed that the government's independent assessors thought the Prison Service's public sector bid to run the prison was superior to Wackenhut's, which was found seriously wanting. The assessment said that there 'appear[ed] to be the lack of an overall strategy to the regime' proposed by Wackenhut. The Prison Service outscored Wackenhut on 'running a secure prison' and 'treating people fairly'. Wackenhut seemed uninterested in the rehabilitation of offenders, as there was a 'failure to address satisfactorily numeracy, literacy and key and basic skills'.

A grim human story lay behind these assessments: Doncaster prison had earned the name 'Doncatraz' because of its miserable atmosphere, with incidents of suicide and self-harm among inmates running above the national averages. Wackenhut beat the Prison Service bid on cost alone – and the difference here was marginal. But the home secretary overruled his civil servants and gave the prison back to the US contractors: the political imperative to keep the idea of prison privatization alive was more important than the inconvenient realities of private prisons.[14] For Wackenhut, making a profit meant cutting costs. Prisoners faced the grim consequences of the new penny-pinching regimes. Wackenhut's Kilmarnock Prison also faced fines and complaints about understaffing, while its Lowdham Grange jail, near Nottingham, was fined £89,000 in 1999 following assaults, indiscipline, and the improper handling of prisoners' complaints.[15]

When the idea of new 'Secure Training Centres' for 12–15-year-old lawbreakers was introduced by Conservative Home Secretary Ken Clarke, Labour's crime spokesman Tony Blair denounced them as 'colleges of crime',[16] and as 'new borstals'.[17] Just over a decade later, MPs evaluated the performance of the 'new borstals', and found they were indeed ineffective: by 2004 the cost of locking up teenagers had risen to £283 million a year, but did not stop crime, since eight out of ten youngsters reoffended within two years of their release.[18] But Blair had become prime minister in those ten intervening years, and along the way had completely changed his mind about child jails, deciding to embrace this ineffective solution with enthusiasm.

At the same time as denouncing Secure Training Centres, Blair was beginning to build a New Labour politics based partly on the fear of child criminals. Blair described headlines generated by the killing of James Bulger by two youngsters as 'hammer blows against the sleeping conscience of the country',[19] suggesting that this terrible and rare killing should lead to new crime policies. Blair also called for curfews for children, and for the need to 'get tough' with drunken yobs. In the run-up to his 1997 election victory, commentators analysed and agonized over Blair's new stance, finding the influence of Christianity, communitarianism, a special connection to 'ordinary' people, and many other philosophical origins for his new turn. They may have underestimated the future prime minister's cynicism: three years into his first term as prime minister, Tony Blair was suffering a dip in his popularity. He hoped to climb out of this dip through a strategy he outlined in a memo headlined 'Touchstone Issues'. After suffering a series of bad headlines, and the humiliation of being slow-handclapped by a mass meeting of the Women's Institute, Blair agonized that he was seen as 'out of touch', and demanded: 'I should be personally associated [with] two or three eye-catching initiatives' on crime, such as 'locking up street muggers. Something tough, with immediate bite that sends a message through the system.'[20] Blair did indeed come up with an 'eye-catching initiative' to stop him looking soft and weak. He announced a plan for police to be able to march drunken louts to a cashpoint and force them to pay on-the-spot fines. This initiative crumbled when, a day later, his own son was arrested for drunkenness in Leicester Square. There was no sign of a deep political philosophy about crime in Blair's memo, just a crude cynical attempt to play to a right-wing gallery with authoritarian gestures.

These events showed the simple machinery behind Blair's politics: building consensus by focusing on crime in general and criminal youth in particular was as essential a part of the New Labour project as was handing public services over to private companies. Consequently, when Labour came to power, all criticism of the new private youth jails was dropped.

They fitted the bill perfectly – at least, for everybody but their inmates. Blair was developing a politics that would later bloom in the war on terror. Firstly, he was building a political consensus against a fearful enemy. This gave him a powerful political position, but it also created new pressures. Although defining politics as a battle with a series of enemies neutralized right-wing attacks on the Labour government for a time, it also created a need to show real solutions to the new problems, or risk being accused of emptiness, 'spin', and posturing. The political opposition, once it had recovered from being outmanoeuvred to the right, could offer its own strategies to deal with the new enemies: youth, yobs, asylum seekers, and later terrorists. Needing a quick policy solution, Blair turned to the private sector. Because these companies desperately wanted to break into new public sector markets, they would not quibble about the effectiveness of the new demands, but would just do the job, despite questions from public servants about the new authoritarian policies. They had strong financial incentives to be 'yes-men' in the new authoritarian drive. There was no money to be made in questioning the approach. They could even encourage ministers by offering new punitive technologies or facilities, giving the government the opportunity to demonstrate initiative. This mutual relationship drove forward the growing security state before the 9/11 attacks, and went into overdrive after those terrible events.

So Labour seized the political initiative from the Conservatives over antisocial youths. In due course Wackenhut was running the Hassockfield Secure Training Centre. In 2001 the Social Services Inspectorate condemned the new borstal. There was a massive turnover of low-paid and poorly motivated staff. In its first twenty months the jail's director, two assistants, and forty-seven other staff resigned. The inspectors stated that staff were 'to varying degrees, bewildered and destabilised by the rapid changes of management'. They found that lessons were uncontrolled and unproductive, reporting that 'swearing went unchecked, missiles were thrown around the room and there was general restlessness and move-ment'. The demoralized staff could not deal with their difficult charges, so 'teaching was unsatisfactory and poor behaviour was a direct conse-quence. Unpleasant comments to adults and other peers needed firmer and consistent responses; spitting was evident and appeared to be a significant problem.' The inspectors also found poor policies to prevent bullying and – ominously – suicide. Hassockfield later had the grim distinction of hosting the youngest ever suicide by a British prisoner, when a 14-year-old boy, apparently with a history of self-harm, killed himself at the centre in 2004.[21]

Wackenhut also managed the Ashfield Young Offenders Institute, a child jail that was so bad that in 2002 the Prison Service sacked the governor and imposed a new one. The director general of the Prison Service, Martin Nairey, declared: 'I considered that the prison was unsafe for both staff and the young people detained there and that urgent action was required'.[22] Children were withdrawn from the facility after the Chief Inspector of Prisons found that staff were 'failing, by some margin, to provide a safe and decent environment for children'.[23] Because the private company had cut back so heavily on experienced staff, the inspectors 'observed a worrying level of delegation of staff responsibility that extended as far as role reversal', with staff having 'begun to rely on' two of the inmates 'to carry out reception procedures'. The young prisoners likened their role to that of 'mini-officers'.

Ashfield and Hassockfield were unhappy institutions, but Wackenhut ran a borstal in America that was even more violent and abusive. In 1997 the firm was given a contract to build and run a youth jail at Jena, Louisiana. Three years later the state of Louisiana settled a lawsuit brought by the Juvenile Justice Project, a non-profit law firm, which led not only to the eviction of Wackenhut from Jena, but also to the end of all profit-making youth jails in the state. The campaigners had exposed such grim brutality in Wackenhut's facility that Louisiana was forced to abandon the whole privatization scheme. A US Justice Department report found that 'Jena fails to provide reasonable safety, improperly uses chemical restraints, and provides inadequate mental health, medical and dental care for the approximately 276 adolescent boys confined there at any one time'. Investigators found that guards routinely used excessive force, and that they abused, mistreated and humiliated the young prisoners. Inmates reported that guards bullied and beat the youngsters, and encouraged favoured prisoners to hurt other inmates, offering bribes of cigarettes and other treats. The investigators found 'remarkable similarities in the alleged manner in which security officers forced compliance by tripping youths, twisting their arms, legs, or ankles, slamming them into cell walls or doors, or taking them violently to the ground'. Wackenhut's charges were also denied proper food and clothes, in circumstances of Dickensian misery. One of the experts sent into Jena by the Justice Department found some inmates in their cellblocks without clean clothes who were 'huddled under a sheet or blanket . . . some reported this was the reason they had not attended school'. The investigator said a shortage of shoes was 'pervasive. On all dorms, many youth had no shoes.' The lack of clothes and proper food came down to simple meanness, according to the Justice Department, because '[a]t least in some areas, the problems seemed to be linked to the reluctance of Wackenhut Corrections Corporation to spend adequate funds for the care of the youth'.[24] Staff turnover was high. Jena had five governors in its short life, while 125 guards and other staff were fired for having sex with inmates; taking money, goods or favours from the prisoners; the excessive use of force; and smuggling in alcohol and drugs. The guards sprayed inmates with tear gas, and at one Thanksgiving endangered lives by throwing a tear gas grenade into a full dormitory. The grenade was designed for outdoor use – and no riot had taken place in the dorm before the grenade was hurled at the youngsters.

The combination of violence and sex became a theme at some of the company's facilities. Riots at Wackenhut's Guadalupe prison in New Mexico left one guard dead in 1999, while in the same year three inmates were stabbed to death at its Lea County jail in the same State. Investigators found that Wackenhut put untrained staff into high-profile roles in the prisons, and delayed calling the police to quell rioting. In Texas, Wackenhut was fined £500,000 for understaffing the Travis County jail. The company tried to make improvements, but lost the contract. Before the firm left the premises, a sex scandal emerged at the prison. Inmates at the 1,000-bed jail alleged that guards traded shampoo and underwear for sex, or simply raped the inmates.[25] A number of guards were indicted and found guilty of sexual offences against prisoners. At the 200-bed Coke County prison, which housed troubled young girls, Wackenhut staff were accused in a lawsuit of making their inmates

> live in an environment in which offensive sexual contact, deviant sexual intercourse and statutory rape were frequent, and which resulted in a hostile, permissive sexual environment, and where residents were physically injured to the point of being hospitalized with broken bones.

Wackenhut denied the charges, but settled the case out of court for $1.5 million, without admitting liability.[26] Two more male guards were sacked from the Wackenhut-run Caldwell County jail in Texas for having sex with prisoners, while five guards at a Fort Lauderdale, Florida institution run by the firm were punished or sacked for sexual offences against inmates.[27]

The federal system of government in the US meant that Wackenhut could deal with these scandals on a regional basis, making promises to do better and offering improvement plans – or by downplaying the accusations, and claiming that they were teething difficulties within each regional prison department. Their business could grow in one region while they lost contracts in another. In Britain all prison contracts were handled centrally, so politicians had to face up to the failings of the firm all at once. This probably delayed the introduction of private prisons in the UK; but once the New Labour government was committed to the programme, problems in the jails did not deter them.

New Labour's enthusiastic embracing of private prisons stemmed partly from a desire to break the monopoly of the Prison Officers' Association. In the minds of ministers and their supporters, breaking the union could represent a liberal cause: public sector prisons had been the sites of some serious maltreatment scandals in this period, with persistent racist abuse of inmates of – for example – Wormwood Scrubs and Brixton prisons. Officials implied that obstruction by guards and their local union representatives was as much a cause of the abuse as, say, overcrowding or under-funding. Certainly, most of the complaints against private prisons centred on neglect and under-supervision, rather than aggressive assaults. But the case of Alton Manning showed that private prisons could also harm prisoners in the traditional manner. In 1995 Manning was a prisoner in Blakenhurst prison, a Midlands jail run by UK Detention Services. After a fight with the private warders, he had been restrained by a neck hold and asphyxiated to death. Such choke-holds are banned by Prison Service rules – but this ruling was ignored by the private providers. There was no investigation into Manning's death until 1998, when an inquest Jury passed a verdict of unlawful killing.

Even after the delayed inquest found that Manning had been illegally killed, the Crown Prosecution Service said that there was 'insufficient evidence' to prosecute. Now that the government ran some prisons through contractors rather than directly, the government could at least have responded to Manning's killing by market methods: they could have refused to give more contracts to UK Detention Services. But Manning and his family suffered from the worst of both worlds. The state simultaneously avoided responsibility for his death, by leaving the initial response in the hands of the private contractor while also appearing to rally to the firm's defence in an attempt to support the privatization programme in general. Grotesquely, the head of the Prison Service, Richard Tilt, responded to the inquest jury's verdict by arguing that black people like Manning were more susceptible to choking to death because of alleged physical differences. Tilt claimed Prison Office Research showed that 'Afro-Caribbean people are more likely to suffer positional asphyxia than whites'.[28] A few Labour MPs, led by Bernie Grant and Oona King, called for Tilt's resignation; but Jack Straw and Tony Blair accepted an apology letter from Tilt, and happily left both him and UK Detention Services in their jobs.

The growth of the private prisons showed that, given the right circumstances, both Tory and Labour governments would hand over new powers to the new security industries. These governments would willingly give profit-making organizations absolute authority over people. The conditions for the growth of the new security industries included, firstly a growing market based on politicians playing to popular fears and insecurities, and, secondly, business-friendly administrations that sincerely believed commercial companies to be better at even the most sensitive duties formerly carried out by the state alone. When these companies made terrible errors – errors that could cost prisoners' lives – governments seemed drawn to make excuses for their subcontractors, fearful that admitting things had gone wrong would be tantamount to admitting that the privatization programmes themselves had been a mistake. The discipline of the market seemed to work in reverse, so that politicians were forced to back rather than sack failing companies.

This pattern – of new firms bidding for business based on new fears – would also appear in the 'war on terror', as well as the 'war on crime'. The same firms, and the same politicians, who had been involved in privatizing the justice system would use these lessons to privatize military affairs, where the consequences of market failure were even more deadly. British and American governments that had hardened themselves to the abuse of prisoners by for-profit prison companies would be ready to accept the possibility of the abuse of 'terrorist suspects' by for-profit security firms.

The burgeoning of the private prison industry also led directly into the worst scandal of the war on terror. A cluster of executives from America's 'correctional' industries were sent to Iraq in 2003 to rebuild the country's prison system, working for the Coalition Provisional Authority. Their involvement was one of the clear indications that the Bush administration believed that the war on terror could largely be subcontracted to the private sector. The US avoided the difficult political questions involved in deciding whether to give responsibility for the prisons to either US or Iraqi officials. In either case, this choice would have involved judgments about who was the legitimate authority, considerations of national responsibility, and engagement with political traditions in both nations. Instead, the US seemed happier to believe that the solution to these complex problems came in an off-the-shelf package supplied by the private sector.

Terry Stewart came to Iraq from his own private jail firm, Advanced Correctional Management, which had bid unsuccessfully to run a women's prison in Texas just before his arrival in Iraq. Before he moved to the private sector, Stewart was head of corrections in Arizona. In 1997 Federal Investigators sued Stewart because they thought he was obstructing an abuse investigation in the jails in his state. Despite their lack of access to the jails, investigators said they found evidence that female prisoners faced an 'unconstitutional pattern or practice of sexual misconduct', and that at least fourteen female inmates had been repeatedly raped, sexually assaulted, and watched by corrections workers as they dressed, showered and used the bathroom.

Stewart was joined by Lane McCotter, an executive of prison company the Management & Training Corporation (MTC). MTC, a Utah-based private jail firm, faced a number of allegations of guards smuggling in drugs and allowing escapes, and of poor healthcare for inmates. McCotter's personal record was even more disturbing than that of his new employer. He had been forced out of the top spot in Utah's Department of Corrections when a schizophrenic prisoner died after being strapped to a chair naked for sixteen hours. Gary Deland, another former Utah head of prisons who had moved into the private sector to run his own consultancy, worked with McCotter and Stewart. Deland specialized in giving evidence in court against claims of jail abuse – for example, he defended the use of cage-like, mobile 'detention trailers' in Texas to punish prisoners on 'agricultural work' details.[29] He testified that these cells on wheels were a perfectly fine accessory to 'chain gang'-style work details, and argued their case in court. This trio was not directly involved in the abuse of prisoners at Abu Ghraib – the American army would begin torturing, aided by another group of private sector 'consultants' (see Chapter 8). But the executives arguably contributed to the grim condition of Iraqi prisons, including those in the Abu Ghraib complex. The miserable physical conditions of Iraq's jails, and the failure to build a new, effective prisons infrastructure to replace Saddam's Bastilles, created the background for the humiliating brutality in post-war Iraqi jails: the poor physical state of the prisons added to the dehumanizing atmosphere of the cells.

General Janis Karpinski was the colonel in charge of the military police guarding Iraqi prisoners. She was one of the few senior officers disciplined for the Abu Ghraib torture scandal, but claims that she was a scapegoat. There is an element of special pleading in some of her arguments: Karpinski should have seen that something was rotten in the jails under her guard when the Red Cross told her they had found male inmates being kept naked except for women's underwear in an effort to humiliate them. Instead, she admits she accepted assurances from intelligence officers that this was acceptable procedure. While Karpinski failed to spot and stop the abuse, she was not the driving force behind it. Her memoir of Iraq[30] identifies some of the other players in Iraq, including the trio from America's private prison industry. Karpinski's account may be coloured by a desire to shift the blame on to others, but her language is striking nonetheless. She describes them as 'the incarceration cowboys', who seemed to be 'the kind of swashbucklers you sometimes see in the wake of a military expedition'. Karpinski recounts Stewart shouting at and grabbing the shirt of an Iraqi general who was asking for payment for his men working in prisons, until bystanders had to separate the men. She says Deland 'went about his job like some kind of cowboy Commando, with a knife strapped to his leg, a side arm on his belt and an automatic rifle slung along his back'. The three men photograph themselves sitting on 'bricks of cash', which formed a 'pile about the height of a barbecue', or 'holding fistfuls of US dollars, with more bills sticking out of their pockets'. The money came at least partly from Iraqi oil receipts. The prison executives' 'can do' approach impressed US officials, who believed that the private sector could rebuild Iraq. Unfortunately, the 'can do' attitude masked a 'can't do' reality. Again and again, the executives used the cash to pay for work that was never done; for prison tiles that were laid, stolen, re-laid and re-stolen; for refurbishment that never happened – in other words, for prisons that remained filthy holes.

After watching the export of what seem like the worst failures of the private prison system to Iraq, the British government decided to recycle the experience and ask the men who had helped build Abu Ghraib to take charge of the British prison at the forefront of the war on terror. In 2004 the Home Office invited a team from Lane McCotter's Management & Training Corporation to bid for British prison contracts. The Home Office wanted bids for a number of jails, including an extension to the high-security Belmarsh prison, where British terror suspects were incarcerated.

Group 4 was one of the leading security firms able to profit from the war on terror. They also worked their way into the government's affections by dealing with prisoners and refugees. Open the pages of the October 2004 edition of Group 4 Securicor's in-house magazine,[31] and you will see the full range of services offered by the modern security company. The cover shows a purposeful looking young man wearing a forage cap and military fatigues, whose job is 'protecting United States troops in Kosovo': the most powerful army in the world believes it needs to shelter in Group 4's strong arms. They have hired Group 4 to mobilize its private guards in defence of Camp Bondsteel, the massive American base established in Kosovo after the NATO war with Serbia. Group 4 staff in battle-dress uniforms carrying M16 rifles patrol the perimeter. The company's magazine happily emphasizes the paramilitary nature of the job, with pen portraits of staff including a 'Force Protection Supervisor', who was formerly a member of a Special Weapons and Action Team (SWAT), and a number of specialists who are ex-soldiers looking to 'return to the military environment'. One of the guards tells the company magazine, 'at first I thought it was crazy that civilians were protecting the military', although she had realized that 'now it makes perfect sense'.

But any modern company knows that getting stuck in one market segment can be risky, so Group 4 chases every possible security-related business. Susan Brophy, one of the firm's Kosovo guards, reveals that she had first worked for the firm as a 'detainee custody officer' in Britain, before moving to France 'when the company opened up an immigration detention centre there'. Group 4 roams across nations and between ministries in search of work: the same magazine contains a piece on a day in the life of an 'incident response officer', supplied by the firm to Manchester Council in a uniform which, but for the absence of a truncheon, is almost exactly the same as a police uniform. The local metropolitan council needs to field what are unkindly called 'plastic police', because the Association of Chief Police Officers introduced a policy limiting police responses to burglar alarms. Under the new regulations the police would not respond to alarm calls from any premises that had given five false alarms in the preceding 10 months. Group 4's police lookalikes were hired to patrol those business locations plagued by frequent false alarms. If these 'plastic police' officers came across an actual break-in or other criminal act, they had to try to 'contain the situation' until the real officers arrived.

Group 4's magazine also contains news that Home Secretary David Blunkett, accompanied by one of his ministers and the head of the Probation Service, had attended the Group 4 launch of a new 'eye in the sky' at the firm's Manchester control centre. The technological breakthrough linked electronic tags to GPS satellite systems. Group 4 said this electronic tracking was exciting, and that 'the new technology will provide an added layer of public safety . . . providing extra intelligence about an offender's movements'. Group 4 Securicor said that the media launch 'was a huge success and created a great deal of positive publicity for the technology and for Securicor', while the firm's 'Head of Justice', David Taylor Smith, said,

> I am delighted that we were chosen to host the launch of this new technology, and in a couple of years [sic] time, we will look back on today's launch as the start of an important new service. Satellite tracking is the next generation of electronic monitoring, adding another component to robust offender management.

From supplying armed guards for the army to prisoner and immigration detention, dealing with street crime, and electronically monitoring ex-offenders, Group 4 was able to display an impressive range of security solutions. In the process, its staff mixed with US President Bush and British Home Secretary David Blunkett. Group 4's glossy magazine shows that the firm has come a long way from its origins as a Danish security firm whose first British business was supplying store detectives in the 1960s.

Group 4's promotional material also unwittingly highlights one of the company's high-profile failures. One year after it had boasted about hosting Blunkett on a demonstration of satellite tracking tags, a leaked memo showed that the scheme was ineffective. Blunkett hired Group 4 to help him 'be at the cutting edge of technology in the drive to make our communities safer'. But internal government memos revealed the Home Office wanted to hush up poor performance in these trials of equipment using Global Positioning System (GPS) satellites to track those on probation for sex and domestic violence offences. Unfortunately these 'eyes in the sky' had remarkably poor vision. The GPS-based system could not penetrate clouds, leafy trees, nearby tall buildings, or trains. The Home Office memos said

> We have not sought to publicise the pilot scheme since its launch in September 2004 due to the risks of negative media coverage of the poor results to date . . . Media attention may highlight some of the difficulties with the technology and raise questions about the cost and low throughput of offenders.

Civil servants reminded the current home secretary, Charles Clarke: 'You were not prepared to take that risk.' Instead the Home Office decided to extend the failing pilot until 2006, while trying to stop 'publicity at the current time'.[32] This was one of a series of embarrassing failures for the firm, which earned Group 4 page after page of derisory press coverage as it acquired public contracts from the 1990s onwards. But public derision did not impede the firm's growth.

Group 4's staff made their first inroads into the public sector in a prison van. The Conservative government tentatively gave the firm some contracts transporting prisoners to and from court in the early 1990s. This could have served as a bridge to greater opportunities in the incarceration business – but Group 4 stumbled by freeing prisoners it was meant to keep under lock and key. On the first day of the firm's 1993 contract, one of its charges fled from the dock of Hull Magistrates' Court. Christopher Hatch was recaptured two days later, but others followed his example and escaped from the firm's custody. Seven prisoners forced the hatches and windows on Group 4's vans, or otherwise escaped its clutches, in the first two weeks.[33] Judges also complained about the long delays in court as they waited for Group 4 to arrive with the accused. In one case, inmates from Lincoln Prison had to tell Group 4's driver the way to the city's court, in a vain attempt to get to the trial on time.[34] Staff shortages over Easter led the firm to use secretaries and clerks to drive the vans in return for a £48 daily bonus. The move breached the company's rules about only using trained, Home Office-certified custody officers.[35]

Sensing the government's weakness, opposition home affairs spokesman Tony Blair accused the Conservative government of presiding over 'an Ealing comedy'.[36] The laughing stopped when Ernest Hogg choked to death in the back of a Group 4 van. Hogg had been sent litres of vodka and white rum by post to drink in his prison cell in the Group 4-run Wolds prison. The drink, disguised as mineral water, was spotted by guards and confiscated; but it was loaded in evidence bags into the Group 4 van taking Hogg to court. The Group 4 transport staff apparently failed to realise that the evidence bags were significant, and handed their charge back his drink. Hogg swallowed the liquor, choked on his own vomit, and was left to die alone by unknowing Group 4 staff. Again Blair launched an attack on the company and the government. According to the future prime minister, 'this farce has now turned to tragedy'. Blair also called for 'an urgent review of present government contracts with Group 4'.[37] Four years later, the newly elected Prime Minister Blair was not sufficiently moved by Group 4's generation of either farce or tragedy to do anything other than continue to patronize the firm. This was partly because Group 4 had entrenched itself in the public sector by pushing around some of the most vulnerable members of society: the company specialized in dealing with asylum seekers, and had thus made itself invaluable to the new government.

The government tried hard to support Group 4's prisons work, but found it difficult to build a political coalition in support of the company's power over prisoners. Ministers found that they were fired at by both sides on the issue. The liberal press and politicians were sympathetic to criminals suffering at the hands of a profit-driven company, while the right-wing press were alarmed at the firm's difficulty in holding on to prisoners. Both the government and Group 4 needed to operate the new private security system out of the public glare. Luckily, one group of detainees was generally outside the circle of sympathy or interest. From the 1990s onwards, the government took upon itself increasingly more powers to lock up refugees judged as 'bogus'. While the Labour opposition grumbled about the ever more restrictive immigration acts, they did not do so very loudly. The Labour opposition seemed to believe that the Conservatives had mobilized a popular xenophobic sentiment on the refugee 'crisis', and tended to duck the issue. At the same time, right-wing politicians and commentators painted the asylum seekers as 'cheats', 'bogus' and 'abusing our hospitability'.[38] In short, they tended to define those seeking refuge as grasping rather than dangerous people. Consequently, the government found it easier to hand these new authoritarian powers to imprison asylum seekers to a private company; it mattered little if the new business failed from time to time. Escaped asylum seekers did not raise the same kind of fears as escaped criminals. As a result, the imprisonment of asylum seekers – vilified as 'economic migrants' – was handed to firms that in fact *were* unashamedly economic migrants. International businesses that traded freely across the world made profit by imprisoning those who were told that they must not travel to seek a better life.

Private industry already had a small foothold in this area. Since 1970 the Harmondsworth immigration detention centre had been privately run by Securicor. It acted essentially as an extension of the air travel companies: airlines supported the centre in order to offset their liabilities for having brought asylum seekers into Britain on their aeroplanes. The sixty or so detainees were even fed on in-flight meals in airline food trays supplied by the travel firms. An increase in the number of people seeking asylum, notably Tamils fleeing persecution, led to increased work for private security companies. Private guards were hired to guard asylum seekers in a converted Sealink car ferry, the Earl William, moored at Harwich. In 1989 the Tamils were replaced by Turkish Kurds, one of whom caused a ripple of interest in that year when he committed suicide by setting himself on fire.[39] But the Harmondsworth centre generally went about its business without attracting much attention. Then, with the 1993 and 1996 Asylum Acts, the Conservative government massively ramped up the number of refugees who would be detained, and handed this new captive market to Group 4. The firm took over Harmondsworth, but also won a new contract, in 1993, for the much larger Campsfield detention centre. The site was an unused prison complex that had previously been used to deliver an unsuccessful 'short sharp shock' experiment on young lawbreakers. Within a month of its opening, the Immigration Service signalled their determination to create a market for its services by seizing half of a planeload of Jamaican passengers, who were accused of intending to settle illegally in Britain, rather than simply to visit relatives. It handed them over to Group 4 for temporary detention at the Oxfordshire camp.

The Campsfield inmates soon began reacting to the boredom and misery of their private detention. In March 1994, up to 100 inmates began a hunger strike. Their protest was largely broken when the strike leaders were moved to prisons. In June, inmates took to the Campsfield rooftops and rioted. Six detainees escaped before the turbulence was subdued by police in riot gear. The politics surrounding asylum seekers had some important differences from that relating to prisoners. While the government was embarrassed by Group 4's prison van failures, and was put under pressure by the Labour opposition's front-bench spokesmen, this was not the case with Campsfield. Instead, the main complaints came only from the left-wing fringe of the Labour party, and Conservative ministers responded aggressively. When veteran left-wing MP Jeremy Corbyn raised the issue of the hunger strikes in parliament, Home Office minister Charles Wardle was unmoved. He said he refused either to be 'blackmailed' by the hunger strikes or concerned by the 'hysterical and at times aggressive behaviour of the rent-a-mob crowd' that frequently gathered outside Campsfield House. Wardle felt free to sneer that the only opposition came from 'a motley crowd of the Oxford Trades Union Council, the Socialist Workers Party, the Revolutionary Communist Party and others of that ilk, including, last Saturday, Mr Corbyn'.[40]

Charles Wardle was apparently no more embarrassed by rioting and escaping detainees than he was by protests; indeed, the minister tried to blame the latter for the former. Wardle claimed that the riot had been partly caused by the 'motley coalition of left-wing protesters' demonstrating outside the jail.[41] In the wake of the 1994 disturbance, Group 4 formed the first ever private riot squad to deal with truculent asylum seekers. Group 4 staff were trained after Home Office consultation to use batons, shields and 'physical restraint' techniques. Staff would get an extra 'shift allowance' of 50p per hour for agreeing to sign up for 'tactical unit' training.[42] This represented a major transfer into the private sector of powers that had formerly been guarded jealously by the police; but because it was taking place in the political netherworld of immigration detention, there was little protest or complaint from the established parties. The asylum system provided the perfect training ground for the private security industry.

The incredible licence apparently given to Group 4 in the detention of asylum seekers was shown in the aftermath of a second riot at Campsfield, in 1997. Over 100 police in riot gear, accompanied by dogs, were used to quell a twelve-hour disturbance at the centre, which started when inmates thought one of their number was being strangled by Group 4 guards. The new Labour administration, like the Tory one, immediately lashed out at the refugees and their supporters. Home Office minister Mike O'Brien said that detainees had been seized by a 'moment of madness', and had destroyed their own facilities in the riot.[43] The government started prosecuting inmates accused of rioting. The prosecution fell apart when Group 4 staff were shown to have lied repeatedly. Inmates had claimed that Group 4 regularly punished inmates who complained too much by 'bumping them out' to high-security prisons. The riot began when one such inmate was being 'bumped out' by means of a grip around the neck. In the trial of the rioters, Group 4 staff said that they had never even heard the phrase 'bumped out', let alone used a choke-hold to do such a thing. Unfortunately for Group 4, police statements taken after the riot, CCTV of the events, showed that the firm's officers had used the phrase regularly, had taken an inmate out using a neck hold, and had lied repeatedly. Guards claimed that asylum seekers had destroyed their own telephone – a self-destructive act aimed at one of their most important facilities. In fact, two guards had destroyed the phone with batons during the melee. Guards who claimed they had been knocked out by inmates who doused them with solvents were shown on CCTV with no injuries.[44] Faced with the Group 4 staff's failure to tell the truth, the prosecution withdrew its case and the nine asylum seekers walked free. In response to such a major failure by their contractor, the Home Office did everything it could to shore up the firm. Soon after the riot, Mike O'Brien turned up personally to present the firm with an 'Investors in People' award: Group 4 might have lost in court, but still received a certificate of good business practice from a government minister as a consolation. After the trials collapsed, Home Secretary Jack Straw tried to deport one of the defendants. The government, it seemed, was keen to show as much support to this private company as they would to an arm of the state.

Group 4 repaid the government's faith by becoming implicated in a yet more serious incident. In January 2002, ministers opened Yarl's Wood, a 900-bed detention centre in Bedfordshire, and Group 4 was given the contract to manage the facility. Some of the tabloid press immediately denounced the new building on an old army base as a place of 'luxury' similar to a 'top hotel'.[45] Unlike most top hotels, however, Yarl's Wood was struck by rioting, and the next month by a fire that effectively burned it to the ground, despite the best efforts of eighty firefighters running fifteen fire engines.[46] Inmates started the riot when a female prisoner was held down by guards following an argument over where she could pray. Unlike most luxury hotels, Yarl's Wood, built by Group 4 and their partner construction firm Amey, was 'astonishingly flimsy', according to the Prisons Ombudsman.[47] The building, he said, was 'poorly designed and not fit for purpose'. In particular, in his rush to generate places from the private consortia, Jack Straw had allowed the building to go ahead without the sprinkler system that could have stopped the fire. The fire service had forewarned Straw that this absence of sprinklers meant Yarl's Wood was a 'disaster waiting to happen'.[48] Since the government was nominally responsible for Yarl's Wood, the complex was exempt from fire regulations, even though the facility was in fact privately built and operated.

Group 4 showed its gratitude to the government by promptly suing the police for nearly £100 million to make up for its business loss. On the night of the fire, police had to wait five hours while Group 4 failed to bring the situation under control. The firm had to endure some humiliation in the prosecutions of some of the rioters. The prosecution – which had initially considered putting the firm itself in the dock – told the jury that Group 4 was a 'national laughing stock', which had 'blundered' into the field of private custodial services. 'You may wonder', Counsel for the prosecution asked the jury, 'whether any large commercial organization could have made a bigger fool of itself even if it had been trying to do so'.[49] With Group 4 suing the police, the police considered a prosecution of Group 4. The stiff courtroom criticism and police anger suggested that the close relationship between the state and its subcontractors was breaking up. But after the heat and smoke of the controversy died down, the government continued with business as usual. It was, it seems, subject to 'customer capture' with the custodial company. Too much had been handed over to the private firms for there to be any retreat, so the government simply ignored such difficulties.

Group 4 hung onto its contracts in Yarl's Wood, as elsewhere. This did not mean the operation had improved. An undercover reporter from the *Daily Mirror* got a job at the newly reopened Yarl's Wood to find widespread racism unchallenged among the firm's staff. 'Jamaicans are drug-dealing pieces of s**t. Algerians are the slimiest bastards in the world . . . They're all terrorists, the ones we get anyway. And the Chinese are evil little bastards', a senior officer told the undercover reporter.[50] He was also told that staff would deliberately 'cause pain', give troublesome inmates a 'good crank', and destroy CCTV evidence. The staff psychologist said that asylum seekers were 'bastards'. The government, however, responded simply with another inquiry, a few promises, and the continued use of private contractors. In the business school jargon, by outsourcing performance-critical activities, the government had allowed an unhealthy shift in the balance of power. Locking up refugees was absolutely essential to the government's performance. By swimming with the tide of bigotry against asylum seekers, the government hoped they had found an easy way of shoring up their own popularity: a Labour government thus made locking up refugees one of its 'key performance indicators' in an effort to win the editor and readers of the right-wing *Daily Mail* newspaper. Handing this responsibility to private firms looked at first like a quick, simple solution – there was no need to worry about the practical or moral questions raised by increasing the incarceration of would-be immigrants; the job could be done by the signing of a contract. But the supplier now held the purchaser in its hands: every embarrassment and failure in the asylum detention business had to be ignored, or the whole system would be in jeopardy. Group 4 and its competitors had come across a captive market – and the government, as well as the asylum seekers, were their prisoners.

Around this time a scandal broke in Europe that contained a serious but largely ignored warning relating to the growth of the new private security state. In 1999 a standoff between the European Parliament and the European Commission grew into a serious confrontation. The elected members of the Parliament were confronting the normally more powerful appointed members of the Commission, as a small wind of democracy blew through the normally unresponsive corridors of the EU. The Commission was forced to resign en masse when an independent report showed that the Commissioners had done little to contain, and much to encourage, a series of corruption scandals. The Parliament pursued these scandals with a rare and surprising vigour, and the Commission's resignation left the EU effectively without any leadership of its civil service. A Eurosceptic British press reported the details of the dispute gleefully, including the fact that one Commissioner – former French Prime Minister Edith Cresson – had hired her dentist for jobs for which he had no qualifications (and on which he did very little work).

But the same newspapers spent a lot less time reflecting on the involvement of a partly British firm in the scandal. EU Commissioner Jacques Santer was heavily criticized by the report for allowing an uncontrollable 'state within a state' to develop in the security office. Most of the work in this out-of-control area was subcontracted to Group 4 Securitas in a five-year contract worth about £5 million. In 1997 the Belgian newspaper *De Morgen* made serious allegations about the contract, revealing that Group 4 had tendered for the contract and had subsequently been leaked details of rival bids by an EU official in a Belgian café. With this information, they amended their bid after the tenders were closed, winning the contract. Then they altered the contract again, increasing their prices. The Commission's report substantiated these allegations, finding 'evidence that manipulation effectively occurred in favour of Group 4'. *De Morgen* also alleged that Group 4, having won the contract by fraudulent means, then took on 'ghost personnel', paid for under the security contract, who actually ended up working as chauffeurs, gardeners and handymen around the Commission. Group 4 also hired some staff who were friends or relations of Commission staff. It seems the head of security – a Belgian with neo-Nazi links – built up his state with a state through the Group 4 contract, buying favours from some high Commission officials. In the somewhat strangled language of the auditors, 'concerning ghost personnel', it was concluded that '. . . other services in the commission employed staff throughout the security office for purposes other than security' and that '31 Persons were placed at the disposal of the Security Office or its intermediaries for periods of up to one year for tasks other than security but were still paid by Group 4.'[51] The European auditors' report also noted that 'a large number of persons were recruited on the recommendation of various persons in authority, and some of them had close relations with the Assistant to the Director of the Security Office'.

The scandal at the European Commission showed that contracting out the security functions of government bodies could have serious consequences: security services were able, almost automatically, to act with authority and autonomy, and to have access to the centres of power in ways that, say, cleaning contractors did not. The security privatization became a vehicle for fraud led partly by a retired policeman with far-right connections. He built a 'state within a state' at the heart of Europe. His security force armed itself with sniper rifles and machine guns – although thankfully his 'ghost' staff did nothing more sinister than work at odd jobs for Commission officials, or act in a boorish and drunken way in front of Europe's political leaders. The Commission experience presented a lesson in the dangers of security privatization; but it was a lesson that would be largely ignored.

At about the same time as the contracts were being 'manipulated' in Group 4's favour in Europe, the firm began developing its political links in Britain. Leading Conservative politician Norman Fowler sat on the board of Group 4 Ltd in the UK from 1990 to 1993. Labour MPs expressed concern over the propriety of Fowler's role. In 1992 the company won the management contract for the Wolds prison in Humberside. Group 4 hired Shandwick Consultants to deal with the subsequent media interest. Shandwick were at that time run by Peter Gummer, the brother of another Conservative minister, John Gummer. Other figures from the British establishment joined the firm. Barrie Gane, ex-deputy head of MI6, joined the company in June 1993. A Group 4 spokesperson said that Gane's 'knowledge of international affairs is particularly useful in the development of our strategy and international growth'. Coincidentally, Group 4 won a contract at around the same time to guard MI6's new headquarters at Vauxhall, London.

The New Labour government that took power in 1997 also began, after a time, a process of integration with the new security firms. I was able to witness the way these companies put money into the new governing party's events during a meeting at the 2004 Labour Party conference. The home secretary of the time, David Blunkett, addressed party delegates on his policies – from antisocial behaviour orders to stricter controls on asylum seekers. The meeting was paid for by Reliance Secure Task Management, a company that 'operate a wide range of contracts in the criminal justice sector'. Their banners and brochures surrounded the Home Secretary. Reliance was involved in running police custody cells, electronically tagging offenders, and transporting prisoners between courts and prisons. They are one of Britain's leading security firms, whose business has since grown as the government has passed more and more business from the police and prison services to private enterprise. Their brochures admitted no difficulties in Home Office policy. Instead, glossy publications promised 'cost effective solu- tions', 'dedicated tasks delivered with a high degree of accountability in secure and sensitive environments', and 'added-value solutions through a tailored approach to secure, practical and cost effective service delivery'. In fact Reliance was facing criticism in Scotland after it had accidentally released some prisoners, while leaving others who should have been freed languishing in prison. Shortly before the meeting, the *Sun* newspaper sent a reporter to work for Reliance, and he was told that staff had a 'headbanger' game for dealing with prisoners they disliked: sudden breaking at speed causing the inmates to 'smack their heads' in the portable cells. The reporter who had become Reliance's latest recruit was also advised to '[t]urn the heating right up and let them roast in the cells. Or come winter you turn it right down and freeze them. That shuts them up' – or simply to 'hit them'.[52]

Some former Labour ministers developed even closer links to the security industry. In 2004 a complicated set of business manoeuvres reordered the main private security firms in Britain. Group 4 bought out some of Wackenhut's international business, but sold some of their own prisons to a new firm called GSL. Around the same time, Wackenhut's UK custodial business, trading as Premier Prisons, was sold to its partners, a privatization firm called Serco. GSL was owned by a venture finance business called Englefield Capital, which in turn retained George Robertson – who had been both a Labour defence minister and the head of NATO – as an advisor. Serco, which operated schools as well as prisons for the British government, took on former Labour education minister Lord Filkin as a director. By 2004, the owners of two of the foremost private security firms in Britain therefore had leading Labour politicians on their payroll.

These new security firms had built up a business exploiting the crackdown on crime and asylum; but they would become involved in the fight against terrorism. The private sector would allow ministers to sidestep concerns about civil liberties. Its willingness to bid for new kinds of security contract would also let ministers sidestep resistance to their moves against historic legal principles within the civil service and judiciary. Nine foreign nationals were imprisoned without trial in the high-security Belmarsh prison on the authority of David Blunkett's Anti-Terrorism, Crime and Security Act – an emergency measure passed after 9/11. The men could not be deported because they came from countries where they would very probably be tortured on their return. But the Home Secretary said that MI5 advised them that the men represented a terrorist risk – although apparently there was not enough evidence to put the men on trial. Under the new Act, the men were subject to administrative detention. This imprisonment without trial faced many legal challenges, until in 2004 the Law Lords caused a constitutional crisis by striking down the law. Lord Hoffman argued against the detentions in the most forceful manner, saying that the

> real threat to the life of the nation, in the sense of a people living in accordance with its traditional laws and political values, comes not from terrorism but from laws such as these. That is the true measure of what terrorism may achieve. It is for Parliament to decide whether to give the terrorists such a victory.

The new home secretary, Charles Clarke, faced a political problem of the highest order: the Law Lords were saying that the detentions he had claimed were essential in the war on terror actually represented a failure in the face of terrorism. Either he had to face down the Law Lords and risk identifying himself as an authoritarian in conflict with the legal establishment, or accept their ruling, which would mean admitting that his crucial legislation against al-Qaeda was in fact disposable.

The private security companies offered a neatly packaged third way, avoiding either of these embarrassments: control orders. The Labour government circumvented those parts of the state that objected to the repressive new anti-terror laws by turning to the private sector. But when the government hired Group 4 and Serco to run the 'control orders', they introduced the special mix of oppression and incompetence in which these firms appeared to specialize. The terror suspects had never been tried in any court; nor apparently had they been questioned by the security services since their arrest about any possible relation with al-Qaeda or its affiliates. Instead, they were condemned by unseen evidence to house arrest. Many of the suspects had to stay at home for 24 hours a day, and were forbidden from speaking to anyone other than their wives and children. The private security firms fitted the detainees with electronic tags and monitored their house arrest. Those subject to control orders had to ring an anti-terrorist call centre at regular intervals to assure the government contractors that they were not engaging in any subversive, violent or dangerous acts. The control orders were later relaxed, but often in incomprehensible ways: one suspect was allowed to travel freely on public transport, but visitors to the house had to be thoroughly vetted by the Home Office. Journalists interviewed him by simply standing on the other side of his open front door. As months passed, many of those who followed the orders became deeply depressed. Some suffered from mental health problems. They were 'sad , broken people',[53] according to one writer who knew them well. However, while those who obeyed the orders were ground down, more determined suspects could easily slip out of the contractors' grasp.

Staff from the BBC documentary programme *Inside Out* went undercover to work for Group 4 at their tagging control centre. They found that many of those tagged – including murderers and sex offenders – went unmonitored for weeks, and occasionally even months. The tags worked on mobile phone networks – except that they often didn't work. Some of the tag wearers disappeared off the company's recording system, and were classified by the company as having 'missing status'. The tagged offenders soon realised that the 'base units' Group 4 had fitted in their homes to service the tags were unreliable, and often failed to work when installed or after a few weeks. Group 4 staff did not have the manpower or the will to investigate properly those who had gone into 'missing' status. Worse, some Group 4 staff were found 'blagging' – or faking records – so that periods of unmonitored absence did not appear in the company's management information. Staff told the undercover reporters that one of the tagged men who had disappeared below the radar for twenty-four hours was a terrorist suspect supposedly linked to the London tube bombings. A few months previously another terror suspect – an Iraqi allegedly linked to al-Qaeda – had simply removed his tag and fled, never to be relocated.[54]

This was the real price of repression on the cheap: the privatized, cut-price house arrests broke the spirits of those that obeyed them, but also allowed the strong-minded terror suspect simply to escape. The absconding suspected terrorists caused some embarrassment to the government, to its 'tough guy' home secretary of the time, John Reid, and to the tagging firms. But by 2007 the private security firms were too much part of the new criminal justice system for the scandal to affect their business.

2

Base Motives

In the 1980s Carling lager's television advertisements showed a series of cheeky and daring stunts, with a slogan suggesting that only one of their maverick drinkers would be brave enough to perform them. In the advertisements bystanders would admire some bold, brave or mischievous act, then comment to each other that the hero must surely consume Carling's leading lager. In 1988 Carling joked about the Tory privatization bandwagon. Their television advert showed a soldier, his base and tank stamped with the slogan 'The British Army plc: The most exciting share offer of the century',[1] and the punchline comment 'I bet he drinks Carling Black Label'.

There are no records to show how many pints of Carling government ministers drank in the next fifteen years, but shares in slices of the British armed forces are now vigorously traded: private firms run nuclear bases, transport tanks into the battlefield, and are ready to fly some of Britain's key warplanes. Everyone from the US vice president to the Norwich Union bought shares in British Army plc. The commercial takeover of British army bases was carried out on the quiet. In 2007 complaints about British army housing hit the headlines. Military accommodation had been poor for years, but the fact that soldiers were also being asked to die in Iraq and Afghanistan made their squalid living conditions seem particularly unfair. The hard fighting in the war on terror threw a spotlight on army housing. Conservative opposition leader David Cameron seized on the issue as a way of criticizing the Labour government's military record, and promised a charter for improvement in living quarters for the services. Cameron carefully avoided mention of the fact that his own shadow foreign secretary, William Hague, supplemented his parliamentary salary with a £65,000-a-year job advising a firm called Terra Firma Capital – a company that made millions of pounds of profit through its ownership of the poorly maintained military housing, squeezing cash out of the Ministry of Defence that could otherwise have been used to improve soldiers' living standards. Hague's employer, Terra Firma, relied heavily on the privatization of military bases for its profits. This was barely mentioned in the press or parliament in a testament to how little the public and media were conscious of the commercial penetration of the British armed forces.

In the 1980s, private companies already supplied the guns, bullets, aeroplanes and bombs used by the armed forces. But Thatcherite ministers in office under her successor, John Major, began the movement of the direct running of military services to the private sector. Management of army bases became the first frontline in the privatizers' campaign to own a slice of the armed forces. During the war on terror, private companies would be well established on the battlefield itself; but they began their conquest of the military market by winning positions in less glamorous military territory, picking up contracts in army bases. The Conservative governments of Thatcher and Major were fully committed to privatization, and successfully mobilized popular support behind the sell-offs and share offers; but the Conservatives also relied on their patriotic and even militaristic appeal for political support. Mrs Thatcher faced down General Galtieri in the Falklands War of 1982. Television audiences were gripped by the image of Mrs Thatcher sitting in the turret of a Challenger tank in 1986, wearing a scarf and goggles that made her look, in the words of the *Daily Telegraph*, like 'a cross between Isadora Duncan and Lawrence of Arabia'. The prime minister proceeded to fire a tank shell, successfully hitting the target 1,000 yards down the West German practice range. Conservative ministers used Thatcher as a model long after her departure.

While the government of John Major tried to soften the image of Conservatism in some areas, neither he nor his ministers wanted to weaken the association of the Tory party with military toughness. Tory ministers struck Thatcher-like martial poses for years after she had left office. In 1995 Michael Portillo was still the darling of the Tory membership – not the touchy-feely, sensitive politician he became after being thrown out of parliament by the voters of Enfield. As defence secretary, he struck the most memorable Conservative military pose, in a 1995 conference speech that ran, 'We will speak of pride, of honour, of valour in battle and, yes, of glory.' Then, repeating the SAS motto 'Who dares, wins', Portillo declared to a nation either startled or roused, depending on their political complexion: 'We dare. We will win.' It would have been hard to strike this pose and then openly begin replacing the SAS with private mercenaries, so Portillo instead began a stealthy privatization of the defence sector.

Given their desire to bask in reflected military glory, the Conservative governments of the 1980s and 1990s could not embark on a wholesale handover of the army, navy and air force to private industry. Using privatization to break up the government's position in utilities and transport, or to chip away at the welfare state consensus, was one thing; messing with 'our boys' was quite another. However, neither could the Conservatives avoid offering something to the powerful business lobbies that backed their government. If businesses demanded access to new military markets, they were sure to make some headway. Equally, Conservative politicians were politically committed to the idea that private industry would bring new efficiency and cost-cuts in any area of state expenditure, including the army. Their friends – and in many cases future employers – ran the firms that wanted to make inroads into military services. Consequently, 'The British Army plc' slowly changed from an advertising executive's joke to an on-the-ground reality. The outright privatization of military services was still a novel and contro-versial idea, and so began as a stealth operation in the distinctly un-glamorous area of military housing.

Housing for squaddies was notoriously poor. The miserable state of married quarters had caused the army real recruitment problems: soldiers and their families despaired at the dilapidated, poorly maintained houses, and refused to sign up for longer service in an army that would force them to live in such grim conditions. So Defence Secretary Portillo had a brilliant idea: sell off all the houses to the private sector, which would inevitably be more efficient than the army, and then lease the houses back. The deal, worth £1.6 billion, was put out to tender in 1996. The scheme covered 57,400 homes on a 999-year lease, with 2,500 'surplus' homes to be cherry-picked and sold off.

The two leading bidders were both closely linked to the Conservative Party. John Beckwith, a Tory fundraiser who ran the 'Premier Club', whose members raised £10,000 each for the party, led a group of American banks in a bid to win the contract; but he lost out to Annington

Homes. This coalition included Hambros Bank, run by Tory party treasurer Lord Hambro. Whiz kid financier Guy Hands was also an important figure at Annington Homes, and also had Conservative connections. Hands was a close friend of William Hague, who became Tory leader after John Major. Indeed, Hands had been best man at Hague's wedding. But the real scandal broke when former servicemen realized how Hands had got his hands on the Annington deal: the financier was involved because his employer, Japanese bank Nomura, was one of the main investors in the scheme.

The prospect of a Japanese takeover of the accommodation sections of British army bases enraged World War II veterans. Harold Payne of the National Federation of Far East Prisoners of War was 'disgusted', while Arthur Titherington, secretary of the Japanese Labour Camp Survivors Association, was 'almost speechless', adding, 'It seems to me that certain senior members of the government have no feelings about the past.'[2] Backbench Tory and Labour MPs were also outraged: Labour's Bruce George said, 'I am not xenophobic, but I do not like the idea of housing for which the MOD is responsible being bought by the Nomura bank. If the Japanese win contracts, many people will be insulted.'[3] Sensitive to these attacks, Annington Homes did what most military suppliers do to gain the edge when bidding for work: they appointed some ex-military men to front the deal. Businessman and former Commando Sir Thomas Macpherson was recruited as chairman. Retired Air Vice-Marshal Sandy Hunter, a former commander of British forces in Cyprus, joined him as deputy chairman, and the deal went through.

Perhaps the veterans and the parliamentarians were too backward-looking. Had they looked to the present and future rather than dwelling in the past, they would have seen the true spirit of Nomura. In 1997 Nomura was suspended from the Japanese stock exchange for a month because of a case involving payments to gangsters. The firm was eventually fined ¥100 million for paying off Ryuichi Koike, a so-called 'Sokaiya' racketeer. The Sokaiya run protection rackets, taking payments for ensuring that firms' annual general meetings run 'smoothly', and threatening to disrupt the meetings by revealing embarrassing secrets. Nomura's president and managing director received suspended prison sentences.

A second financial scandal in 1998 was masterminded from the UK. British Nomura traders tried to wipe 15 billion Australian dollars off that country's stock exchange by using concerted and planned trading in stocks and shares. The brokers hope to push the market down as a whole, then sweep in and make profits by buying up the now cheap stocks, and so make a profit on Australia's losses. An Australian judge found that 'Nomura engaged in deliberately misleading conduct designed to achieve illegitimate ends'. Tapes revealed that the traders themselves had joked about banking fraudster Nick Leeson, and being 'clapped in jail the next time you set foot in Australia'. The traders all stood to win millions of pounds of bonuses on the back of Nomura's profits by undermining the value of Australia's businesses. The Securities and Futures Authority fined Nomura £250,000 for this share-rigging fraud in October 2000. In the same month Nomura sacked two of its senior London salesman for unauthorized dealing in web company Scoot.com. Nomura alerted the Securities and Futures Authority, who stripped the traders of their licences for 'gross misconduct'. The firm faced more scandal when a former Nomura trader called Isabelle Terrillon won a £70,000 out-of-court settlement for sex discrimination and unfair dismissal, although her employers did not admit liability. She told the court that her boss had told her to 'wear short tight skirts in the office', while one of her colleagues had asked her to 'strip down and give him a massage' in the middle of a meeting with clients.

Labour's Bruce George warned that the MoD housing sell-off was 'bananas' and a 'pantomime', because 'the MoD will retain the responsibility for managing, providing social services and maintaining the security of the estate, but it is getting nothing out of it. The gainers will be the Tory party and the property speculators.' Michael Portillo, then the darling of the Tory party, disagreed, telling the Commons, 'We achieved an excellent sale.'[4] It turns out that Michael was wrong and Bruce was right. In 1997 the government's independent financial watchdog, the National Audit Office (NAO), investigated the deal and found that the £1.7 billion paid for the homes by Nomura was between £77 million and £139 below their real worth. Even though the army was swindled on the cost of the houses, they also had to lease them back and pay to tart up the still squalid stock. The MoD planned to spend £816 million on maintaining the homes over the next twenty-five years, plus £470 million on upgrading the shoddy dwellings, even though the houses were all owned by Nomura.

NatWest bank advised the army on how to carry out the sale.

NatWest, who itself was among the advisers paid £11 million to design the deal, decided that it was a good idea for the army to be responsible for the upkeep of houses it no longer owned. The bankers 'considered that excluding maintenance would avoid over-complicating an already novel sale transaction'.[5] The main novelty seems to have been an extraordinary new way to cheat the taxpayer. In 2000 the Audit Office took a new look at the management of military accommodation, and found that the army was paying £40 million a year to rent houses from Annington, and then keeping them empty. In 2002 Nomura took a £600 million dividend out of Annington Homes, the front company created to buy the army houses. This meant that Nomura grabbed a 323 per cent profit in the first five years. Nomura's consortium paid £1.66 billion for the 57,000 army houses in late 1996. The bank put only £226 million into the deal and made a total profit of £730 million. When Guy Hands left Nomura to found his own investment company, Terra Firma Capital, he took the Annington Homes investment into the new company.

This sorry tale looks like just one more of the botched privatizations from the 1990s. A lot of money was wasted, and some people got stuck in grim houses, but nobody died. But the Annington Homes saga was also significant because it represented an advance guard of Thatcherism conquering new military markets. Privatizing the privates' quarters created a bridgehead that would ultimately lead to business influence on the battlefield. In truth, not many people outside the army cared about soldiers' quarters; nor indeed did many inside the army above the lower ranks lie awake at night worrying about soldiers' houses. While the top brass might call upon soldiers to do and die, the military establishment had allowed their housing to drift into a miserable state long before Annington Homes came on the scene. Tory patriotism did not extend to pride in how soldiers were treated. Labour's left wing, caught up in battling privatization and cuts in unionized public services, did not make military housing their priority. Consequently, the Annington Homes tale remained a minor scandal. However, in hindsight we can see that the selling off of soldiers' quarters was an early, stealthy move by the corporations into military markets. The privatizers then marched boldly into other, more significant military bases.

A larger and more dangerous privatization took place near Plymouth. Just outside of the city are the Devonport royal dockyards, which have maintained ships for the British navy for hundreds of years. They were founded by William of Orange in 1691, and remain one of the Royal Navy's main refitting yards. The base edged up to the front in the new Cold War in the 1980s, when it began refitting British nuclear-powered submarines. In the middle of that decade, Michael Heseltine asked Peter Levene to review their 'efficiency'. He recommended that a private firm manage the docks, their 20,000 workers, and their contracts to maintain the ships of the British navy. Labour's defence spokesman, Denzil Davies, denounced the moves, arguing that '[a] franchise might be suitable for a fast-food burger bar but is totally unacceptable for refitting and repairing Royal Navy vessels'. In 1985, 20,000 of the dockyard workers struck and demonstrated for a day in protest. Even the Conservative Party-dominated Defence Select Committee opposed the deal.[6] While the handover was held up, the unions, buoyed by support in the House of Lords, decided to try and stop the privatization in the courts – a move that looked dramatic, with government ministers receiving writs, but was ultimately unsuccessful.

Once again, a NAO report revealed that the expected financial benefits had failed to materialize. Labour's new defence spokesman, Martin O'Neill, complained that 'this unnecessary process was being carried through in order to prove the resolve of the MoD to be as ideologically sound as the other privatising ministries'. The firm that took over Devonport was a US-owned company called Devonport Management Limited (DML). DML in turn was largely owned by a US multinational, Halliburton. In 1995 the former US defence secretary and future vice president, Dick Cheney, became Halliburton's chief executive officer – an appointment that caused controversy in the US, as Cheney had commissioned Halliburton to explore and then carry out large-scale military privatizations before leaving office, when Bill Clinton ousted his president, George Bush Sr. Cheney returned to the White House as vice president in 2000, this time serving under the son of President Bush, George W. Bush. The way his old firm Halliburton won new contracts in the war on terror – building the prison complex at Guantánamo Bay, Cuba, for example, or taking charge of the oil infrastructure in occupied Iraq – caused an international outcry. But his firm's role in one of the worst British privatization scandals is less well known.

In 1997, one of the last acts of the Tory government was the final and total sale of Devonport's dockyards to Cheney's Halliburton. They may have been influenced by the fact that Halliburton was a financial supporter of the Conservatives, having donated some £18,000 over the past few years to the party. Halliburton's British partners, BICC (later renamed Balfour Beatty) and the Weir Group were also Tory donors, with Tory lords serving on their boards. The Conservative commitment to privatization was by itself enough to ensure the sell-off, but the cash and connections probably helped. The Labour Party made some final, low-key protests about the privatization. After Labour came to power in 1997, all of these protests disappeared as the pro-privatization New Labour government learned to live happily with an American multi-national running Devonport. Ministers began mixing with Dick Cheney himself, giving honours to his executives and more contracts to his firm. Even Labour's pre-election protests about the final sale of Devonport were based more on political expediency than principal: Labour had a stronger commitment to the rival Rosyth docks, which sit in a Labour-voting Scottish constituency; the Devonport docks were located in an area thought of as Tory marginal territory. This judgment turned out to be wrong in practice, because after 1997 Plymouth's two seats became firmly Labour. It was also wrong in principle, because the real scandal was about to break – and it had everything to do with the realities of privatization and nothing to do with a 'north–south divide'.

The 1997 sale included a job refitting Britain's 'Vanguard'-class sub-marines. These four nuclear-powered vessels each carry some forty-eight Trident nuclear missiles around the seas of the world. They represent the UK's sole nuclear weapons system. Refitting and refuelling these vessels involves stripping and replacing their radioactive parts once each decade, in a specially built dock. When Halliburton had some trouble controlling costs at Devonport, it decided to squeeze more money out of the Ministry of Defence by effectively holding Britain's nuclear deterrent hostage. The NAO found that a project costed at $904 million in 1997 had increased by over 50 per cent by 2002.[7] According to the NAO, the MoD believed it would win a legal case against Halliburton over the extra charges, but did not go to court because delays 'would have adversely affected the effectiveness of the UK's strategic nuclear deterrent'. They did not dare go to court because, even though they were convinced they would win any case, putting Britain's only nuclear weapons in the middle of a court case would have compromised the UK's position as a nuclear power. The supposedly hawkish Dick Cheney was willing to bargain with the most significant weapon owned by America's chief ally in order to squeeze more cash out of the government.[8]

Halliburton claimed that the British government caused the price-hike by demanding better safety standards than those in the firm's original tender. For example, the MoD demanded that a crash barrier be built around the 'central pool' where the submarines were dismantled. Naval official John Coles said the barrier was needed to stop ships 'crashing into that building' and releasing radiation. The British government, on the other hand, argued that Halliburton had been sloppy with both safety and pricing from the very beginning. The NAO stated that it was

> clear to the [Defence] Department that the nuclear safety requirement on this project would, from the outset, be stringent. The Department considers that DML was slow in putting in place the management processes needed to demonstrate its compliance with those principles and in producing good quality safety cases for the Inspectorate, resulting in less time for the consideration and resolution of the issues raised.

The company vehemently disagreed with the report. A short statement issued by the company said, 'DML disagrees that poor performance by itself or its sub-contractors was a major cause of the cost increases as it estimates that such poor performance only increased costs by $30 million.' But the report bears out the British navy's worries prior to the privatization that Halliburton was not properly qualified to work on sensitive nuclear projects, stating that 'the Department had concerns about DML's ability to manage the project. Initially DML had no experience of managing a major construction project that was subject to civil nuclear safety standards.' When the cost overruns became apparent, lawyers for the MoD told them that if they took the company to court, 'the argument was very much in the Department's favour, and the Department had very good prospects for defeating DML's claim'. But while the navy was confident of victory in the courts, Halliburton was still able to blackmail millions out of the MoD because, in the words of the NAO, the government had 'little room for manoeuvre', because it 'had nowhere else to go'. The navy could not face 'further delays' caused by a court case or while finding a replacement.

The Ministry of Defence decided it would not take Halliburton to court. The ministry believed they would win, but a court case would mean the failure of the contract, which in turn would put Britain's nuclear weapons out of business. A parliamentary committee found that 'because of the importance of these facilities to the maintenance of the effectiveness of the United Kingdom's strategic nuclear deterrent, the Department could not accept the contract's failure and the resulting late delivery of the facilities'. A parliamentary committee examining the report said that Halliburton had the navy 'over a barrel' when it came to asking for more money. As part of the original 1997 contract, Halliburton's lawyers had negotiated a maximum liability of $55 million on the contract, while cost overruns had since risen by five times that amount.

Halliburton's safety record was as worrying as its willingness to financially squeeze the navy. In October the Devonport operation was fined $94,000 by the Health and Safety Executive (HSE) for exposing twenty-four workers to asbestos. Plymouth magistrates were told that some of the men affected 'already think their days are numbered'. The HSE representative said that 'at the end of the day up to 24 young men must now agonise for 40 years whether at some stage they are going to suffer symptoms of mesothelioma, asbestosis or cancer'. Reports from the Nuclear Installation Inspectorate showed that safety problems continued on the refitting of the nuclear submarines. The moving crane that pulls nuclear flasks out of Trident submarines had recently crashed into HMS Vanguard, and 'a few litres of slightly radioactive liquid were spilled onto the floor' of the dock.

Safety began to worry local residents when the government said that Halliburton could massively increase the amount of radioactive tritium the company could release into the waters of the river Tamar. Tritium is a radioactive isotope that builds up in the cooling systems of nuclear submarines. The older craft used to discharge it at sea, but the Vanguard-class vessels 'recycle' it. Vanguard submarines do not flush Tritium, so they will not leave a nuclear footprint that can be detected by the enemy; such recycling is thus a security issue, not an environmental one. In order to refit the vessels, Halliburton needed to find a home for their excess tritium. So in May 2000, DML asked the Environment Agency for a licence to increase the amount they could dump. Their original submission proposed a staggering 666 per cent increase in the limit put on tritium emissions into the Tamar, and a 500 per cent increase in the limit on emissions into the atmosphere through a chimney. The Environment Agency tried to rein Halliburton in by proposing smaller limits, but they seem to have been little match for the multinational company. Under the deal finally struck, the Devonport docks were able to increase their liquid emissions by 500 per cent and their gaseous discharges by 400 per cent. A local campaign held meetings in the summer of 2000 with around 400 angry residents – an impressive number for a city that was otherwise completely supportive of its military docks.

The MoD's own research showed the depth of local hostility to Halliburton. Four of the navy's eleven decommissioned nuclear submarines were floating idly in Devonport's docks. The defunct reactors needed to be removed, and the MoD decided that they should be safely stored on land, in a plan known as Project Isolus (short for 'Interim Storage of Laid-up Submarines'). Devonport was itself a possible site, and Halliburton a possible contender to handle this nuclear scrap. In 2001, the MoD's own consultation on Isolus, carried out by Lancaster University, found hostility to private contractors handling nuclear waste both in Plymouth and at Rosyth in Scotland, where British firm Babcock ran the nuclear docks.

The report was commissioned by the MoD, which is desperately searching for ways to get rid of the engines of defunct nuclear submarines. Contractors at the two privately run nuclear shipyards at Rosyth and Plymouth are bidding to store the radioactive scrap on dry land, to the alarm of residents. According to Defence Minister Lewis Moonie, the MoD commissioned the report from Lancaster University to show that they had 'been open and consultative from the start'. The MoD commissioned Lancaster University's Centre for the Study of Environmental Change to run a consultation – using all of the appropriately modern devices, including 'four stakeholder panels' and a 'citizen's jury' – in an effort to avoid direct contact with angry locals. Unfortunately for Moonie, the consultation came up with conclusions that matched those reached by local campaigners against the nuclear waste. While Moonie claimed he welcomed the document and would 'consider carefully' its recommendations, the MoD press release did not reveal the substance of the report.

In fact the MoD-commissioned study revealed that there was 'a very strong feeling, especially in areas which saw themselves as potential sites, that the most appropriate place to store the wastes was London, particularly at a site close to the Houses of Parliament'. The researchers added that this was 'not facetious, but represented several powerful lines of reasoning' – including the idea that '[i]f the wastes are safe, then they can be stored in or near centres of population. If they are not safe, no site can be expected to accept them.' In a blow to the ministry's plans, and in line with the views of Plymouth campaigners, the study found that only 'very few stakeholders articulated the view that Devonport is the most practicable place to dismantle the submarines and store the wastes.'

The consultation revealed public opposition to the navy's two private contractors – Babcock in Scotland and Brown & Root in Plymouth. The MoD's consultation revealed that the MoD was

> seen as secretive and pursuing [its] own agenda. Contractors, for example, are perceived as profit driven, whilst regulators are seen as powerless, in cahoots with or at least siding with those they are regulating, overly constrained by their remits, and biased towards the status quo.

The Lancaster team discovered that the public was fantastically hostile to the nuclear privatizers, as the 'strongest expressions of mistrust came in relation to contractors, who were seen as fundamentally compromised by their necessity to prioritise profits. This brought them in direct conflict with the strongly articulated position that safety should be prioritised over costs.' The team also received submissions from whistleblowers, including what was described as 'a detailed report from an ex-subcontractor of Babcock Rosyth Defence Limited' indicating that 'they were not suitable for this work'. The report also noted that DML, the Devonport contractors undertaking work on the submarines, and owned by Brown and Root Ltd, 'were not seen as having a good reputation for being environmentally and socially responsible'.

Recommendation 3 of the report was that 'appropriate bodies should be informed of the strength of feeling against building further nuclear powered submarines, especially in relation to the absence of a final disposal route for the radioactive wastes'. Responding to the report, Defence Minister Moonie demonstrated his open style of government by concluding that private firms would continue to handle the waste, that nuclear submarines would still be built, and that planned land-based nuclear storage would be announced next year. Moonie did delay the onshore dismantling of HMS Renown at Rosyth, but stated, 'I have no reason to suppose that the company will not be granted the necessary approvals' in good time. In short, the public had been consulted on nuclear submarine scrap storage, only to be thoroughly ignored.

In 2004 the campaign found a new and surprising supporter in Michael Meacher, the environment minister who initially authorized the increase in discharges. After leaving office, Meacher told a Plymouth public meeting that he felt 'deeply suspicious' of the evidence he had been given that the nuclear discharges were safe. The European Commission is also prosecuting the British government over the tritium releases, charging that they breach the 'Euratom' treaty against nuclear pollution. The British government says that, as a military site, Devonport is immune from the treaty. Putting private firms in charge of Britain's legacy of nuclear military waste kept the problem at arms length from the government, but it merely masked the problem of what to do with Britain's persistent but unwanted legacy of military nuclear waste. In 2004 the HSE reported that Halliburton's plans to get rid of one type of atomic goo were lost in a maze of subcontracting that made no sense.

The HSE's 27 May 2003 report into the Devonport nuclear dockyards received no press coverage at all – which is a shame, because the report actually shows that the Halliburton-run nuclear docks has churned out more and more radioactive gunk with fewer and fewer places for it to go. The dockyard decommissions Britain's nuclear submarine fleet, producing 'ion exchange resins' in the process. These take the form of radioactive slime left over after water treatment of the submarines. As 'intermediate level nuclear waste', they need careful disposal. Halliburton's strategy is to leave them for thirty years, until they decay into a less dangerous state, and then have them buried. Halliburton subcontracts responsibility for this radioactive waste to AEA Technology, which treats it at a 'ModulOx' plant at Winfrith, near Dorchester. But this plant is just a pilot. As the HSE point out, 'the strategy described above relies on AEA Technology's resin treatment facilities being available for a number of decades'. But the plant represents a small pilot scheme, and the Winfrith site is supposed to be cleaned up in twenty years.

The HSE is concerned that the plan 'does not appear to be consistent with the decommissioning strategy for the Winfrith site'. It also points out that levels of carbon-14 in the resins is higher than expected. The ModulOx plant, requiring a licence from the Environment Agency, drives off this controlled substance. Halliburton is working on the assumption that an increased carbon-14 disposal authorisation will be granted', leading to the warning of 'significant risks associated with Devonport's proposed strategy for resin wastes due to the apparent mismatch with the current decommissioning strategy for the Winfrith site and to the assumption that an increased carbon-14 disposal authorisation will be granted.

The nuclear inspectors and Environment Agency believe that 'Devonport needs to resolve this matter without delay, including consideration of contingency options if appropriate, to avoid unnecessary storage of waste in a non-passively safe form'. Of course, Halliburton could just ignore these warnings, safe in the assumption that the government would have to grant the licences and let the bigger ModulOx plant be built – or yet more waste would be left lying around with nowhere else to go.

In 2000, Halliburton suffered a rare setback in its expansion into Britain's military business. In 1990, Mrs Thatcher's government had handed over the management of Aldermaston to a group of private contractors. Aldermaston was both the home of Britain's nuclear deterrent and the birthplace of Britain's anti-nuclear movement: Lord Penney had brought together the team of scientists who built Britain's A- and H-bombs at the Berkshire base on 1 April 1950. Marches to the Aldermaston base in the late 1950s became the focus for building the Campaign for Nuclear Disarmament. Fears of nuclear destruction motivated the anti-Aldermaston marchers, while fears of Soviet ambition kept the base alive, as Britain's ongoing commitment to 'mutually assured destruction' kept the complex in business. This in turn created opportunities for private business. Just one month before Thatcher left office, her government announced that a consortium called Hunting-BRAE would run the Aldermaston base.

Hunting, like Halliburton, was a firm that worked for the oil industry and the military – it worked on oil pipelines and owned tankers, while a subsidiary made cluster-bombs. The 'BR' in Hunting-BRAE came from Brown & Root, one of Halliburton's leading subsidiaries, which was also part of the consortium. Like Halliburton, Hunting was a donor to the Conservative Party. In 1994 Hunting Engineering – its bomb-making subsidiary – was also a client of a lobbying firm Decision Makers Ltd, of which leading Tory MP Dame Angela Rumbold was an executive director. It was a promising start, but in 2000 the government announced that Hunting–BRAE would not be asked to re-tender for the contract: the government had ignored warnings from Greenpeace when they were given the Aldermaston contract. The environmental campaigners' argument that Halliburton's poor record meant they should not be trusted with Britain's atom bomb factory fell on deaf ears. In 2000, however, Halliburton and Hunting were kicked out of Aldermaston, as even the MoD could face no more leaks or failures.

In 1994 the director-general of the HSE, John Rimington, announced that if Aldermaston were covered by the same rules as a civil nuclear station, it would not receive a licence and would be closed down. As an example of the plant's weak procedures, Rimington highlighted a 1992 incident when a 'billet' of plutonium decayed into a fine powder, contaminating workers in a store area. The workers did not wear protective suits because it had not occurred to management that such a thing could happen. Hunting–BRAE had been running the plant since 1990 under a pilot for the plant's privatization, and in 1994 had won the official contract. But Rimington did not blame the contractors for the safety lapses he described at the plant. He said that weak safety management stemmed from decades of poor management carried out when the plant had operated under a shroud of Cold War secrecy. The HSE review was seen as a 'benchmark' for Hunting–BRAE. Sadly, the new consortium rapidly slid below this benchmark. In 1998, Hunting–BRAE was fined £22,000 for contaminating two workers with plutonium: the men were observing the cleaning of 'glove boxes', but without safety suits.

The following year the Environment Agency fined Hunting–BRAE when they released tritiated groundwater into a local brook. An Aldermaston worker tipped off the Environment Agency about the firm's regular dumping into one of the tributaries of the Thames. The firm had not asked for a licence for the river discharges, but had set its own arbitrary limit for the amount of tritium to be dumped – a limit which the Environment Agency said had no scientific basis – and then started exceeding that same limit. Outside the official record, a leaked report revealed 100 unreported safety lapses in 1998. The same document included details of a 1993 incident when uranium shavings from a lathe came close to 'criticality' – the point at which they could cause an explosion.[9] Other incidents and problems included a series of fires, a month during which all the firefighting pumps were unfit for service, and eight examples of environmental contamination outside the plant in 1998.

However, while Hunting-BRAE lost the contract, the government did not lose enthusiasm for privatization. A new consortium made up of US arms giant Lockheed, Serco – a specialist in prisons and military privatization – and British Nuclear Fuels Ltd took over the management of the base. Local MP Martin Salter was a long-term critic of Aldermaston's pollution record. Salter argued that it was 'naive' to think safety had got worse when the privatization began – he did not think the performance of the contractors was worse than the years of secret MoD operations at the site. But Salter was sufficiently worried about the quality of the new management company to raise a debate in parliament.

Hunting-BRAE was central to the next advance of the privatization army. The contractors used the bases as a first step in their march to privatize the battlefield itself. The company's next base was to be built much closer to the battlefield, in the Kosovo conflict. Military action against Serbian forces in Kosovo was promoted positively, as a humanitarian intervention to defend a minority under assault from Serbian-backed forces. But there was an element of the later politics of insecurity in the Kosovo conflict, in the depiction of Milosevic as the leader of a 'rogue state' – an unpredictable and dangerous destabilizing threat to the Nato countries. In July 1999 the MoD awarded a £110 million contract to build 'semi-permanent' bases for 5,000 troops in Kosovo to a group called The Hiberna consortium 'made up of Hunting-BRAE, WS Atkins, John Mowlem and MACE shipping'. This Kosovo contract was modelled on LogCap, a US army deal with Halliburton. Under LogCap, Halliburton built Camp Bondsteel in Kosovo. LogCap and Halliburton's subsequent army base building in Iraq were criticized for 'feather-bedding'.

Under their 'cost plus' contract, Halliburton made money by excessive work: they cleaned officers' rooms more than twice a day, and drove around convoys of empty trucks – a practice drivers referred to as 'shipping sailboat fuel'. Halliburton also simply overcharged, asking $100 for a bag of laundry. But the Hiberna consortium did not follow the US example, finding instead their own, more typically British way of making money. Instead of excess, the British contractors decided on parsimony. The supposed winter base for British soldiers was not built in time. The consortium blamed this on 'bad weather conditions', as if this was an unexpected problem in winter. So American troops in Kosovo lived in overpriced luxury, in heated tents with attached burger bars, while British squaddies shivered in cold comfort in their tents, waiting for the contractors to build their huts.

Hunting-BRAE's work housing British squaddies in Kosovo contained a grim irony. The company made cluster bombs – munitions which, when fired, shoot out many small 'bomblets', many of which do not explode on impact. The unexploded 'bomblets' become, in effect, landmines. Anti-landmine groups argued that cluster bombs should therefore be banned alongside other landmines. Many civilians, including children, fell victim to the bomblets that lay dormant after fighting ceased. As it turned out, some of the few casualties among British troops were also caused by unexploded bomblets from a cluster munition – two Ghurkhas were killed in this way in June 1999. So the firm that housed British soldiers also killed them. Finally, in 2003, the running of the Kosovo camp finally passed to another contractor, the Anglo-American DynCorp. DynCorp already had experience in the Balkans. As we shall see, the firm ran a private police force in the region, whose officers became embroiled in a scandal over the trafficking of prostitutes.

None of the military base privatizations of the 1990s look like glorious successes. Indeed, many of them are marked by embarrassing failure: squalid soldiers' houses at home; winter quarters unbuilt because of bad weather abroad. Add polluting nuclear facilities, fines, and legal wrangling, and a picture of failing policy starts to develop. However, these unappealing advertisements for military privatization did not stop the process. Indeed, the election of a 'New' Labour government saw a rapid increase in the shift of military affairs into the commercial arena. The Labour Party elected in 1997 rapidly abandoned its social-democratic impulses, let alone any residual socialism, but it did not lose the urge to 'reform' or 'modernize'.

Emptied of its socialist content, 'reform' came to mean increases in commercialization and competition, rather the regulation of them. The arrival of an enthusiastic but decidedly un-socialist New Labour government gave a second wind to the privatization plans that were in fact being toned down by its weary Tory predecessor. Labour ministers who had once been part of the 'peace movement' threw away their CND cards and committed themselves to new military adventures. But their lack of a traditional, right-wing 'patriotic' political past paradoxically meant that they felt more able to break with military traditions and speed up the privatization of the armed forces, at the same time as sending those forces into battle with alarming frequency.

3

Projecting Power

The end of the Cold War sent a shiver of fear through the boardrooms of the big defence contractors. Weapons makers really believed that arms sales would fall as peace broke out – but they worried unnecessarily. The peace dividend shrank: conflicts buried under the ice of the Cold War thawed into very hot battles. At the same time, the US and her allies, no longer burdened by serious opponents on the world stage, were drawn to new ventures in far-off lands. 'Projecting power' became the new slogan, meaning that the military must develop the equipment for expeditionary forces, rather than relying on the kind of kit designed for an army facing Russian troops across the European plain. Military thinkers began worrying about 'asymmetric warfare'. During the Cold War, there was a nice symmetry between Nato and the Warsaw Pact, which was predictable and easy to comprehend – ICBM matched ICBM, and tank division faced tank division. But the army intelligentsia feared their smaller and weaker enemies: 'terrorists' and 'rogue states' were unpredictable; the enemy was sometimes hard to identify. Power projection was seen as the key to winning an 'asymmetric war'; the victorious Goliath needed to be able to reach out and destroy the new generation of Davids. This military doctrine crystallized and expanded when al-Qaeda blew its way into the headlines in 2001. With Islamist terrorists reaching into the heart of the Western world and killing thousands, there was now an urgent need to develop the ability to reach out directly with precision and force into areas of the world previously considered marginal.

The new privatization and the new desire to project power in the war on terror went hand in hand, became ever more intimately linked. Private companies helped to plan, build and man the new expeditionary forces for the new gunboat diplomacy. Using their foothold in the military bases that they now controlled, executives from the military-industrial complex set out to occupy the battlefield itself. The new Labour government reinvigorated the Conservative Party's privatization drive, rather than rejecting it. In particular, Labour resuscitated an ailing Tory policy known as the Private Finance Initiative (PFI). Under this scheme, the government would sell schools or hospitals to private contractors and then lease them back, with the commercial consortia supplying both the building and staff formerly controlled by the state. The PFI and public–private partnerships in health, education and on the London Underground all attracted great controversy – but huge military PFIs were commissioned with little public comment outside the business pages.

Plans for British military privatization were made at a meeting of British and American politicians, officials, soldiers and businessmen in Oxfordshire in 2000. The meeting was chaired by future US Vice President Dick Cheney. Nine months later, Cheney's old firm won a contract to provide 'sponsored reserves' – British soldiers who were employees of a US multinational. The 'Joint US–UK Conference on Privatising Military Installations, Assets, Operations and Services' ran over two days in April 2000 at Ditchley Park, an ultra-establishment conference centre that provides the ruling class with the space to think in private. The conference was jointly chaired. Dick Cheney, who was then chairman and chief executive of Halliburton, and the managers of the Devonport submarine base shared duties with Field Marshal Lord Vincent, a former chief of defence staff who was then chairman of Hunting plc, the firm building – or failing to build – barracks for British troops in Kosovo. Other veterans of base privatizations were present. Ian Andrews, chief executive of the Defence Estates Agency, and John Wilson of the Defence Housing Executive represented the civil service in the miserable privatization of soldiers housing (see Chapter 2).

One of the UK's top military contractors, Serco, was well represented at the conference. Steve Cuthill, the managing director of Serco Defence, and retired Major General Malcolm Hutchinson, who managed Aldermaston for Serco, were both in attendance. A Serco-Lockheed consortium took over the Aldermaston atomic base from Lord Vincent's Hunting. The official inspection of their management of Aldermaston showed that systems had improved when they took over, although the firm's ability to learn safety lessons was 'limited in effectiveness' and they had 'yet to develop fully satisfactory arrangements' to make sure staff 'who carry out safety related activities are suitably qualified and experienced'. Serco also managed other facilities, including Fylingdales (the early-warning base on the Yorkshire moors), and a military college.

British attendees at the conference also included the men who could give the firms more participation in future combat zones. John Spellar, then an armed forces minister, came along with a host of MoD top brass, including Peter Ryan, the Director of the MoD's 'Public–Private Partnership Unit'; Colin Balmer, the MoD's Principal Finance Officer; and Alistair Bell, the director of the Defence Logistics Organization. The conference was organized by the semi-official US military think-tank, the RAND Corporation.

According to the conference summary, both the US Department of Defense and UK MoD 'are increasingly interested in leveraging private sector capital and expertise to provide defense activities'. The meeting ended with an 'action plan' to increase military privatization. Martin Kitterick, a partner of accountants PriceWaterhouseCoopers, which advises the MoD on military sell-offs, told the conference about two schemes – the Heavy Equipment Transporter Project and Future Strategic Tanker Aircraft Programme – that were 'pushing back the boundaries of the Private Finance Initiative and raising difficult issues for the MoD'. In January 2001 the £300 million Equipment Transporter contract was awarded to Brown & Root, a subsidiary of Dick Cheney's Halliburton. Brown & Root also bid for the Future Strategic Tanker deal, although they later withdrew from the competition. Cheney resigned as chief executive of Halliburton in August 2000, to be George W. Bush's vice presidential candidate. Retired US Navy Admiral Joseph Lopez, a Brown & Root chief operating officer, accompanied Cheney to the conference.

The 'difficult issues' noted by Kitterick were raised by the sponsored reserves scheme, according to which soldiers are recruited by, and become employees of, private companies. In the heavy equipment transporter scheme, drivers of special tank transporting lorries become employees of Halliburton. But since they might have to transport tanks into battle zones, the drivers are also members of the army reserve: should they be caught in a battle, they would be transformed from drivers working for a US multinational to British soldiers. The private firm is contracted to supply the army not only with driving services, but with a set number of physically fit army reserves, although they will be under military command during actual fighting. Halliburton's tank transporters scheme came on stream after the 2003 invasion of Iraq. The scheme drew some embarrassing press when one of the tank transporters was first put on show for defence correspondents. The 'all terrain' vehicle flipped on its side while trying to make a turn in a supermarket car park. After this incident, the heavy equipment transporters fell below the Fleet Street radar. While there was widespread criticism of the way the vice president's old firm had won lucrative contracts in Iraq for the US government, the fact that British soldiers hired by Halliburton were driving around tanks at a tidy profit for the firm went unnoticed.

Halliburton's tank transporters went into service for the British army in November 2003, sending sixteen of the heavy trucks into Iraq with No. 3 Tank Squadron. The MoD decided that all of Iraq represented a 'theatre of operation', and so sent the Halliburton-hired sponsored reserves into the Middle East wearing army uniforms, carrying weapons, and 'under military control, military law and subject to military discipline'. This did not disguise the fact that some of Britain's newest soldiers were hired, and at least partly trained, by a US multinational. The 'sponsored reserves' concept in the end probably only mobilized a few hundred armed men – but it acted as an important bridge in military doctrine. In 2000 British ministers and a future US vice president agreed to a scheme that would put soldiers employed by private companies on the battlefield. This concept turned a supplier of equipment into a supplier of soldiers; it normalized the idea of using commercial gunmen. This provided a policy bridge to the much more widespread use of mercenaries in Iraq and Afghanistan. When the beginnings of the war on terror raised the military temperature to boiling point, the idea of commercial soldiering was already in the pot, thanks to the sponsored reserves scheme.

The Oxford conference participants agreed that 'concepts such as sponsored reserves in the UK and technical representatives in the US also blur the line between military and contractor'. But the top British and US politicians, soldiers and businessmen did not worry that battlefield privatization was introducing commercial conflicts of interest into war, or even creating new mercenaries. Instead, the conference participants were simply unable to decide where business should end and army begin. The conference report stated,

Each of the three working groups attempted to define military core competencies that should be excluded from privatization. However, each of the three groups had difficulty drawing a clear dividing line between the activities that must be performed by military personnel and those that could be performed by civilian or contractor personnel.

PriceWaterhouseCoopers consultant and MoD adviser Martin McKitterick argued that privatization and the new kinds of warfare were intimately linked. He said that the 'changing shape and scale of conflicts under its peace-keeping role' was a 'driver for change' and that 'involving the private sector is often a component for implementing such change'. The planners believed that innovative, profit-driven firms would be better at changing the shape of the battlefield than hidebound senior officers. When the US-led military actions in Afghanistan and Iraq were launched, US Defense Secretary Donald Rumsfeld was committed to breaking radically with military doctrines, and proposing much greater use of lighter, faster and more flexible troops. He wanted to break with older concepts of 'overwhelming force' and massive Cold War-style set pieces. The participants in the RAND conference thought the private military contractors could be used to break the resistance of hidebound army officers to new military doctrines, and to shake up rigid bureaucracies at the Pentagon and in Whitehall. Using the private military companies would allow the political leadership to shake up the army command and shake off their attachment to old ideas like the need for 'overwhelming force'. Introducing a commercial element into the process would help shift the military to new ideas of faster and lighter warfare. The new doctrine of lighter, quicker war in turn made war more likely. In this way the use of the private military companies helped bring the politician's dream wars closer to reality.

While the US has had some notable privatizations close to what conference attendees called 'the bullet line', they were generally jealous of Britain's overall lead in military sell-offs. Dick Cheney told the Oxford gathering, 'My general impression is that our British colleagues are far ahead of us in the US in the extent to which they have adopted changes in culture, attitude and style of operation that are required for successful privatization efforts.' Cheney had personal reasons for holding this view: he made clear to the conference that a large portion of his company's military business at the time was the 'ownership and operation of the

Devonport Dockyard in the UK'. But all were agreed that Britain really was in the lead over privatization. Martin Kitterick confirmed that most of the MoD 'has been very progressive in its attitude toward involving the private sector in its activities' and that their 'track record is impressive'.

Lord Vincent of Hunting PLC pointed out that Thatcherism was one of the main reasons for the UK's lead in privatizing the army. He argued that since recruits were now expensive to train, the pressure was on to find cheaper alternatives, but that 'when Margaret Thatcher began her energetic drive for privatization, it began to open our eyes to some of the opportunities that were available'. Labour built on Thatcher's enthusiasm for military privatization. When US representative Mahlon Apgar thanked all those who had helped arrange the conference, he acknowledged that 'in many ways most important of all' were 'our British colleagues at the Ministry of Defence, especially Mr John Spellar, Mr Roger Jackling and Mr Peter Ryan, who enthusiastically supported the project'. Spellar was the Labour defence minister at the time, and Ryan was the head of the army's 'public–private partnership' unit, while Jackling was the MoD's second permanent under-secretary.

One of the main arguments at the conference was that the army would to get into bed with business in order to get privatization off the ground, since too much attention to the rules would stymie the process. One conference participant explained the way the private sector drove British policy:

> We must rewrite the rules. The UK did this by setting up a task force with two teams: a policy team of a dozen civil servants, backed by external consultants; and a projects team headed by a creative financier and staffed by a dozen 'best in class' private sector professionals. They not only rewrote policy and guidelines for public–private partnerships but championed the 'change management' programme in the MoD and throughout the government.

Financiers and consultants became the army's new special forces – commercial commandos who could breach the defences of the MoD. Contracts became the military's new secret weapons. Ignoring the rules became UK policy, as 'the UK MoD adopted the slogan "deals not rules" to encourage cultural change'. Apgar argued that, in the US, what he called 'excessive interest' was taken in privatization by legislators, and that

'Congressional hearings' were a 'high-powered microscope' revealing problems like 'the $700 hammer and the $3,000 telephone', thereby killing off privatization. The conference believed that its task was no less than 'organising a new military–industrial structure'. This involved a variety of cosy, non-competitive practices like 'longer-term contracts', 'not setting all prices in advance', and 'emphasis shifting to selection of partner rather than selection of bid'.[1]

The conference ended with a pledge to take the 'next steps'. These included a resolution to make permanent links between US and British business and military interests, to 'establish a permanent, ongoing forum, such as this Conference for continued US–UK exchanges'. The Oxford gathering also decided that the private sector should make policy, as the participants developed 'a strategic vision for the military's privatization efforts, with the assistance of private sector experts'.

There were two additional project schemes involving sponsored reserves: the water-borne strategic sealift scheme and the airborne future strategic tanker scheme. Heavy equipment transporters drove the army's tanks onto the battlefield, while strategic sealifts were used to sail tanks and troops onto the beaches of foreign interventions. The PFI deal aimed to provide six roll-on-roll-off ships, so that the Joint Rapid Reaction forces could roll rapidly onto a foreign shore. Private contractors were offered £950 million in a twenty-five-year contract to have these ships ready. They could be sailed commercially, delivering cargo around the world until the army needed them for a 'major operation'. Then the craft had to be ready to carry twenty-five Challenger tanks, twenty-four warrior armoured cars, and an extra cargo of "Braveheart" self-propelled guns. The private shipping firms would provide officers and crew, who would be transformed into active-duty sailors when the ships sailed into combat.

The blurred lines between contractors and sailors began worrying at least one Labour MP, Stephen Hepburn, as well as the seafarers' union NUMAST. The companies who won the sealift contract, known as the AWSR consortium, originally planned to use cheaper foreign crews, relying heavily on Filipino sailors, who could be paid lower rates than British seamen, when the ships were on civilian missions. More expensive British crews would only be mustered when the war became imminent. But after vigorous prodding by Hepburn and others, the MoD altered the contract so that the ships would always have British crews, on either civil or military sailings. However, campaigners for British shipping were disappointed by the contract: SS Anvil and her sister ship were built in Belfast's Harland & Wolff shipyard, but the other four craft were made by Flensburger Schiffbau-Gesellschaft, near Hamburg.[2]

The strategic sealift ships went into operation in time for the Iraq war. From summer 2003 the private fleet landed the British mechanized troops who would invade Iraq into the Gulf. Appropriately, the AWSR consortium included James Fisher Shipping, which is a 'shipping partner of choice for many of the world's oil majors'.[3]

The future strategic tanker project involved Britain's most important warplanes. The tankers comprise a distinctly unglamorous and almost unreported airborne refuelling fleet that was in fact crucial to the conflicts in Kosovo, Afghanistan and Iraq. The proposed privatization of the planes showed that the new military contractors wanted to run services right in the heat of the battle. The still ongoing attempt to commercialize these warplanes showed that the Ministry of Defence was at least as comfortable with business school jargon as the language of military command, and that their ministers were happier at a sales conference and crass industry sponsored 'entertainments' than they were visiting troops on the battle-field.

The existing airborne refuellers do not look much like warplanes, because they are adapted models of civilian airliners. The RAF has nineteen VC10s and nine Tri-Stars. The VC10 was originally a civil airliner, flying BOAC passengers to Australia and the West Indies in the 1960s.

In 1978, however, the RAF decided that it needed aircraft that could refuel their Tornado jet fighters in mid-air, giving the planes a longer reach. The air force made do by refitting second-hand commercial passenger aircraft called VC10s – some from the bankrupt East African Airways, some from Gulf Air, and some retired from British Airways. Other second-hand craft were cannibalized for scrap to keep the VC10s that still functioned in the air. The passenger seats of the former airliners were ripped out and replaced with fuel tanks, while a special hose was fitted into the cargo area at the back. This hose would extend during flight between the VC10 and Tornado jet, and pump the fuel between the two airborne craft. The Lockheed Tristars were also civilian aircraft, bought second-hand from British Airways and converted into airborne petrol stations. The VC10s and Tristars began flying for the RAF's 101

Squadron in 1982 and 1985, respectively: some of the most important planes in the RAF's hangars were very old passenger airliners, bought second-hand from bankrupt airlines and kept in the air with scavenged parts from the scrapheap. Yet these unglamorous looking, slow moving old craft were what kept the sleek military jets in the air.

Compared to glamorous new craft like the Eurofighter, the tankers looked old and distinctly unsuited to modern warfare; but they became very important as the theatre of war moved to a new location with new scenery and new actors. The Cold War script for air fighting never got beyond a rehearsal: there were no dogfights between Nato and Warsaw Pact jet fighters, and there was no need for Western jet aircraft to intercept incoming Soviet bombers. Instead, the air forces were used largely to attack often poorly armed ground troops and militias. Consequently, the refuelling planes, which allowed the jets to project their power, became more important. By refuelling craft in mid-air, they allowed Britain and the US to attack far-off lands without the need for local – and politically sensitive – airbases. US warplanes could reach Afghanistan or Iraq from Diego Garcia with the help of refuelling craft. While the governments of closer countries might have political objections to acting as the launch-pads for these interventions, the residents of Diego Garcia had been bundled off the island between 1967 and 1973, and were therefore in no position to object. The tanker planes were a 'force multiplier', able to 'extend the range of fighters and bombers'. The refuelling craft took Tornados from Germany to bomb Kosovo in 1999. After acquitting themselves well in the first 'liberal intervention', they became a key tool in the war on terror. They flew intensively for three months in 2001, and kept US navy and marine aircraft refuelled to attack Afghanistan. They then helped British and American craft attack Iraq in 2003. So while the Eurofighter – an enormously expensive flying white elephant designed to do battle with planes form the now defunct Warsaw pact – continued sucking up military budgets, the MoD realised that the tanker fleet also needed attention. The tanker planes had to be renewed, which in the new military landscape meant that they had to be privatized in a multimillion-pound PFI deal. Two consortia bid for the contract: one based on EADS, the European firm behind the Airbus; and one centred on US plane giant Boeing.

The £13 billion privatization of the refuelling aircraft inevitably involved the sponsored conferences and junkets that mark this military contractorization. In November 2003 the war on terror was at its bloody height. Afghanistan had been bombed; Iraq had been invaded and occupied. British and American troops were involved in regular firefights with their enemies. This turned out to be one of the bloodiest months for allied troops since the invasion: over 100 were killed, as were uncounted Iraqis, as the post-war insurgency began to take shape. British soldiers were also busy driving their ageing 'Green Goddess' tenders around Britain to break a strike by firefighters. But Armed Forces Minister Adam Ingram still had time to slip away to Brussels for a conference on military Private Finance Initiatives. While his soldiers were risking their lives in foreign wars or being drawn into British industrial relations, the Armed Forces Minister thought his time was best spent at a conference on military privatization. The event was driven by money and marked by tawdry luxuries. Delegates from companies who wanted to wind military contracts paid £3,504 per head to mingle with MoD officials at events including 'Champagne Brainstorming Roundtables' and a 'Belgian Beer tasting evening'. The Minister took seven top MoD officials to the conference,[4] including Dr Richard Williams, head of the PPP unit; Brian Dewdney, head of the Pubic–Private Partnering Group at the MoD's logistics organization; and Simon Kershaw, an MoD official working on the future strategic tanker scheme to privatize the refuelling warplanes.[5]

At the height of the 'war on terror', military officials and politicians took a light-hearted look at their weapons. Kershaw's PowerPoint presentation slides about the future strategic tanker aircraft project were boyishly enthusiastic. He said the scheme had 'the Spice Girls factor'. Illustrating his point with a picture of the pop group, and quoting their breakthrough hit, Kershaw claimed that the privatization could provide 'what you really really want'[6] to the RAF. Potential bidders for army privatization contracts were told that Dewdney would 'answer the key question – Which services will be selected for PPP/PFI projects in UK military logistics'. Serco, which had been one of the bidders for the future strategic tanker project, sponsored the event. Executives from companies bidding to run the refuelling aircraft, including Serco and Boeing, were joined by other military privatizers, including Halliburton's Peter Smart, and Sir John Stokoe, a former major general now supplementing his military pension with a job as a director for Amey plc, a firm specializing in the Private Finance Initiatives.

The organizers obviously felt their conference was a success because they ran the event again in 2004. Yet again, the British Minister and his officials found relief from the pressures of running troubled military interventions in Iraq and Afghanistan by immersing themselves in the tacky glamour of a sales conference paid for by military privatizers. The 2004 conference was in Berlin. Serco sponsored the conference again. Adam Ingram, the MoD's Brian Dewdney and eight of his fellow senior officials working on British military privatization came along to enjoy mixing with privatizers at cheesy corporate entertainments like a 'Berlin-Themed Cabaret Cocktail Reception'. This event was sponsored by EADS, one of the bidders for the contract to run the RAF's tanker plane, who promised: 'This fun-filled themed evening will explore Berlin's vibrancy and diversity to the full, encompassing everything from the glamour of Marlene Dietrich to the rise and fall of the Berlin Wall.' While British politicians would lash out at any critics who failed to take their arguments about the battle against terrorism seriously, they were prepared to let their own hair down while inspecting the weapons of that battle.

Decadent cabaret and champagne brainstorming between the military and private executives may have seemed seedy, but Dr Timothy Stone of accountants KPMG - the MoD's top adviser for the tanker deal – saw a more serious potential conflict. Under the tanker PFI, the private consortia would own the planes and lease them to the RAF. They would also provide some of the ground crew and possible air crew. They would include 'sponsored reserves' – private staff who could convert to RAF officers during hostilities. The RAF was unenthusiastic about sponsored reserves, but accepted their involvement at the insistence of Gordon Brown's Treasury, who thought the new privately funded soldiers were an exciting innovation. Stone explained that the warplanes would be run 'like Hertz & Avis'. Dr Stone's presentation makes clear that Ministry of Defence officials talked about war in the strangled language of management consultancy, sales conferences and business schools. The original plan was that the planes should be used for civilian charters, and then rapidly converted to refuelling tankers when war called. In this way they RAF could cut costs, because there would be 'third party revenue'. All the RAF needed to do was realize that 'refuelling is a service not an airframe'.[7] In the new military service economy, the armed forces did not need to own their planes when the work could go out to contractors. Dr Stone noted that there were possible problems. Firstly, his PowerPoint presentation said the 'Military need to go to war at short notice' but 'civilians like long contracts'.

Instead of prioritizing the military's needs, Dr Stone seemed to suggest that the army should compromise and try and fit in with the needs of the contractors. Secondly, there were 'restrictions on usage' of the planes. Dr Stone, whose presentation predates the Iraq war, told his audience that this included 'e.g. not flying to Iraq on civilian operation'. The MoD's chief adviser could see the ensuing embarrassment if the planes needed to bomb Iraq were busy at Baghdad airport delivering supplies for Saddam's regime.

The scheme soon became involved in a third conflict that had not been envisaged by Dr Stone: Boeing flew into a corruption scandal in the US that infected their British bid. Boeing was also tendering for a £17 billion scheme to lease military tanker aircraft to the US air force. The government claimed that there was no relation between the US Boeing tanker scheme and the British bid. But President Bush thought the schemes were intertwined. When Bush visited Britain, he reportedly lobbied the prime minister to give the tanker PFI to Boeing. Bush was backing Boeing in the US, and having 'compatible' planes for the two refuelling fleets would be a military advantage, as well as reaping huge rewards for a US firm.

The US scheme came under fire in 2003, when senators realized that Boeing's scheme to lease 100 refuelling tankers to the US air force would cost up to 40 per cent more than simply buying the planes. Even supporters of the scheme recognized it as a subsidy to Boeing. Norm Dicks, the Member of Congress for Washington State, home of Boeing, wrote to George Bush arguing that the lease of the firm's 767s for the refuelling fleet should be part of the 'economic stimulus package' to compensate for 'the loss of work at Boeing' following 9/11.[8] Senators argued down the price by arranging to buy most of the planes, leasing only a few. In the US, politicians debated whether to buy or lease the refuelling craft. In Britain, PFI was the only game in town, and the only debate concerned which of the two consortia should supply the planes.

After the cost problems came the corruption. Darleen Druyun, an American military official who had worked on the US tanker deal, took a job with Boeing. She apparently gave Boeing figures from the rival bid to supply tankers from European arms firm EADS – figures she picked up while working for the military. When the scandal broke, Druyun was sacked along with the firm's chief financial officer Mike Sears. It then emerged that Boeing had invested millions in Trireme, a fund led by Richard Perle, a key presidential adviser and influential hawk who sat on the US Defence Policy Board. Perle in turn had used his influential position to lobby in favour of Boeing's contract.[9] Boeing also invested millions in Paladin Capital, a firm run by former CIA boss James Woolsey, another Defence Policy Board member, although Woolsey denied actively promoting Boeing's deal. Some of the people caught up in the US scandal were also familiar faces in the UK. Boeing's Phil Condit and Jim Albaugh directly lobbied trade minister Patricia Hewitt in favour of Boeing winning the British tanker plane deal. Jim Albaugh had also personally contacted then-defence minister Geoff Hoon to recommend Boeing's tankers for the RAF. Condit has since resigned. Albaugh was also involved in the lobbying in favour of Boeing's US deal. Boeing's vice president, David Spong, also appeared to be involved in both deals.[10]

The UK spokesman for Boeing's consortium told me that the firm's difficulties were 'just a hiccup at the moment' for their PFI scheme, and that 'companies have their experiences, just like families'. But the bad experience became a permanent separation when Boeing was knocked out of the UK competition. Losing Boeing left just one bidder for the scheme. Without the leverage of competition, the RAF had difficulty controlling costs, and the contract remains unresolved. The supposedly dynamic solution of privatization left the RAF stuck with the same ageing planes waiting to fly to the next war.

In the US, the scandal blew up because of the perception of a 'revolving door' between the government and arms firms. While there is no evidence of impropriety in the UK, there was certainly movement between the RAF and the contractors. Keith Archer-Jones was the managing director of the Boeing bid. Until 1999 he had been an RAF group captain (equivalent to an army colonel) in charge of the existing fleet of ageing VC10 refuelling planes, and with responsibilities for 'smart procurement'. I asked TTSC if Archer-Jones's position meant that the contractors were just selling back to the RAF something they already had. Their spokesperson said that Archer-Jones's RAF background meant that he 'knows what he is doing', and that the consortia 'had to hire people with relevant experience, because commercial staff don't have relevant experience'. No doubt serving RAF staff also have the relevant experience, but under the scheme they will be replaced with private contractors. I asked Airtanker, the rival consortium,[11] about their ex-services staff: the firm apparently have just 'a couple of squadron leaders' on the books.

The privatized 'power-projecting' missions brought companies right onto the battlefield. The contractors assured governments that they could summon up the necessary military transport to launch expeditionary missions just by signing contracts: leasing military transport boats, trucks and aeroplanes with commercially provided crews promised governments the ability to invade far-off lands without the need to buy expensive vehicles, or train and maintain extra military staff. These schemes promised that a lighter, leaner military would also have a longer military reach, which is precisely the message that ministers who wanted to commit to an aggressive 'war on terror' wanted to hear. In fact the companies made enormous profits, but delivered schemes with variable rates of success. By the time this had become clear, however, the wars in Iraq and Afghanistan were already underway.

4

Nation-Building the DynCorp Way

'Nation-building' became one of the central themes of the war on terror. For fifty years after World War II, politicians used the phrase 'nation-building' to describe the way those countries in the developing world that had freed themselves from their colonial masters set about creating their own national institutions and traditions. This definition of the phrase was still common in the mid 1990s, but with the end of the Cold War a new meaning soon occupied the phrase: 'nation-building' soon came to mean the developed world imposing political and social forms on those parts of the globe judged to have failed in their development. From the 1990s onwards, the debate about nation-building centred on how far the most powerful nations should intervene in, and directly shape, affairs inside other sovereign states. Enthusiasts for US nation-building, like Frances Fukuyama, argued that 'failed' states would become the breeding grounds for all kinds of monsters that would then attack the West. Fukuyama wrote that 'The chief threats to us and to world order come today from weak, collapsed, or failed states. Weak or absent government institutions in developing countries form the thread linking terrorism, refugees, AIDS, and global poverty.'[1] In Fukuyama's widely accepted model, the greatest danger to the US state came from their rivals' weakness, not their strength.

During the Cold War, the West faced the powerful Soviet and Chinese blocs, and could negotiate some form of armed standoff with these dangerous, but generally predictable and rational enemies. Peripheral countries had often been backed by one or other of the Cold War powers, who pumped money and other support into these marginal nations in order to gain territorial advantage. The end of the Cold War and emergence of one victor meant the rivalry was gone, and so these taps were turned off: the support for weak countries ended. Losing the financial, military and political support of one or other of the rival superpowers was too much for some of the weaker states, and in some cases their governments and political structures collapsed. US military think-tank the RAND Corporation has said that the Cold War's end led to a 'rash of state failures'.[2] This disfiguring condition required a liberal application of the soothing lotion of military intervention. A whole new set of dangers lurked, growing inside those countries where central government was collapsing. Enthusiasts for nation-building saw disease, warlords, drug barons and terrorists finding purchase in the collapsing countries. The failed states were acting like Petri dishes, breeding new microbes that would come back and threaten to undermine the West by poisoning its youth with narcotics, or attacking its citizens with bombs. Nation-building was proposed as an international act of hygiene to cleanse the dangers lurking under the world's rim.

Nation-building also provided a way of fitting 'non-state actors' into Western foreign policy. Disaffected men building bombs in their bedsits for Islamist outrages, or criminal gangs selling narcotics grown in the Third World to the dejected poor or thrill-seeking rich of the First World would, at first glance, seem to be a police problem – one to be solved by the standard procedures of investigation, arrest, and trial. But the world's policeman used these 'non-state actors' as the argument for international military and political intervention. Supporters of nation-building suggested that only by entering failed states – by force if necessary – and rebuilding their political, military and economic systems on approved lines could the breeding grounds for terrorism and crime be wiped out.

Looking back from 2007, enthusiasm for nation-building looks distinctly odd. The interventions in Afghanistan and Iraq were the highest – or perhaps the lowest – points in the war on terror. In one case, a nation that arguably was both failing and harbouring terrorists was attacked and occupied. In the other case, a state which, while brutal and weakened, was neither obviously failing nor demonstrably supporting the main terrorist enemy was subjected to a military intervention. But what came to unite Afghanistan and Iraq was the shoddy quality of the reconstruction: instead of replacing failing states, the US-led interventions created failing states. The new Iraq and the new Afghanistan had weak central authority, and delivered little in the way of basic services to their citizens. Their populations were forced to shelter either with or from warlords and militias. In both cases, government authority barely extended beyond the capital, while grievances against the occupiers became nationwide. Ironically, the interventions created the conditions for terrorism to grow – even in the case of Iraq, where it had previously found little purchase. However, before the Iraq intervention these desperate failures of US-sponsored nation-building were not widely predicted. Instead, the concept had grown in popularity. It was a solution in search of a problem, proposed to deal with warlords, drug lords, narco-terrorists, and human rights abusers across the globe. Nation-building was prescribed in Latin America, Europe and the West Indies. The fact that the proposed architects of nations were the worst kind of cowboy builders was not widely appreciated.

But the drive towards US-sponsored nation-building after the fall of the Berlin Wall did not take place without argument. There was vigorous opposition to the use of US force to reshape the internal affairs of 'failing' states, mostly from the traditional Republican right. Democratic President Bill Clinton took the first and most important steps along the new road, against vigorous opposition from his Republican opponents, who derided his foreign policy as marked by 'mission creep' into international 'quagmires', accusing him of airy idealism and a lack of realism about US foreign policy goals. Clinton sent US troops to support the UN's 'Operation Restore Hope', which sought to stabilize a government in Somalia – a nation torn apart by Cold War rivalries and local disputes. The operation set forces under the UN flag against local warlord General Aidid. A US mission against Aidid's men, named 'Operation Gothic Serpent', went badly wrong. The gothic serpent was itself badly bitten: eighteen US Army Rangers were killed in street fighting in the capital, Mogadishu, as were hundreds of Somalis. The losses were a shock to American politicians – a shock that was magnified when a Somali crowd dragged the mutilated body of one of the US soldiers through the streets the next day. President Clinton ordered the withdrawal of US troops from Somalia shortly afterwards.

The Somali intervention had been an attempt to show that, now that there was no serious Cold War enemy, the US would intervene directly in the affairs of other nations. The mission was supposed to help throw off the so-called 'Vietnam effect'. US authorities remained nervous of serious foreign entanglement, since their defeat in Vietnam almost twenty years before the events in Somalia. Clinton's intervention was designed to march through this fear, under the banner of aid and rights. The failure of the Somalia intervention represented a major blow to these new ambitions. One year later, Clinton planned another 'humanitarian intervention', in Haiti – a policy that was vigorously contested by the Republican opposition. In his first television debate with his Republican challenger Bob Dole, in 1996, Clinton was accused of being involved in 'nation-building' – which was deployed by Dole as a swear word – and 'mission creep'. He faced the isolationist slogan 'Americans shouldn't have gone there in the first place'.[3] In the presidential debates of 2000 between the Democrat Al Gore and Republican George W. Bush, the battle-lines were more or less the same. Bush said that he and Gore 'have a disagreement about the use of troops. He believes in nation-building. I would be very careful about using our troops as nation-builders.'[4]

The standard interpretation of the Republican turnaround on nation-building is that the events of 9/11 shocked the US right out of their isolationism. The attacks created a new coalition, allying the no-longer-isolationist Republicans with liberal hawks and neoconservatives, all now keen to try to reshape the world by force, and so beat the terror threat. The sight of the collapsing Twin Towers and the penetrated Pentagon turned isolationists into interventionists. The 9/11 attacks did indeed bolster a new coalition behind nation-building interventions, but another metamorphosis of the interventionist animal was already underway – a change that had begun with the Somalia debacle.

Clinton remained committed to building international US authority through direct interventions, but he was clearly affected by Republican criticism of the use of US troops to do the job. Instead, after Somalia, Clinton's government began increasingly to contract out the nation-building work to private companies. This meant that the US could indeed sponsor nation-building, but that if its involvement in complex local issues led to deaths or other scandals, there would be less political cost to the US military machine. In the decade before 9/11, private military companies became an essential part of 'humanitarian interventions'. By privatizing nation-building, the Clinton administrations had managed to hide problems of corruption, incompetence and violence. Consequently, when this kind of privatized reconstruction became a central part of the war on terror, all of the conditions for incompetence, profiteering and failure were in place, but remained unrecognized in the mainstream political debate: the failures of the private sector in Iraq were predictable from events in Haiti, Colombia, or the former Yugoslavia; but precisely because the work had been hived off to the private sector, they were not part of the national political conversation.

Following the scuttle from Somalia, Clinton girded his loins for the invasion of Haiti. The US had given military and political support to the grisly dictatorships of François Duvalier and his son Jean-Claude. The two dictators, known as 'Papa Doc' and 'Baby Doc', ruled Haiti for forty years, up to 1986. The Duvaliers and their ruthless secret police, the 'Tonton Macoutes', made the lives of the poor black Haitian majority a misery. In 1991 the charismatic Jean-Bertrand Aristide was elected as representative of the poor people's Lavalas or 'Avalanche' movement, before being deposed in a coup that represented a return to dictatorship as usual. In 1994 Clinton authorized the landing of troops in the country to restore Aristide, persuading the existing dictator to shuffle off into Panamanian exile. Here was, on the surface, an exemplary liberal intervention: US military force deposed a dictator in favour of a demo-crat, with few casualties. The US clearly had interests in a country only a boat-ride away from their own shores – especially since thousands of refugees from the country's violence and poverty were in fact sailing boats to the US. Clinton also wanted to use the invasion to shake off 'Somalia syndrome', and show that American power could be used on the international stage.

The Haitian intervention, unseating a foreign dictator often described by the US as a 'warlord' to bring stability to a nation, is obviously a relation of the invasions launched as part of the war on terror. The Haitian intervention could have been held up as an impressive example of the benign use of US force in the run-up to the invasion of Iraq; or rather, could have been had the US not effectively made the reinstated Aristide into their political captive. The restored Haitian government was forced to carry out IMF austerity programmes in a country that was already the poorest in the western hemisphere. Popular discontent with these economic programmes meant that Aristide was able to return to power on a renewed mandate in 2001; but US forces stood by as Aristide was unseated by a second coup, and gave political support to a new government that persecuted his Lavalas movement. Liberal intervention, it turned out, was not so liberal.

It did, however, have one special feature: taking on board Republican criticism about using the army for nation-building, Clinton had hired a private firm, DynCorp, to train the new Haitian National Police. Subcontracting the intervention had political advantages, but it was not an unambiguous success. Within two years of the force's creation in July 1995, Human Rights Watch reported that its members had been responsible for at least fifteen deaths and dozens of cases of mistreatment. The organization's director reported that it was 'alarming to see members of this new, US-trained police force, resort to abusive practices reminiscent of Haiti's repressive military'.[5] The misbehaviour of the privately built police force was a small warning of later problems in Iraq and Afghanistan – but the diffuse responsibility between contractor and government meant that neither really suffered much serious public criticism as a result.

DynCorp was on a business journey that would take it into the lucrative territory of military privatization. The firm's origins lay in companies founded by US pilots returning from World War II. These businesses coalesced into the Dynalectric Corporation, which held many contracts servicing US air force planes. The company changed its name to DynCorp – a name that became well known in the war on terror because of the company's high-profile contracts supplying men wielding guns. But they got their important breaks by supplying men wielding spanners: other military contractors specialized in selling things, but DynCorp had a lead in selling services. Instead of supplying planes, DynCorp supplied support services for them. In the 1970s and 1980s, this seemed like a small niche market, but in the following two decades it became a much more important area of military supply, as defence chiefs began substituting private employees for their own troops. DynCorp won significant contracts in military support operations. For example, Dyncorp took over the controversial 'Logistics Civil Augmentation Program' when the much-criticized Halliburton lost the deal in 1997. Under this contract, private firms 'augmented' the US army by running their bases, often at great cost to the US Department of Defense.

DynCorp's emphasis on 'services' meant that it became an important subcontractor in that other close cousin of the war on terror – the war on drugs. This gave the company the chance to change its private engineers into private soldiers. Like the war on terror, the war on drugs was battle against an abstract enemy. It was used to justify foreign military actions by arguing that they were the best way to deal with the disruption caused by the presence of illegal stimulants within the US itself. This foreshadowed the way in which the war on terror was used to justify foreign battles as a response to terrorist destruction in the US. Both enemies were also defined with sufficient vagueness to squeeze many foreign policy aims under their banner. The US Drug Enforcement Agency makes much of the link between the two campaigns.[6] The US government invented the term 'narco-terrorist' to dramatize the idea that the bomb-makers were very often funded by drug sales.

The 'war on drugs' launched by President Nixon in the 1970s had by the 1990s metamorphosed into another way to rebuild US confidence in foreign interventions, as well as providing an indirect method to throw off the 'Somalia syndrome', most obviously in the form of the US-authorized paramilitary operations in Colombia. The Latin American nation was one of the world's leading cocaine producers, and cocaine-funded criminals were intimately entwined in the country's political, economic and legal systems. Colombia was also a major site of US investment – and a leading oil producer – facing a left-wing insurgency. A bloody civil war was being – and continues to be – fought between radical guerrillas and a government augmented by right-wing death squads. Fighters of the Revolutionary Armed Forces of Colombia (FARC)[7] do battle with right-wing paramilitaries like the United Self-Defence Forces (AUC).[8] Proceeds from cocaine production un-doubtedly help fund the battles, although wider social tensions are arguably more important. If the US government was serious about the war on drugs, it would have broken off relations with Colombian President Uribe. In 1991 the US Drug Intelligence Agency called Uribe a 'close personal friend' of leading drug gangster Pablo Escobar, and said that the future president was 'dedicated to collaboration with the Medellín [drug] cartel at high government levels'.[9] If it was serious about the war on drugs, the US would also have focused on Colombia's right-wing paramilitaries, which it knew were linked both to drug crime and to the army. US officials sent telegrams back to Washington describing the 'body count system' leading to the army's human rights abuses, the use of paramilitaries as proxies in the war to protect oil pipelines from the guerrillas, and the link between drugs and the right-wing death squads. The US government in fact focused most of its efforts on supporting the Colombian government and army and on defeating the FARC.

But much of the US support was not direct. Having learned the lesson about US troops being caught up in nation-building, the US subcontracted the job to private military companies. In particular, it gave work to DynCorp. The company already had a commitment in neighbouring Peru which had aroused little interest among politicians and the press. In that country a US-backed administration faced an insurrection by Maoist guerrillas know as the Shining Path, who outshine Colombia's FARC when it comes to indiscriminate brutality. The US Drug Enforcement Administration contracted DynCorp to maintain helicopters and train pilots used to spray herbicides on coca plants in these countries. But this soon threw them into conflict with the local guerrillas, who lived among coca-growing peasants. In 1992, in a little-reported incident, three DynCorp staff died when their helicopter was shot down by Shining Path guerrillas in Peru.[10] This was one of the earliest instances of the new breed of US contractors being killed abroad in what was arguably a fighting mission.

DynCorp's role in Colombia was more clearly defined, and better reported. In practice, DynCorp staff – mostly ex-military men – flew active missions, mostly into territory controlled by the guerrillas rather than by the paramilitaries, and engaged in firefights with the left-wing insurgents. While DynCorp and its US employers offered many different definitions of their role, one of their pilots had a more straightforward opinion. Carlos Weiss, a Peruvian helicopter pilot who had flown missions against guerrillas in his own country, was especially blunt: 'of course I was a mercenary. I was a mercenary in Colombia. It was a typical mercenary operation. That's why I say I was a mercenary. I was paid to do a job: fight a war that is not mine'.[11] Much of DynCorp's work involved flying planes spraying herbicide onto coca farms; but soon after Weiss had spoken out, DynCorp staff became engaged in a direct shootout with FARC guerrillas while trying to save one of their downed pilots. Reporting of the firefight made clear that DynCorp staff flew helicopter gun-ships as well as the fumigation planes.[12]

Shortly after DynCorp's firefight, a short burst of combat was ignited in neighbouring Peru. On an anti-drug mission, the Peruvian air force shot down a light plane, killing its occupants. But, far from being drug dealers, the occupants of the plane were in fact US missionaries. The attack killed Americans Veronica Bowers and her daughter Charity. Their plane was identified and targeted for the Peruvians by a CIA flight manned by unknown contractors.[13] The privatization of the proxy war in Latin America meant that the US government could push the war on drugs forward without too much political embarrassment, but it also opened the door to errors by the contractors.

DynCorp's involvement in the war on drugs created a space in which this private company could lead government policy in new, dangerous directions. Its high-profile anti-narcotics work came under political and legal pressure, so the firm persuaded the US government to make new and bizarre claims about international terrorism to head off any legal challenges to their profits. DynCorp's principal anti-narcotics activity was the aerial spraying of a weed-killer – a variant of Monsanto's 'Roundup' – on suspected illegal crops. But the sprays intended to eradicate coca bushes, marijuana plantations and poppy fields often fell on food crops, or directly onto South American peasants. An American lawyer, Terry Collingsworth, filed a lawsuit against DynCorp on 10 September 2001. The legal claim was a class action representing Ecuadorian farmers living on the border with Colombia, who said that DynCorp's spray planes were shedding a noxious chemical load in their country. Instead of eradicating Colombian cocaine, the farmers said DynCorp was killing their crops and poisoning their children. DynCorp fought back, using the events on the day following that on which the lawsuit had been filed.

The company persuaded Rand Beers, a US secretary of state, to file a paper with the judge claiming that the lawsuit would disrupt the battle against the FARC guerrillas. Beers tried to link this to the 9/11 attacks by claiming, 'It is believed that FARC terrorists have received training in al-Qaeda terrorist camps in Afghanistan.'[14] DynCorp wanted to use the Beers statement to stop the lawsuit, claiming that it aided Osama bin Laden. This represented a major shift in US policy: not only did Rand Beers's statement link the war on drugs with the war on terror, it also tried to relate the FARC with al-Qaeda. This attempt to shoehorn America's enemies together into one vast international conspiracy was a taste of things to come in the war on terror: attempts to link unrelated opponents like Saddam Hussein and Osama bin Laden became hallmarks of the response to 9/11. But, in this corporate-inspired political recipe, the flavours clashed too strongly. The allegation of links between the FARC and al-Qaeda were too outlandish even for the Bush administration, and Beers was forced to withdraw his assertion and 'correct' his deposition of a few days earlier by dropping the allegation that Colombians had been trained in Islamic terror camps.

Colombia was in the US 'back yard', but Clinton had ambitions to extend the country's military grasp into areas outside its traditional sphere of influence. Clinton's efforts in this direction laid the basis for the ambitious attempts to project power in the war on terror. Most significantly, Clinton sought an active role in the former Yugoslavia – an area previously seen as part of the Russian sphere of influence. Yugoslavia began breaking up as part of the general collapse of Communist parties' rule in Eastern Europe in the 1990s. A vicious war broke out over the disputed Bosnian territory. Serbia and Croatia, where opportunist ex-communist leaders had transformed themselves into nationalist ultra-presidents, fought to seize territory on a complex battleground, in what was partly a war of aggression, partly a civil war. International attempts to foster peace either failed or added fuel to the fires of war. The US and its allies then intervened more decisively, in the form of Nato's Operation Deliberate Force. This 1995 bombing campaign, aimed at weakening the Bosnian Serb army, paved the way for the settlement of the Bosnian war in the shape of the Dayton agreement.

This US-sponsored peace treaty, signed by Serbia's Slobodan Milosevic, Croatia's Franjo Tudjman and President Izetbegovic of Bosnia, brought an end to open warfare in the territory for a time. The US had shown that it could shape an area formerly considered part of the Soviet sphere of influence through military force. But these were still tentative steps on the beat of the world's policeman; US intervention was carried out from the relative safety of the pilot's cockpit. Putting US boots on Bosnian soil was a different matter.

In 1996, President Clinton took on new international responsibilities by agreeing to contribute to the post-war UN mission in Bosnia and Herzegovina. He clearly felt that getting into nation-building would also help build the US nation. By sending personnel to build a new political entity in the Balkans, the US would show that it was able to put forces on the ground into previously hostile territory. Involvement in the Balkans was a display of Cold War victory. But Clinton was under pressure from the 'isolationist' Republican right, who suggested that he was risking US lives for hopeless liberal causes. The 'realist' republicans suggested that foreign entanglements were idealist nonsense. They were especially angry that this US intervention was taking place under the banner of the UN. Tom Delay, the Republican leader of the House of Representatives, who would later become a vocal supporter of the Iraq war, backed soldiers who refused to serve in the Balkans.[15] The Congressman led votes in the House against Clinton's deployment. Faced with Republicans backing a symbolic mutiny of troops deployed in the former Yugoslavia, Clinton found a creative way around the problem: he subcontracted the operation. Clinton gave DynCorp a contract to send retired US police officers into the region as the US contribution to rebuilding the local state. This seemed like a clever move, but Clinton was sidestepping one kind of trouble only to put his foot firmly into another.

DynCorp was already an influential actor in the US contribution to Bosnian reconstruction. An indication of just how influential came when, in 1996, a plane carrying Clinton's secretary of commerce, Ron Brown, fell from Bosnian air space to crash in Croatia. A rising star in the Democratic Party, he died alongside a number of corporate executives who were accompanying him on a trade mission, including the representatives of top firms like Bechtel and ATT. Daniel Bannister, chief executive officer of DynCorp, was scheduled to be on the plane, reflecting the company's importance. But the DynCorp boss was forced to cancel his journey at the last minute, and was saved from death by his change of travel plans. Bannister told television news,

> I think the good Lord decided for whatever reason that I should have stayed here and not gone on the trip, and I didn't. And now I've got to figure out what his message is and respond accordingly, whatever it is.[16]

If Bannister was right, it seems the good Lord wanted some of his company's staff to become embroiled in sex trafficking and cover-ups, because that is what DynCorp did next in Bosnia.

Some of the US police officers sent to Bosnia had some very questionable backgrounds – especially at the top. Dennis Laducer, the former assistant sheriff of Orange County, became the deputy commissioner of the International Police Task Force in Bosnia. He left behind more than the California sunshine when he moved to the cold Balkans. Laducer was sacked from the California Sheriff's department in 1997, following several claims by his junior staff of sexual harassment. Lieutenant Wendy Costello alleged that Laducer had ground his groin into her buttocks, and made other inappropriate advances ranging from sexual propositions to attempted kissing and groping.[17] Two other staff also alleged sexual misconduct, and the county had paid out in excess of $1 million to settle their lawsuits, without admitting any wrongdoing. The claimants said he was known as 'Laducer the Seducer', and alleged that he had made threats about their careers linked to demands for sexual favours. Initially Laducer counter-sued the women, accusing them of a 'conspiracy' to bring him down; but his case was dropped, his job taken, and the women given hundreds of thousands of dollars in payouts. When the tape of his first interrogation surfaced, Laducer was heard admitting to pinching and grabbing his female staff. But, he said, 'It's just people communicating. It's just reaching out for people.' Asked if he had told Lieutenant Costello that he would 'lick her face' he responded: 'That is a phrase I use [but] I don't mean it to be sexual.'[18]

Michael Stiers, deputy police chief of the Colorado city of Aurora, became another deputy commissioner for the DynCorp-run US contribution to the International Police Task Force in Bosnia in 1999. He left Colorado with a lawsuit hanging over him relating to sexual misbehaviour by his officers. In 1997, one of his Colorado officers, Barbara Wimmer, launched a lawsuit against the Aurora police department and against Stiers in person. Wimmer had broken off a relationship with a fellow officer, who she testified had then stalked her, and on one occasion raped her, as well as breaking into her house. She said the stalker had also assaulted and choked her. Despite repeated requests for a transfer, the Aurora police department chiefs made her work within 20 feet of her aggressive ex-boyfriend. In 2000, while Stiers was leading the DynCorp police operation in Bosnia, a United States Federal Grand Jury awarded Wimmer $1 million in compensation. Stiers was personally told to pay $250,000 to the harassed female officer for his part in the scandal. The judge told the jury that they could only make Stiers liable for punishment if they believed his behaviour was 'so outrageous in character and so extreme in degree as to go beyond all possible bounds of decency and to be regarded as atrocious and utterly intolerable in a civilised community'. Their award showed that they did indeed believe that the new Bosnian police boss acted atrociously and intolerably.[19]

DynCorp scoured the US for law enforcement officers to send to join Laducer and Stiers in Bosnia. Some were early retirees; some were younger policemen and women looking for a new challenge; some where keen to leave behind something unpleasant in at home; some were looking for a new cause. As well as the obviously bad lieutenants, there were some definitely good cops on the planes to Eastern Europe. Kathryn

Bolkovac was one of the idealist officers. A veteran police officer from Lincoln, Nebraska, Bolkovac wanted to join the international mission partly because of her heritage. Her grandfather had fled Croatia when he was 16, and she felt this was her chance to return and help the region. Bolkovac, a 38-year-old mother of three, as well as a police officer with long experience of dealing with crimes against women, was as different from 'Laducer the Seducer' as possible. Unfortunately, her profession-alism and idealism ran straight into DynCorp's corporate cynicism. When she found evidence of sex crimes and corruption within the international police force in Bosnia, including the DynCorp operation, the company tried to sideline and silence her; and when Bolkovac refused to play ball, they sacked her.

Bolkovac worked on the Human Rights Team in Bosnia, dealing with sexual abuse. She was deeply frustrated that her investigations into prostitution and trafficking seemed to have been sidelined by the DynCorp-run police force. The fact that UN, Nato and DynCorp staff seemed to be among the clients of the brothels made her more angry: officially, DynCorp and the officials of the international police mission condemned this behaviour. Dennis Laducer told Human Rights Watch, 'I meet with each monitor and tell them not to go to these clubs. "Don't use the women there." I say it fifteen times; it's supporting organised crime. "I will send you home," I tell them.'[20] In practice the firm seemed more concerned about covering up its own embarrassment, ignoring staff involvement with prostitution, and hushing up obvious cases by quietly repatriating staff caught red-handed using brothels. Indeed, Laducer himself was later seen leaving one of the most notorious brothels in Bosnia, and was sent back to the US.

Russian and other Eastern European criminals were trafficking girls from Romania, Ukraine, Moldova and Russia, and within the former Yugoslavia itself, and forcing them to work as prostitutes. Disturbed that the international police force would not take these issues seriously, Bolkovac sent an email to many of the most senior officers in the UN mission, which began, 'Do not read this if you have a weak stomach or guilty conscience.' In the following text, Bolkovac outlined what she had learned from her interviews with thirty-five women who were forced into sexual services. 'They are locked in rooms and withheld food and any outside contact for days or weeks', she wrote. 'After this time they are told to dance naked on table tops and sit with clients and recommend the person buys a bottle of champagne . . . which includes a room and an "escort" to the room.' Bolkovac told her DynCorp and UN colleagues,

> If the women still refuse to perform sex acts with the customers they are beaten and raped in the rooms by the bar owners and their associates. They are told if they go to the police they will be arrested for prostitution and being an illegal immigrant.

When some of the women still refused, the reaction was swift and brutal:

> One is forced to dance naked on a table in the bar and drink vodka. The bar owner then breaks a light bulb over her head and tells her to hold the hot wires while she dances. She is jerked off the table by her hair and raped by the owner.

Bolkovac was trying to shock the UN into action against slavery. Instead, she shocked DynCorp into action against her. Within days, Michael Stiers demonstrated the managerial skill he had developed in Colorado: he told Bolkovac she was unable to perform her work properly, and suspended her from duty. DynCorp then accused Bolkovac of falsifying her time sheets, and sacked her for 'gross misconduct'. Perhaps DynCorp could not be completely blamed for corruption among its staff – corrupt police officers, and prostitution rings serving military bases, are hardly unknown. But they could be – and were – held accountable for trying to cover up these crimes by victimizing their best employees.

Bolkovac sued the firm for unfair dismissal, and this led to a surprising revelation. When I began covering the Bolkovac case for the *Observer*, I discovered that DynCorp was not an American firm after all: all of Bosnia's DynCorp staff were employed by a subsidiary of the firm, DynCorp Aerospace, based in the British military garrison town of Aldershot. Bolkovac was able to use the new 'whistleblower protection law' to sue the firm in an industrial tribunal in Southampton, on the English south coast. The tribunal found that there was 'no doubt' that Bolkovac had been unfairly dismissed. The firm had acted in 'complete defiance' of their stated disciplinary code, and had then tried to excuse the sacking with evidence that was 'sketchy to the point of being non-existent'. The tribunal's chairman said that Bolkovac had become a 'marked woman' for her stand, adding, 'It is hard to imagine a case in which a firm has acted in a more callous, spiteful and vindictive manner towards a former employee.' DynCorp was forced to pay Bolkovac £100,000 – but this meant little, as the firm continued to grow as governments ignored the grim lessons of this case, and signed more private security contracts.

As if the Bolkovac case were not shocking enough, DynCorp became involved in a parallel claim over Bosnian misbehaviour. Texan Ben Johnston worked for DynCorp in the former Yugoslavia on one of their more traditional contracts, servicing US army Apache and Black Hawk helicopters at a Bosnian base. At first Johnston tried to keep his head down at the base, because they were 'a rougher crowd than I'd ever dealt with. It's not like I don't drink or anything, but DynCorp employees would come to work drunk.'[21] He soon noticed the mechanics were often bad workmen, and always ready to bill the army for unnecessary repairs.

Soon his fellow workers invited him to Bosnian brothels, based in former discotheques that had been renamed with suitably American names – like 'Las Vegas' – to attract the new punters. But Johnston soon came to believe that the DynCorp engineers were using their relatively high salaries not just to sleep with girls, but actually to buy and sell them. 'I heard talk about the prostitution right away, but it took some time before I understood that they were buying these girls', he recalled. He complained to a senior member of staff about the trade in girls who seemed to him to be underage. Unfortunately he did not realize that this manager was 'the guy who would take new employees to the brothels and set them up so he got his women free'. DynCorp staff were working with gangsters to buy and import girls into the brothels at $600 a time. The manager in question had even videotaped himself having sex with two of the trafficked females. One of the women could be heard on the tape saying 'no'.

Unable to make any headway by complaining to his managers, because he thought DynCorp were '100 per cent in bed with the mafia over there', Johnston went instead to the army's Criminal Investigation Division (CID). The military investigators found evidence that DynCorp employees were illegally buying and selling guns, as well as girls. They unearthed the tape of a DynCorp manager having sex with apparently unwilling women. One DynCorp manager had made the tape, and another had acquired a copy that he was using as a kind of insurance, to protect him from being sacked. One DynCorp manager told military investigators how men from the firm worked with a 'man we call "Debeli", which is Bosnian for fat boy. He is the operator of a nightclub by the name of Harley's that offers prostitution. Women are sold hourly, nightly or permanently.'

The CID investigation threw up clear evidence of rotten behaviour; but the military policemen consulted their legal advisers, the grandly named Office of the Staff Judge Advocate. After talking to this grand legal wizard, the officers believed that the legal treaty that put US forces onto Bosnian ground also gave contractors some kind of legal immunity. The CID's legal advice was that 'under the Dayton Peace Accord, the contractors were protected from Bosnian law which did not apply to them. They knew of no US federal laws that would apply to these individuals at this time.' This was a stark warning of things to come during the occupation of Iraq: the contractors were not soldiers, and so could not be disciplined by military courts; however, like all US forces in Bosnia, they were exempt from local laws. The military CID carried out an investigation, but made no prosecutions.

This left only DynCorp to deal with the sex traffickers on their payroll. The firm made some slight gestures, saying that it had fired five employees for crimes linked to prostitution. But these men were simply shipped back to the US and sent on their way without prosecution. The DynCorp admission merely illustrated the scale of the problem without offering any real solution. But while DynCorp was soft on the criminals, it was hard on the whistleblowers: like Bolkovac, Johnston was sacked as soon as his complaint had any effect. Shortly after the CID investigation, DynCorp told Johnston he was out of a job because he had 'brought discredit to the company'. With the military unwilling to take any action, and the company shooting the messenger who had brought the bad news, Johnston was left to fight on his own. Disgusted by his treatment and the company's behaviour, Johnston sued DynCorp for damages. The firm denied wrongdoing, but quickly and quietly settled out of court shortly after it had lost the Bolkovac case.[22] It was cheaper, it seemed, for DynCorp to supply poor quality officers than to weed out those who were unsuitable. The firm had a financial incentive not to see the crimes and misdemeanours of its staff exposed to public scrutiny. Some employees picked up on DynCorp's laxness, and happily abused their positions. Steve Smith, a police officer from Santa Cruz who worked for DynCorp in Bosnia, explained to the *Washington Post* that police caught misbehaving in Bosnia might have to stop working for DynCorp, but they could otherwise continue their careers in law enforcement. There was no tool to force the corrupt cops back onto the straight and narrow. In Cruz's words, 'there are no professional consequences unless they want to keep working for DynCorp. The problem is that you have no hammer.' As a result, he said, the bad apples realized that they were 'making $85,000 in a place where everyone else is making $5,000, and they're chasing whores, they're shacking up with young women, and they're basically just having a good time'.[23]

There were two lessons to be learned from DynCorp's Bosnian disgrace. Firstly, seeing contractors as a way of avoiding responsibility for 'reconstruction' was a mistake. Handing over political and military interventions to profit-making firms created a host of problems, and at best should have been treated with caution. Secondly, if governments are committed to using the private sector for post-war reconstruction, they should think very hard before using a firm with as bad a record as DynCorp's. Unfortunately, neither lesson was learned, either in London or Washington. In fact, DynCorp's record tempted British and US politicians into believing that they and other private firms could be central to the war on terror. The company's lobbyists and brochures clearly encouraged the Blair and Bush governments into believing that they could launch new aggressive military campaigns and rely on DynCorp and other companies to stabilize the resulting shattered nations. In 2002, British Foreign Secretary Jack Straw published a consultation paper suggesting that private military companies should be central to any new international action. Straw's paper mentions DynCorp eight times, saying that it is among the firms that 'maintain a reputation as respectable organizations'[24] – giving a whole new meaning to the word 'respectable'. The US government was even more enthusiastic about DynCorp. Like Jack Straw, US officials became even more enthusiastic about the firm after 9/11. DynCorp got an enormous boost from the war on terror. Within a month of the start of the Iraq war, DynCorp was sent in to help the US overlord Jay Garner help 'conduct assessments of how to establish local policing'.[25] DynCorp managed to stay a lot longer in theatre than Garner. He was quickly replaced, having suggested that Iraq should have quick elections, after which Iraqis themselves could rebuild Iraq. His replacement as US administrator of Iraq, L. Paul Bremer, held off from calling elections, while making sure US firms were able to seize control of reconstruction. DynCorp's suggestion for establishing local policing seemed principally to involve giving more contracts to DynCorp.

The initial US policy for Iraq involved a corporate reconstruction, with all existing organs of the Iraqi government more or less dissolved. The army was sacked, and the Baath party proscribed. For two years the allies did not seek to rebuild a state based on elections, instead opting for building it upon contracts. Coalition Provisional Authority officials shipped in from Britain and the US handed out the organs of the state as a series of business deals with largely Western companies. The Iraqi police more or less deserted their posts to a man after the invasion, leading to an orgy of crime – especially looting. DynCorp promised they could rebuild the force. By April, DynCorp claimed it had been awarded a ten-year contract to 'support law enforcement' in Iraq, worth up to $50 million in its first year. It promised up to 1,000 advisers to restore law and order.

There were two key elements to the police plan. Firstly, a set of new police academies would push new Iraqi recruits through a short eight-week programme. Secondly, a series of advisers would look after these rookies and any established officers still on the scene, with mentoring on the job and in police stations. The use of advisers in the stations was intended as vital protection against corruption and human rights violations by the new officers. As it turned out, DynCorp took a reported $750 million in Iraqi contracts, but simply failed to put the advisers onto Iraq's streets. The mentoring scheme was almost useless, and put only around fifty retired police officers into Iraqi police precincts, to little effect. The training at the new police academies was so poor that the US army took responsibility for the main training base away from the firm. The academy, based in Jordan for security reasons, rarely failed any of its students, expelling less than 1 per cent of around 50,000 trainees for 'security reasons'.

The combination of short training and poor mentoring was entirely unable to stop the new Iraqi police force from becoming thoroughly infiltrated by Shiite militias, who used the uniforms to carry out sectarian torture and assassination. DynCorp was unconcerned about the obvious failure of the rebuilding of the Iraqi police. A company spokesman told the *New York Times*, 'We are not judged on the success or failure of the program as they established it.'[26] The company not only failed to train the new police, but some of their staff were also implicated in law-breaking. Three men working for the firm on the police academy contract cheated the US government out of £0.5 million, in a fraud over fuel supposedly used in officer training. DynCorp sacked the men, but, despite their failure to ensure proper auditing, remained otherwise unembarrassed by crime at the academy.

DynCorp wasn't able to make a mess of the new Iraqi police force all by itself – other companies stepped in to help. The Parsons Corporation won many contracts from Iraqi 'reconstruction', including $75 million to rebuild the Baghdad police academy. At the end of 2005, the official US auditor of Iraqi projects, Stuart Bowen, said that the Baghdad police college was 'the most essential civil security project in the country – and it's a failure [and a] disaster.'[27] Thanks to some very expensive jerry building, so much 'urine and fecal matter' poured from upper floors that the filth filled light fittings and dripped on wannabe officers. The flows of muck even compromised the concrete structure, so that much of the building was in need of demolition and rebuilding. While Iraqi police cadets suffered in the sewage showers of the Baghdad academy, DynCorp built an entirely separate luxury residential police camp outside the capital. DynCorp took $43.8 million from the US State Department to build a luxury base for over 1,000 police trainees at Adnan Palace, but left the school empty for 'security reasons'. US auditors found that DynCorp had spent around 10 per cent of the cost on an Olympic-sized pool and twenty luxury Hollywood-star-style trailers, without any authorization from the State Department.[28] The State Department cancelled the job in September 2004, but work on the trailers seems to have carried on until 2006, thanks to 'weak and sometimes non-existent contract administration'. While inspectors could locate the luxurious ghost town at Adnan palace, they could not account for $36.4 million of weapons, body armour and other equipment supposedly supplied by DynCorp, thanks to vague invoices and unclear paperwork.

Raining human waste on the heads of badly trained and badly supported rookies was no way to build a police force. Instead of being bound together as one force that could express the legal will of the nation, this shoddily cobbled-together force fragmented into just another series of gangs trying to hold on to a little power, a little money, or a little security in a fragmenting Iraq. The police didn't become just one more armed group fighting for space among the gangs of Iraq – they actually broke down into different gangs. John Chapman, a Texan deputy sheriff hired by DynCorp to train Iraqi police, gave a sense of how low the firm's training was aiming. He was asked by the *New York Times* what would count as success for recruits in the police. 'Show up for work', Mr Chapman said, 'Anything besides show up on payday.' US Marines certainly had low expectations of the trainees. US Marines were expecting 150 DynCorp trainees to arrive at their base near Baghdad in 2004. The recruits were expected at 9 p.m. At the morning briefing their officer presented PowerPoint slides to his troops. The first slide described the imminent arrival of the helicopter of police recruits with the headline '2100: Clown Car arrives'. The second said '2101: Be ready for negligent discharges' – meaning accidental and uncontrolled shots from the police officers' AK-47s. Faced with DynCorp's graduates, the Marine commander's slide suggested the appropriate military manoeuvre was 'Recommend "Duck & Cover" '.[29]

US Army Captain Philip Carter gave his diary of life with the new Iraqi police force to the *Boston Globe*. Carter said the squad cars, weapons and other materiel he gave to the police were regularly 'skimmed' by officers and resold. As they were taught in buildings where apparent 'skimming' by contractors led them into a rain of piss, they could hardly be blamed for responding in kind. Carter also revealed that the police officers themselves became part of the contraband, writing, 'Local politicians liberally borrow bodyguards, weapons, and vehicles from the police in order to outfit themselves and their entourages.'[30] As the ill-assorted police unravelled into private armies for individual politicians, the Iraq Study Group, made up of senior US political establishment 'wise heads', found that the Iraqi security forces had 'neither the training nor legal authority to conduct criminal investigations, nor the firepower to take on organized crime, insurgents, or militias'. Useless as a crime-fighting organization, the police could be pretty handy when it came to committing crime, and 'routinely engage[d] in sectarian violence, including the unnecessary detention, torture and execution of civilians', according to the Study Group.

The failure of the new, DynCorp-built Iraqi police force was dramatically demonstrated when British soldiers blew up a Basra police station in late 2006. The British forces were trying to wrest control of the new police force away from a sectarian murder squad. The only way they could handle Iraq's new constabulary was by attacking the supposedly reconstructed force with explosives. But the problems with the Iraqi police were, it seems, no barrier to DynCorp winning further contracts. The company became literally central to the Western-backed Karzai government in Afghanistan when the US hired DynCorp to provide bodyguards for the president himself. DynCorp's guards defended Karzai from a number of assassination attempts, losing men in the process. But it also built a reputation for aggression against the wrong people: Karzai's DynCorp guards reportedly slapped and manhandled one of the president's ministers whom they had failed to recognize. But while guarding the Afghan president put the company into the press spotlight, as many journalists were also intimidated by the company's men, the company's police work was probably more important. As in Iraq, DynCorp held a massive contract to rebuild the nation's police. In November 2006 the inspector general of the US State Department and the inspector general of the Department of Defense formed a kind of auditors' tag-team to wrestle with DynCorp's work on the Afghan National Police. They found that the firm had soaked up $1.1 billion in five years. For all the money spent, the Afghan National Police were simply not able to fight crime effectively or to resist a resurgent Taleban. The auditors said that the police's 'readiness level to carry out its internal security and conventional police responsibilities is far from adequate'.

Most importantly, the auditors found that DynCorp's contract replicated all the worst aspects of the Iraq experience: DynCorp sent working or retired US policemen on sabbaticals to train Afghanistan's police in secure centres for eight weeks. But they then came up with only an inadequate number of trainers to mentor and train the new officers on the job: all the classroom learning could easily come to nothing in the field. Law-enforcement experts agreed that on-the-job training for new staff was the best way to make sure that classroom lessons actually fed into police practice, and to spot officers who were not going to make the grade. But DynCorp skimped on this vital part of the programme, with just a few hundred field trainers concentrating on working with senior officers. The auditors mostly blamed the contract itself, rather than DynCorp – although they made some mention of 'mentors initially provided by DynCorp' who 'did not meet all of the strategic planning and executive mentoring requirements'.[31] But many police experts who visited the country, and some Afghan ministers, said that DynCorp's trainers were expensive and not up to the job. Panicked by the failure of the police training, the US tried to supplement the fully trained officers with an 'auxiliary police force' to shore up security against a resurgent Taleban. The auxiliaries received two weeks training, against the two months given to regular officers – which was itself a lot less than the six months given to new police recruits in the Bosnian reconstruction. DynCorp was given extra money to train the auxiliaries, whom observers said included young boys and opium eaters.[32]

There has been a recent growth in nostalgia for the British Empire, with both Gordon Brown and Tony Blair hinting at the positive achievements flowing from Britain's domination of the world. The sight of troops fighting again on the historic battlegrounds of Iraq and Afghanistan, combined with a certain amount of jealousy at the new quasi-imperial rule of the US, has led to a growth in warm feelings about a period when large areas of the world map were coloured red. Whatever the crimes of empire, the British elite had born some of the burden of its administration. Thousands of sons of the elite were sent to run the empire, abusing the servants and the gin in the process. Firms like DynCorp offered the hope that Britain and the US could now order events in far-off countries simply by signing contracts, without having to sacrifice their favourite sons. The companies seemed to suggest they would take up the new imperial burdens – that intervention would be as painless as shopping. The DynCorp experience shows that that promise was an illusion.

5

Soldiers of Fortune

In her important study of the history of commercial warfare, Janice E. Thomson writes that, in the past,

> states did not monopolize violence even within their territorial borders. Urban militias, private armies, fiscal agents, armies of regional lords and rival claimants to royal power, police forces and state armies all claimed the right to exercise violence.

Thomson explores the difference between the modern sense in which war is the business of national armies while crime-fighting is the proper work of an authorized police force, and the quite different arrangements of previous centuries:

> The contemporary organization of global violence is neither timeless nor natural. It is distinctively modern. In the six centuries leading up to 1900, global violence was democratized, marketized and internationalized. Nonstate violence dominated the international system. Individuals and groups used their own means of violence in pursuit of their particular aims, whether honour and glory, wealth or political power. People bought and sold military manpower like a commodity on the global market. The identity of suppliers or purchasers meant almost nothing.[1]

Writing in 1994, Thomson wanted to address the puzzle of 'how did we get from there to here'. Ten years later the puzzle is solving itself, because we are travelling back from 'here' to 'there'. In the decade after Thomson's work, military manpower presented itself as an increasingly popular commodity on the global market. Political changes arising from the end of the Cold War, and the sales techniques used by some mercenary firms to address the new market, created new military businesses. In the run-up to the war on terror mercenaries of the old school rebranded themselves as 'private military companies'. After some early embarrassment, the new mercenarism was encouraged by the British government. The new mercenary firms manoeuvred into position so that when the British and US governments needed new forces to fight the war on terror, the private armies were able and willing to take to the field.

Mercenary soldiers wielded their swords, pikes, axes and guns for much of the later Middle Ages. Soldiers for hire ranged from the Irish gallowglass to Germany's *Landsknechte*. Large-scale mercenarism was practised by the 'free companies' across Europe for much of the fourteenth and fifteenth centuries. In the 1400s, Italians dissatisfied with foreign mercenaries responded by raising their own soldiers-for-hire, called the *condottieri*. Resonating with modern times, *condottieri* literally means 'contractors' – the euphemism most often used to describe private fighters in Iraq. The most crucial political and military events were determined by mercenaries. Rival foreign mercenaries and Italian *condottieri* battled at Marino in 1379: the outcome decided whether the pope would be Italian or French.

Graham Greene wrote one of the most striking speeches in cinema for Harry Lime, the anti-hero of *The Third Man*, who declares that, 'In Italy, for thirty years under the Borgias they had warfare, terror, murder, bloodshed', but produced the glories of the renaissance. By contrast, Lime claims that Switzerland had 'brotherly love, 500 years of democracy and peace', but only produced 'the cuckoo clock'. It's a great moment in film, but the Swiss could wield more fierce violence than Greene allows. Switzerland actually contributed to Italy's years of warfare: the Vatican's Swiss Guard are the remnants of one of the foreign mercenary forces that plied their services across Italy. Since the thirteenth-century Swiss revolt, the pikemen and pole-axe-wielding fighters from the country of the cuckoo clock were valued as some of the toughest fighters for hire available in Europe.

Mercenarism was so central to Italian politics that the issue features heavily in Machiavelli's *The Prince*, one of the most important political works written during the Italian Renaissance. Machiavelli complains that Italy 'has been ruled for many years by mercenaries' with disastrous results, since 'the ruin of Italy has been caused by nothing else than by resting all her hopes for many years on mercenaries'. Machiavelli had personally tried to organize a militia from the people of Florence, offering an early version of the national armies that later supplanted the mercenaries he despised. He drew on this experience to show that mercenaries were a threat to good rule, arguing that the mercenary captains

> are either capable men or they are not; if they are, you cannot trust them, because they always aspire to their own greatness, either by oppressing you, who are their master, or others contrary to your intentions; but if the captain is not skilful, you are ruined in the usual way.

Machiavelli's criticism stands today: effective mercenaries will feel their power and act in their own interests. A mercenary force that can use violence effectively will not feel subservient to its government paymaster, and can ignore or bend instructions to its own interests. The ineffective mercenary, on the other hand, will let the government down 'in the usual way', by delivering a military disaster or failure.

Machiavelli's view that mercenaries are 'useless and dangerous' was a breach with the orthodoxy of his time, but his description of them would become another century's common-sense: 'disunited, ambitious, and without discipline, unfaithful, valiant before friends, cowardly before enemies; they have neither the fear of God nor fidelity to men'. Over the next 300 years, nation-states slowly grew or fought their way into being. These nations replaced the patchwork of empires, city-states and principalities of Europe. With the rise of the nation-states came the rise of national armies, drawn directly from their own peoples; motivated – in theory at least – by love of country rather than love of money. Foreign paid fighters, also known as free lances, were absorbed into national armies.

It took a long time for the mercenaries finally to pack up their weapons and leave the continent, and the European nations continued to shop in the marketplace of violence through other forms of commercial warfare and conquest in the rest of the world. Privateering, piracy, and the business of empire all used commercially supplied violence. Nonetheless the move away from mercenary soldiering was an essential part of the rise of the modern nation-state. The creation of national armies driven by a

patriotic ethos was closely linked to the rise of national self-determination, and in turn to the rise of democracy. The idea of national armies
having a role in politics summons visions of coups, crackdowns and other
anti-democratic activity; but this was not the case in the transition into
the modern era. When national armies replaced the patchwork of feudal
forces and mercenaries, they helped create the conditions for popular
rule.

In the English Civil War, there were certainly mercenaries on the
battlefield. The Earl of Essex hired the colourful Croatian Captain Carlo
Fantom[2] to fight for parliament against the king. Captain Fantom was
honest about his motives: 'I care not for your Cause: I come to fight for
your halfe-crowne, and your handsome woemen.' Fantom was a
Catholic, but happily admitted: 'I have fought for the Christians against
the Turkes; and for the Turkes against the Christians.' He was held in
high esteem for his fighting skills and for his military training, building the
parliamentarians' cavalry by teaching 'the way of fighting with horse'.
Fantom also surprised his fellow soldiers with his apparently bullet-proof
skin. Musket balls set his shirt on fire, but left his body unblemished. He
claimed to have eaten a secret forest herb that transformed ordinary
soldiers into a 'shott free' species called the 'hard men'. The Earl of Essex
was so enthusiastic about his mercenary that he twice stopped the man
from being hanged for 'ravishing' women.

The most important military innovation of the Civil War, however,
was Cromwell's New Model Army, which promoted its officers on the
basis of skill, rather than social standing or money. The Earl of Essex's
forces were absorbed into the New Model Army. It seems that Captain
Fantom was unable to deal with the new, motivated, egalitarian,
puritan army. He crossed the battle-lines to join the King's forces
at Oxford. The royalists finally hanged Fantom – for 'ravishing'
women. The New Model Army cared about its cause more than
about half-crowns and handsome women. When the New Model
Army debated the future of Britain at Putney, the soldiers declared:
'We were not a mere mercenary army, hired to serve any arbitrary
power of a state, but called forth and conjured by the several
declarations of Parliament to the defence of our own and the people's
just rights and liberties.' The age of democracy and the end of
mercenarism came together. There was less room for bullet-proof
Balkan, rapist soldiers of fortune in this new world.

The move of the modern and increasingly democratic nation-states away from mercenarism took place over decades and centuries, but was definite and discernible. Significant commercial warfare ceased in Europe. Corporate soldiering was employed to build the empire – as with the East India Company – but even this form of mercenarism was finally abandoned. By the twentieth century, the 'advanced' world only occasionally employed mercenaries beyond their territory, and at the edges of their foreign policy. The leaders of the war on terror seemed to recognize this relationship between the end of mercenarism and the rise of the modern system of international relations based on concepts of sovereignty. They began slashing away at the essential assumptions of international politics at the same time as reintroducing fighters-for-hire.

Tony Blair spent the last years of his premiership trying to make an impact with 'big issue' speeches that would establish his legacy. It has sometimes been difficult to take Blair's intellectual commitment seriously, as he has picked up and dropped his 'core values' from a rotating wheel of ideologies: the 'Third Way', the 'stakeholder society', communitarianism, ethical socialism – all were described as the basis of his ideas, then quietly forgotten and replaced. However, Blair in office did show a consistent enthusiasm for backing military action, especially joint military action with the US, and viewed the international system as a fetter on this worthy cause. In 2004 Blair made a keynote speech justifying the action in Iraq. He claimed he had been 'reaching for a different philosophy in international relations from a traditional one that has held sway since the treaty of Westphalia in 1648'.[3] This treaty is generally seen as establishing a prejudice in international affairs against interference in another nation's domestic business. The treaty not only signified the end of the destructive wars that had ravaged Europe, it also represented the triumph of sovereignty over empire, of national rule over the personal writ of the Habsburgs.

Blair summed up the Westphalian system he wanted to see trashed as the one where 'a country's internal affairs are for it and you don't interfere unless it threatens you, or breaches a treaty, or triggers an obligation of alliance'. The Westphalian principles were far from firm. For hundreds of years after the treaty, European nations happily marched into the countries of the south and set up colonial administrations, by the simple trick of pretending they weren't nations at all, merely empty, primitive or undeveloped space. But the peace of Westphalia at least created a basis for national self-determination, even if the colonies would have to fight their way into the status of nationhood through the long struggles of the nineteenth and twentieth centuries. The prime minister wanted to argue that national self-determination and the principle of sovereignty took second place to 'humanitarian' intervention; but the 'humanitarian' threshold for intervention seemed to be entirely a matter of his personal judgment, while the instrument of intervention seemed to be defined simply as the most powerful nations.

This new philosophy seemed to boil down to arguing that Britain and the US, now that they had lost any possible threat to their own territorial integrity thanks to the collapse of the Soviet Union, would march their armies wherever they wanted. Rather than creating a new world order, Blair seemed to want an old one. The only innovation involved substituting Britain and the US for the Habsburg dynasty. Blair wasn't the only ideologue irritated by the Westphalian system. Lewis Attiyatullah, a pseudonymous writer described by the US State Department as an 'al-Qaeda affiliated author' regularly posted messages on the internet promising holy war. Attiyatullah also hoped that 'the international system built up by the West since the Treaty of Westphalia will collapse', although he hoped it would collapse in favour of a powerful Islamic super-state.

The treaty of Westphalia ended two wars – the Thirty Years War and the Eighty Years War – which raises the uncomfortable thought that Blair looked back on these decades of warfare, which wasted Europe and caused millions of deaths, with a nostalgic, warm glow. While Blair's prime motivation for taking on the Westphalian system was to liberate himself from restrictions on his freedom to invade, it is worth noting that the long wars before the two treaties making up the peace of Westphalia were the high point of mercenarism in Europe. Large and destructive armies were raised for money in the conflicts. The mercenary armies changed sides, fought for their own interests, and used the civilian populations for plunder. The new international system proposed by Blair looked like a very old system, with strong nations attacking weak ones at will, and fighting their wars with a complex, changing, and self-interested commercial military. Mercenaries became as essential a part of the new world order as they had been in pre-modern Europe, thanks to a major political shift by the British and US leaderships. The politicians picked up and developed changes that had been pioneered by the military companies themselves, turning these private initiatives into national policies. In the second half of the twentieth century mercenaries plied their trade on the edge of foreign policy; but after the end of the Cold War the companies began to march towards the centre of world affairs.

After 1945, mercenaries had found a place at the fringe of the world system. They were represented by a lunatic fringe, as well as a more sober faction. The lunatic fringe was typified by the appropriately named 'Mad' Mike Hoare. After serving as a captain in the British army in North Africa in World War II, Hoare set himself up as a soldier for hire, working for a variety of African leaders trying to carve out territory for themselves as the old colonial rulers retreated. Hoare fought for the secessionist Katanga province in the Congo, and on the Biafran side against Nigeria. His war fighting was marked by colourful violence of the Captain Fantom variety, like punishing a rapist in his ranks by shooting off his toes. Hoare's career ended in 1978 when he tried to launch a coup in the Seychelles. Hoare was nominally acting for one Seychelles politician, and claimed he had backing from the South African government. The coup came unstuck when his 1000 mercenaries – who travelled disguised as a beer-drinking club called 'Ye ancient order of frothblowers' – had their cover blown. A zealous Seychelles airport official spotted an assault rifle in the froth-blowers' luggage. After a short shoot-out and an escape by hijacked plane, Hoare and his compatriots were imprisoned by the South African authorities, who denied knowledge of the plot. There were other freebooting fighters in the 'Mad Mike' mould, including Frenchman Bob Denard. Like Hoare, Denard fought in the Congo, and like Hoare he also favoured island coups. Denard was finally imprisoned in 1995, after he had overthrown the government of the Indian Ocean islands of the Comoros for the fourth time.

The less lunatic element was well represented by Sir David Stirling. He had been the founder in World War II of the Special Air Service, but after the war went private with his Guernsey-based 'Watchguard International Ltd'. Special Air Service (SAS) veterans are still some of the most sought-after private soldiers, and the SAS model of a highly mobile elite military force to be applied at key points acted as an inspiration for many mercenary activities. Stirling's private firm set out to supply military services to established Third World governments, with the knowledge of the Foreign Office. Stirling believed his private military company could help shore up existing, approved governments, but should not be used to overthrow unstable regimes. His company was built as a hired force to battle a Nasserite republican uprising in North Yemen, and to shore up royalist forces. Watchguard went on to train and build the armed forces of a number of the Gulf sultanates. Stirling also involved himself in other military business, like selling British jets to Saudi Arabia.

While 'Mad' Mike and Sir David represented different extremes of the post-war mercenary scene, the division between the two wings was certainly not absolute. So Bob Denard might have looked like an adventurer, but he also often enjoyed the backing of the French government. Sir David might have seemed respectable, but he was drawn into an absurd, adventuristic attempt to topple Colonel Gaddafi in 1970. Stirling's two political initiatives also now look slightly un-hinged. Stirling founded the Capricorn Africa Society, which called for an African federation under the enlightened rule of men like Sir David Stirling. In the 1970s he set up GB75, a secret organization ready to break strike action and beat back union power in Britain.

All of these mercenary organizations had some common features. They might work with the knowledge or even tacit approval of the British government, but they were actually engaged by lesser states or organiza-tions. They were not hired by the most powerful nations or leading companies in the world; nor did they often act in the most significant military theatres. They applied their fighting skills for money at the fringes of the system. The war on terror was to change all this, and bring the mercenaries onto the most important battlefields, to act directly for the leading governments and corporations. The military companies them-selves saw the possibilities for change with the end of the Cold War, and began to bring themselves into the centre of political life. British and US governments looking for a 'revolution in military affairs' to match the new terror threat were clearly pleased by these commercial combat initiatives, and brought the firms into their own military planning.

Defense Systems Ltd (DSL) was a firm very much in the mould of Stirling's Watchguard, and was chaired by another SAS officer, Alastair Morrison. DSL won a contract to defend BP's pipelines in Colombia in the mid 1990s. The British oil firm's Ocensa pipeline wound through territory where the National Liberation Army (ELN)[4] was active. The ELN was Colombia's smaller guerrilla army, made up of enthusiasts for Ché Guevara, and whose tactics included frequent kidnapping of foreign executives and attacks on oil installations. BP was dissatisfied with the protection provided by the Colombian police, and wanted DSL to beef up security, both independently and by working with the Colombian security services. BP and DSL were both accused of working too closely with Colombian forces – which was especially worrying, because the Colombian army had a reputation for ruthless violence against peasants whom they suspected of supporting the guerrillas. The Colombian army was also regularly accused of working with right-wing death squads. The British companies rejected these accusations, but newspaper investigations[5] threw up disturbing evidence.

The *Guardian* newspaper found that BP had supplied the Fourteenth Brigade – notorious for human rights abuses – with night-vision goggles to help them fight better in darkness. They found papers that showed that DSL had written a proposal to form 'intelligence cells' among communities around the BP installations, to try and track down guerrillas. DSL had a subcontract with an Israeli security firm called Silver Shadow, which had written a proposal saying that DSL and BP should work with the Colombian military to protect the pipelines with 'direct supply of anti-guerrilla special weaponry and ammo', night-vision goggles, unmanned observation 'drone' planes, and special radios. They had also offered 'a state-of-the-art investigation-intelligence and psychological warfare 18-day seminar' to DSL and BP staff. The oil firm and their security company made clear that these options had not been taken up, but they did make payments to their Israeli subcontractors, and they did at least comply with the suggestion to supply night-vision goggles to Colombian soldiers.[6]

The important point about the DSL contract with BP is that the company was not working for a small foreign government. Here was a military firm working for a major British multinational. During the Cold War, companies found security by working with the national security forces of nations linked to one or other of the great power blocs. With the end of the Cold War, some multinationals believed that they were becoming stronger than the less coherent states – especially since these states could no longer rely on the option of sheltering under the military umbrella of one or other of the competing superpowers. The multinationals – in this case BP – seemed attracted to the idea of having their own paramilitary force to supplement weak national forces. BP was acting like a feudal lord hiring a mercenary band for protection. The private military companies were moving from the fringe to the centre of the international economy. Colombia was something of a laboratory for the new military services: while DSL worked for a major multinational, another company, DynCorp, worked directly for the US state in quasi-military actions in the country (see Chapter 2).

DSL's employer, BP, is influential with both the British and US governments, so it seems likely that their enthusiasm for mobilizing a private army against 'terrorist' groups in Colombia had some effect on the future commanders of the 'war on terror'.

As one of Britain's leading companies, BP is always going to have a strong relationship with any government – but the firm seemed particularly intimately involved with the Labour Party. Nick Butler was simultaneously treasurer of Labour's oldest think-tank, the Fabian Society, and a BP economist. Butler helped to rebuild Labour's centre ground leadership, helping both Blair and his predecessor Neil Kinnock, and remained an adviser to the former when he became prime minister. The traffic between the company and the Labour Party ran in both directions. In 2001 one of Blair's closest aides, Anji Hunter, left 10 Downing Street to become 'communications director' for BP. In the most striking demonstration of such links, Labour recruited Lord Simon, chairman of the BP board, as a government minister. One of Lord Simon's last acts as chairman of BP was to launch a defence of the company's human rights record in Colombia, claiming that it was not helping the Colombian military to violate human rights, but was actually ensuring that the army maintained 'reasonable behaviour'.[7] He then took what lessons he had learned from BP into government, becoming Labour's trade minister.

While the association between BP and DSL brought the use of mercenaries right into the heart of the Anglo-American establishment, another group of companies were busy making mercenarism respectable, despite some distinctly unimpressive results. Tim Spicer, a former lieutenant colonel in the Scots Guards who had served in the Falklands, Northern Ireland, and as press spokesman for the United Nations Protection Force during the Bosnian intervention, set up Sandline in 1997. His new enterprise was a private military company based on London's King's Road, although registered in the Bahamas. Spicer wanted his firm to have the establishment style of a Watchguard or DSL, but its first big contract ended with an ignominious exit from a tropical island. Julius Chan, the prime minister of Papua New Guinea, hired Sandline. Chan's nation was home to around 6 million people, made up of very many diverse communities living on the western side of the Pacific island of Papua and surrounding territories. Papua New Guinea's territories extended to Bougainville, one of the Solomon Islands, where a separatist rebellion cut away at central government authority. Chan wanted Sandline to spearhead an assault to break the Bougainville Revolutionary Army, which had been demanding independence and a better share of the island's great mineral wealth since 1988.

Spicer's team armed themselves with an impressive array of firepower. They came not only with Russian-made helicopter gunships, but also an aircraft he later described as a 'sky shout' plane. According to Spicer, '[i]t has a tape recorder and a speaker system that is an incredibly powerful system and can broadcast from the aircraft to the ground'. 'Its use is for psychological warfare', he explained. Sandline intended to shout at the Bougainville rebels, as well as shooting at them.[8] As it turned out, Spicer was out-shouted and outgunned by the citizens of Papua New Guinea. When his team arrived in Papua, the army rebelled against the scheme and imprisoned the mercenaries at the point of a gun. Riots and demonstrations spread across the capital, Port Moresby, in support of the troops. The soldiers and demonstrators thought the deal was an imperialist adventure, designed to seize Papua New Guinea's mineral wealth. Spicer was held at the point of a gun, and only released some days later.

These events seemed to stand somewhere between the island adventures of the 'Mad' Mike/Bob Denard type and the government contracts of the Watchguard model. Some of the mercenaries in the Papuan events had been supplied by Executive Outcomes, a mercenary company based in South Africa and linked to a long history of sometimes brutal fighting on their own continent, although Sandline also had an apparently legitimate contract with a government. But there were some distinctly new features to Sandline's Pacific fiasco. Like DSL in Colombia, Sandline seemed to have some links to the mineral industry and a big-name western company. The massive Panguna mine on Bougainville was one of the most contested locations in the secessionist revolt. Environmental damage caused by the mine had provoked anger among Bougainville's people, and the islanders protested that they saw little of the economic benefits of the massive facility. The Bougainville mine was partly owned by Rio Tinto Zinc (RTZ), one of the world's largest extractive companies.

Tim Spicer 'visibly blanched' under cross-examination in the inquiry into the Papua New Guinea events when counsel said that his firm was trying to use its military force to get its hands on the country's mineral wealth. Spicer was confronted with a letter saying that Sandline wanted to be paid in shares in the mine. The letter from Spicer to the Papuan minister of defence said, 'We are proposing . . . that we form a joint venture with your Government, ourselves and RTZ to reopen and operate the Bougainville mine once recovered.'[9] RTZ claimed that it had not been approached about this offer, but Spicer's firm certainly had contacts with smaller players in the mining and extraction industries. Tony Buckingham, a businessman who had moved between the boards of oil-drilling, diamond-mining and mercenary companies, helped Spicer with the Papua contract. Buckingham provided a link to the political establishment. At one point he persuaded UK parliamentary lobbyist Andrew Gifford and former Liberal leader David Steel to join him on the board of one of his firms, Heritage Oil. At the same time Buckingham furnished a business link to military firms like Sandline and Executive Outcomes.[10] While Spicer's firm had not only failed in its mission to take on the Bougainville rebels, but even precipitated the fall of the government that had hired it, the subsequent inquiry revealed that the company was nonetheless on its way to respectability. The international legal system agreed. Sandline sued the government of Papua New Guinea for not fulfilling its contract. The firm was unable to win on the battlefield, but it did win in court. In 1998 the International Arbitration Tribunal awarded the firm £20 million of compensation. In the final settlement, the government also had to return the firm's helicopter gunships, rifles and other materiel that had been impounded on the island.[11] When the government of Papua New Guinea delayed payment, the firm chased the country, freezing some of its international accounts with a Luxemburg court order. Thanks to the freeze on international funds, some aid payments to Papua New Guinea were suspended. Bill Skate, the country's prime minister, declared, 'The people we are dealing with turn my stomach in disgust. Sandline is attempting to hold the people of this nation to ransom', adding, 'It was bad enough that the Chan government paid them $US18 million so they would go and murder Papua New Guineans on Bougainville. Now they want to stand in the way of this nation receiving the financial support we are currently in need of.' Prime Minister Skate may have felt sick, but the company got its cash.[12]

For Sandline, Papua New Guinea was a military failure but a financial success. Its other big mobilization, in Sierra Leone, brought it to the centre of British politics. Sandline had close relations with the South African mercenary firm Executive Outcomes, which had a large pool of battle-hardened fighters recruited from the more notorious of the apartheid-era 'special forces', such as the '32 Battalion'. Sandline relied on this pool of fighters to bulk up its own ex-British officers on deployment in Papua New Guinea. The two companies seemed linked by contracts and relationships with the mineral firms under Tony Buckingham's stewardship. Sandline sometimes appeared to have a partnership with – or to work as an agent for – Executive Outcomes.

Executive Outcomes had been in business in Sierra Leone since 1995 at the latest. This former British colony in Africa had struggled with coups, counter-coups and rebellions since independence in 1961. In the 1990s the primary conflict was between the government – which had rotated between various military juntas as well as the democratically elected President Kabbah – and the Revolutionary Untied Front (RUF). The RUF had no ideology or programme beyond opposition to the government based in the capital, Freetown. It used great cruelty, mobilizing child soldiers and killing and maiming many civilians. The RUF was a warlord's army rather than a political organization, and maintained itself through sales from diamond mines in the territories it controlled. The RUF also had support from Charles Taylor, a warlord from neighbouring Liberia. Executive Outcomes approached the Freetown government in 1995 and offered military assistance to resist the RUF's approaches. Sources at the company speaking to the *Observer* characterized the deal with the Sierra Leone government as follows: 'We said: "You're in deep shit." They said they couldn't pay. We said they could pay us when they could afford it.'[13] The payment for this speculative deal was to be made, it seems, from Sierra Leone's mineral industry – although the company has rejected suggestions that it would be made directly from mining concessions. Executive Outcomes' presence in Sierra Leone also made it easier for mineral firms linked to Sandline gain a foothold there. In 1996 Diamondworks, a Canadian mineral company, announced that it would use Executive Outcomes to protect its mines in Sierra Leone. The announcement was made by Michael Grunberg, who had acted for Sandline in Papua New Guinea, and who has regularly fronted Sandline's public affairs since then.[14]

At some point in 1997, Sandline overtook Executive Outcomes in working both for President Kabbah and in guarding diamond mines in Sierra Leone. In fact, Sandline wound itself up the following year because of its embarrassment about the Papua New Guinea fiasco, and because of growing pressure within South Africa to outlaw mercenary operations. In 1998 the *Observer* suggested that Britain's ambassador to Sierra Leone had helped Sandline import 35 tonnes of weapons into the country to help the Kabbah government beat the RUF rebels. This would have been in breach of a UN arms embargo – the UN wanted an agreed international settlement to restore Kabbah, not a freelance commercial operation. The British government's reaction to the *Observer* revelations was swift and angry. One Foreign Office minister, Baroness Symons, told parliament that the story was untrue. Another Foreign Officer minister, Tony Lloyd, called the article 'ill-informed and scurrilous'. He said that there were no 'British officials' talks with hired killers', nor 'links to notorious mercenaries'. A year later, Foreign Secretary Robin Cook would declare, 'The main interest of Sandline International and its sister group of companies has been not democracy, but diamonds.' The newly elected Labour government, committed to an 'ethical' foreign policy, was denouncing Sandline, referring to it as an organization of diamond-hungry mercenaries and hired killers. Customs and Excise launched an investigation into Sandline's embargo-busting activities, raiding Spicer's house.

There was a slight problem, however. Responding to the raids, Sandline made clear exactly how many times it had met government officials, and exactly how much support it had received for its arms plan. Indeed, when Tony Lloyd addressed a Foreign Office conference on backing Kabbah in Sierra Leone, Rupert Bowen – a former MI6 officer turned director of a firm linked to Sandline – was in the invited audience. The company said that it had had support from Foreign Office officials and colonels in the field, and had imported the arms 'with the full prior knowledge and approval of Her Majesty's Government'.

While the new, would-be-ethical government denounced the mercenaries, the old structures of government had worked with them to shift the balance of military power. Sandline helped mostly Nigerian soldiers restore Kabbah to power in the capital, Freetown. Cheering crowds welcomed the end of RUF rule on the streets of the city. The British government was faced with a choice. It could believe that Kabbah could have been restored to power by an agreed UN-supported effort, and reject the underhand mercenary scheme. Indeed, UN forces did come to the country in 1999, and Robin Cook appeared to be working along these lines. By contrast, the government could decide that it was committed to 'what works', not to tired old principle. After all, even if Sandline's intervention had led to chaos in Papua New Guinea, even if mercenary helicopter-gunships killed civilians as well as rebels, and even if breaking the UN's authority was a dangerous game, the mercenaries had got rid of the hand-chopping warlords. Prime Minister Tony Blair was definitely keen to walk down this path. He declared that the 'good guys [had] won', and said that complaints about mercenary deals were misplaced, adding that 'a lot of the hoo-ha is overblown'.

Work began on re-evaluating the position of mercenaries in 1999. However, the Green Paper outlining the government's proposed stance on the issue was delayed for three years. Tony Blair personally ordered that the Green Paper be held back because he thought memories of the 'Arms to Africa' affair were still embarrassing, and there was a general election to be fought. Even after the election the government showed its nervousness by holding back its position paper. It finally published a paper on private military activity in 2002. So, just as the war on terror was launched, the government was poised between rejecting and legitimizing the use of mercenaries. In June 2001 Tony Blair demoted Cook and put Jack Straw in his place. As home secretary, Jack Straw had overcome his 'repugnance', and put private guards in charge of prisoners. Now, as foreign secretary, Straw was set to give the thumbs-up to putting private soldiers in charge of war.

The central theme of Straw's Green Paper[15] was that the market could regulate the private military companies: all the sins associated with soldiers of fortune belonged to the past; now there were also new mercenaries to work for New Labour. The document was keen to contrast 'mercenaries' who were 'disreputable thugs' with the new 'private military companies'. All of New Labour's prejudices – in favour of the market, of privatization, of 'what works', and of 'thinking the unthinkable' – were put to work in the foreign secretary's argument, without any embarrassing intrusions from reality. Straw's enthusiasm for mercenaries was based on the idea that they could make it easier to fight the new wars erupting in the wake of the end of the Cold War. Straw said that the basis for considering change was that 'we find ourselves in a world of small wars and weak states'. Soon, thanks in part to Jack Straw, that would all change: with the Iraq War, we would find ourselves in a world of big wars and even weaker states, which would be used in turn as further justification for the use of mercenary forces.

Straw also suggested that the need for 'humanitarian intervention' meant that there was a bigger market for mercenaries. Straw's paper said that an important part of the background to the new trade in violence was the 'increasing need for intervention by the international community'. He asserted that 'the cost of employing private military companies for certain functions in UN operations could be much lower than that of national armed forces'. He cited no evidence on the relative prices of mercenary versus national troops – possibly because experience has shown that such savings are illusory, even when leaving aside all the other political and social costs of using private armies. It was clear that Straw, a leading policymaker in the war on terror, believed that the new soldiers of fortune provided a readily usable, cheap and efficient force available to fight the new small wars and interventions. The mercenary companies were not only in a good position to profit from future wars; their existence actually made these wars more likely. Politicians like Straw thought that wars were easier to launch because they had a new pool of fighters to mobilize. The existence of the private armies lowered the bar on launching military action.

Straw's Green Paper looked at all the fundamental dangers of using mercenaries, and in every case argued that the invisible hand of the market would wash away all potential problems. By keeping a smart corporate office and using a serious-looking letterhead, soldiers of fortune became trustworthy businesses. Straw's paper claimed that 'private military companies are different from freelance mercenaries since they have a continuing corporate existence and will wish to maintain a reputation as respectable organizations'. A reliance on such companies' concern over their reputation, and on their commitment to corporate social responsibility, trumped concerns about the potential for violence and misbehaviour. The Green Paper accepted that mercenaries of the old school were 'guilty of abuses of human rights', but business-like attitudes meant that this was no longer an issue because, with private companies, 'there should be greater incentives to discipline. A company normally wants to have a continuing corporate existence: if it acquires a bad reputation, it will rule itself out of certain business.'

Brand reputation meant that private military companies (PMCs) would not switch sides or pursue their own agendas, because 'it is the kind of behaviour that would in the long run ruin a PMC's reputation and its business prospects'. Even the fact that military firms seemed drawn to 'economic exploitation' of 'readily available mineral resources' was actually an advantage, not a problem: the paper argued that 'the association of PMCs with mineral extraction has a positive side', because 'an interest in mineral extraction will give a PMC a vested interest in peace and stability'. Just as the Labour Party believed Enron was a responsible, respectable firm, and took its cash, so Straw thought the PMCs reflected the latest trend in corporate morality. Most pathetically, perhaps, Straw's paper looked at whether the presence of mercenaries actually prolonged wars. This problem, like any other addressed by the new model Labour Party, could be addressed with bureaucratic targets and contract clauses. The paper cited concerns that because mercenaries 'are paid to deal with conflict situations some argue that they have no interest in bringing conflict to an end'. The answer, however, lay in proper management techniques, as developed by consultants: if they 'write performance clauses into the contracts they should be able to give the PMCs a clear incentive to complete whatever tasks they have been employed for'. The UN Special Rapporteur on mercenaries' worries about human rights and sovereignty are airily dismissed by the British Foreign Office paper as the 'sometimes inchoate concerns of Mr Balles-teros'.

The Green Paper considered many 'options for regulation' of the new military firms, but these were never debated again. Programmes to monitor or control private military companies were not proposed, and the issue was never debated in parliament or otherwise taken forward. Instead, the government − exhausted by these moral contortions − decided it had done what it needed to do. The Green Paper led to no new laws or rules, but it did legitimize the new mercenaries. The stage was set for their widespread use in the upcoming Iraq intervention. It insisted: 'Today's world is a far cry from the 1960s when private military activity usually meant mercenaries of the rather unsavoury kind involved in post-colonial or neo-colonial conflicts.' In fact the new mercenaries would be ready to be engaged in the most unsavoury neocolonial conflict for decades.

6

Propaganda War

On 10 October 1990 a 15-year-old Kuwaiti girl, identified only as Nayirah to 'protect her family', gave chilling testimony about the brutality of Saddam Hussein's Iraqi troops during their invasion of neighbouring Kuwait. 'Nayirah' told a meeting of the United States Congressional Human Rights Caucus that she had worked as a volunteer in the Al-Idar hospital, and that 'while I was there, I saw the Iraqi soldiers come into the hospital with guns. They took the babies out of the incubators, took the incubators and left the children to die on the cold floor.'[1] This shocking story became one of the louder rallying cries for the US-led war that expelled Saddam's forces from Kuwait in 1991. Saddam's invasion of Kuwait was clearly an act of unprovoked aggression – but raising enough sympathy for the authoritarian, undemocratic and exploitative Kuwaiti government among Western populations to make the mobilization of hundreds of thousands of troops half a world away was not an easy task. The terrible tale of the murdered infants became the central image that shifted sympathy enough to translate into support for war. President Bush Sr referred to the story at least ten times in the following weeks, reminding US citizens with horror about the 'babies pulled from incubators and scattered like firewood across the floor'.[2] Senators, news reporters, and exiled Kuwaitis referred again and again to Saddam's soldiers' terrible slaughter of the innocents, and US public opinion shifted behind war against Saddam.

There were two remarkable things about the dead baby story. Firstly, it wasn't true. Secondly, it became a story thanks to the hard work of a commercial public relations firm, Hill & Knowlton. Nayirah was in fact the daughter of the Kuwaiti ambassador to the US. No credible authority was able to confirm the mass incubator killing after Iraqi forces were expelled from Kuwait, and many witnesses explicitly denied it. Her testimony was part of a campaign paid for by the Kuwaiti oil sheikhs through a front group, Citizens for a Free Kuwait, and run by Public Affairs giant Hill & Knowlton. The campaign stood out as a remarkable piece of privatized propaganda for war. Hill & Knowlton's Kuwaiti campaign was investigated and picked over on prime time TV – albeit after the war was over.[3] That a private PR firm should be so central in the drive towards war stood out as shocking and extraordinary; but it turns out that, far from being an aberration, the private PR drive for war became the norm in the new war on terror.

Over the next fifteen years, governments and other agencies began turning repeatedly to the private sector to provide the frontline information warriors in the propaganda war. When it came to the war on terror, two issues turned privatized propaganda into a central front in the new Anglo-American campaign. Firstly, the 'war on terror' provided a deeply ideological battlefield. The US president and British prime minister made clear that this was a battle of ideas. The war on terror was intended to include campaigns to win over foreign populations, persuading them to reject anti-Western and Islamist ideas. It included a battle to win over British and US populations to unquestioning support of their leaders for a strategy that rolled a whole series of contentious security, military and political strategies into one supposedly unitary battle against savagery and 'terror'. Public relations are as important to the war on terror as guns. Secondly, the British and US governments were thoroughly committed to the idea that the private sector superior in all ways to the state as a provider of services. The Anglo-American elite was drawn to use the private sector because it reduced governmental accountability and responsibility for the intellectual warriors against the enemy, in the same way that privatization reduced overt involvement in other areas of battle. These strategies were rehearsed in the first Gulf War and in the now-hidden, now-open battle against Saddam that followed. After 9/11 the privately run propaganda war became a key feature of Western strategy.

Public affairs companies attracted controversy long before the Kuwait affair. They are essentially public relations outfits focusing on issues of public policy, legislation and regulation. Using all of the PR man's tricks in the political arena is by nature contentious: when the hidden persuaders are trying to persuade us of what should be legal and what should be outlawed, rather than just of what colour our shirts should be, controversy is inescapable. The history of Hill & Knowlton itself provides a good illustration of the worrying world of commercial public affairs. The firm began when former journalist John Wiley Hill opened a public relations office in 1927. Hill grew his business into one of the world's largest communications companies, thanks to two lucrative areas of work: Hill threw his talents both into trying to stop people striking and to keep them smoking.

Hill had one set of contracts with the US steel industry, which in the 1930s was resisting attempts to organize trade unions. This resistance included gunfire: in 1937 company police fired on pro-union demonstrators, killing ten in the 'Republic Steel Massacre'. Hill oversaw the production of thousands of booklets and pamphlets claiming that the cops had fired in self-defence, and that the unions represented 'communist infiltration'. From 1953 Hill's firm expanded further, thanks to a joint contract with tobacco firms aimed at downplaying growing evidence linking cigarettes to cancer and other health problems. In these two campaigns Hill established some basic principles. Firstly, companies could best get their message across by using apparently independent intermediaries or front organizations. So the Steel companies funded anti-union 'citizens' councils', and the cigarette companies paid for a 'Tobacco Industry Research Council'. Secondly, companies needed to focus on simple, clear, credible messages to try and dominate the debate.[4] Public affairs companies ultimately wanted to influence legislators, and tried hard to be politically connected; but they also had to make their messages look like they came up from the grass roots.

People were killed by the strikebreaking policemen's bullets and by the tobacco firms' cigarettes, but selling a war during peacetime took the public affairs firm into a new area. Commercial advertisers had cooperated with the government during World War II, when they pulled together the voluntary War Advertising Council, producing patriotic publicity. The War Advertising Council ran campaigns persuading US citizens to back the military effort by buying war bonds, or by collecting scrap metal, used tyres and old paper for recycling for the army. This body continued into the Cold War as the Advertising Council, encouraging Americans to remain confident in the contest with Soviet Communism through exhibitions extolling 'People's Capitalism'. Advertisers and the publicity industry also cooperated with the overseas propaganda organization, the United States Information Agency. These activities were regulated by the

Smith–Mundt Act of 1948, which specifically banned the use of state funds for propaganda aimed at US citizens: legally, propaganda had to be aimed abroad, not at home. In the war on terror, the US would return to this Cold War model of using people with advertising backgrounds to help build a general sense of US superiority. But Hill & Knowlton's Kuwait campaign broke very new ground: this was a publicity campaign aimed very specifically at launching a specific hot war, not vaguely supporting values in a long Cold War, and was largely directed at the US population itself.

The US ensured a powerful position in the post-Vietnam War world by backing a series of 'regional strongmen', and only supplementing this international structure with doses of direct intervention when strictly necessary. In 1990 Saddam was one of these strongmen. Sometimes men use steroids as a short-cut to building muscle. The US's regional strong-men were built up on the steroids of arms sales, as well as economic and diplomatic support. The use of steroids can lead to ''roid rages' of uncontrollable anger, and Saddam seemed to succumb to a military ''roid rage' when he sent his forces into neighbouring Kuwait. US ambassador April Glaspie's assurance eight days before the invasion that the US took 'no position in the event of any border conflict between Iraq and Kuwait' may have encouraged him.[5] The history of US support for Saddam made direct US military intervention against the Kuwait inter-vention a difficult sell. So too did the nature of the Kuwaiti regime: undemocratic, authoritarian, isolated, and reliant on an army of badly treated foreign workers.

The Kuwaiti government sought to overcome these obstacles and win backing for the intervention it needed to put it back on its throne by hiring the men who had helped sell cigarettes and anti-union campaigns. They paid Hill & Knowlton over $10 million to sell the war. The firm could offer political connections: Craig Fuller, a close friend of and former chief of staff for George Bush Sr, headed the firm's Washington office. Fuller later left the firm to become the head of public affairs for Philip Morris – the Marlboro men – reinforcing the association between selling wars and selling cigarettes. Hill & Knowlton set to work on two classic PR strategies: first, they founded a front group, 'Citizens for a Free Kuwait', to campaign for war; second, they set out, in Fuller's words, to 'develop a clear, concise message and tell the story effectively'.[6] That message, pumped out in brochures, free footage for television stations and lobby meetings, finally crystallized in the incubator outrage. In an illustration of the smoke and mirrors at work in the campaign, the Congressional Human Rights Caucus meeting on Capitol Hill looked exactly like an official Congressional meeting, but in fact had no statutory basis. Unlike in a real Congressional hearing, the participants could not be prosecuted for perjury. Some were embarrassed when the story came under question: Amnesty International, which had given credence to the tale, retracted its support. But Hill & Knowlton, President Bush, and the government of Kuwait felt no need to look back after they had got their war. The affair was also the first step in the development of private war propaganda, which was to grow greatly after 11 September 2001. This new development of privatized propaganda mostly happened in the US in the ten years before 2001; but there were transatlantic connections. Hill & Knowlton were at this time a subsidiary of a British firm, WPP. After the second Gulf War, more British firms became involved in this publicity battle.

When George W. Bush launched the war on terror in 2001, Hill & Knowlton won less government work than their competitors, and had to wait longer for the contracts they did win; it is likely that their relatively well publicized role in the first Gulf War tarnished their brand for the new conflict. But they still had a presence. In 2006 the State Department gave the firm a $4 million contract to win over hearts and minds in Afghanistan. In particular, the firm was tasked with dissuading Afghans from growing opium poppies. Nato forces had ousted the Taleban, but were now fighting fierce gun battles with forces allied to the former fundamentalist government, who had found new support thanks to the failures of the reconstruction. At the same time opium production was soaring, challenging Western-sponsored rule in the country. The war on terror and its predecessor, the war on drugs, were merging, and Hill & Knowlton were hired to stop this happening. The firm was subcontracted to help run the new, supposedly independent Afghan government: the contract stipulated that the PR firm should have staff working inside three Afghan ministries to 'build capability'.[7]

The company arrived late on the battlefield of the war on terror because of delays caused, it seemed, by their reputation resulting from the Iraq incubator incident. Their other presence in the new ideological war was subtler. Jeff Raleigh, formerly a Hill & Knowlton executive, became a member of the Afghanistan Reconstruction Group, advising the US ambassador how to build popular support for the new Afghan government.[8] Victoria 'Torie' Clark moved from Hill & Knowlton to become Donald Rumsfeld's press spokesman. She was responsible for 'embedding' reporters – a tactic of placing journalists inside allied military units, which helped win sympathetic press for allied actions in Afghanistan and Iraq.[9] Don Meyer, who worked with Clarke at Hill & Knowlton, also worked for Rumsfeld, hoping to craft the PR response to 9/11, and the strategies for the Afghan and Iraq wars, before returning to the firm.[10] Laurie Fitz-Pegado, the Hill & Knowlton executive who had helped coach Iraqis giving evidence to Congress in 1990, including Nayirah, also had a walk-on role on the propaganda stage in the war on terror. American commandos rescued a wounded female US private, Jessica Lynch, from an Iraqi hospital, in one of the most dramatic and heroic battles in the overthrow of Saddam. On first telling, the tale spoke of wicked Iraqis abusing a defenceless female soldier, and of heroic US troops rescuing her. Fitz-Pegado, now working for another PR firm, publicized a book containing a dramatic version of this morality tale. On second glance, however, 'Saving Private Lynch' turned out to be an entirely different narrative. Contrary to Fitz-Pegado's second Gulf story, Iraqi medical staff said that they had looked after Lynch as best they could, and would have happily handed her back to allied forces without being shot at or harassed by the US snatch squad.[11]

While Hill & Knowlton had to wait for work in the war on terror, other firms ran to the front, brochures and briefings at the ready. They were following in the footsteps of military PR pioneers who had worked on the Iraq issue in the ten preceding years. Iraq was the key territory in the development of the privatized information war long before 9/11, and became even more important in that development after the terrorist attacks: most of the hijackers of the aeroplanes that smashed into the Twin Towers were Saudi; none were Iraqi. Iraq nevertheless became central to the war on terror. Thad Anderson, a New York City law student, got hold of some notes made by Stephen Cambone describing his boss, US Secretary of State Donald Rumsfeld's instructions within a couple of hours of the fall of the World Trade Centre.[12] The notes report Rumsfeld as saying: 'Near term target needs – go massive – sweep it all up, things related and not.' This suggests that Rumsfeld was not concerned merely to find those responsible for the attack, but to respond with a massive show of power aimed even at those 'not related' to the terror attacks. The notes also say, 'Best info fast. Judge whether good enough [to] hit [Saddam Hussein] at same time – not only [Osama bin Laden]'. So shortly after the Towers had fallen, Rumsfeld was suggesting a massive attack against the apparently unrelated Saddam Hussein. These notes, and the shoe-horning of Iraq into the 'war on terror', show that while this was a response to the 9/11 attacks, the intention was to use the anti-terror crusade to deal with existing and unrelated perceived strategic threats to the US. The leadership in the White House aimed to marshal its allies under a banner of the war on terror, but to use the crusade against all those it felt were its enemies, whether 'terrorist' or not.

One month after Mohammed Atta and his associates had used passenger aeroplanes as weapons, Rumsfeld filled in some of the gaps in the notes of his immediate reaction to the mass murder. In a Department of Defense briefing Rumsfeld mused, 'Maybe, just maybe, the world will sufficiently register the danger that exists on the globe and have this event cause the kind of sense of urgency and offer the kind of opportunities that World War II offered, to refashion much of the world.'[13] So the war on terror became a way of packaging a wide-ranging strategy to 'refashion . . . the world', rather than a police operation to chase down those behind the New York killings. Bush's former anti-terror adviser, Richard Clarke, made a similar point. On the morning of 12 September 2001, Clarke arrived at the White House expecting 'a round of meetings examining what the next attacks could be . . . Instead I walked into a series of discussions about Iraq.' Clarke describes himself as 'incredulous', and then recalls that he 'realized with almost a sharp physical pain that Rumsfeld and [his deputy Paul] Wolfowitz were going to try to take advantage of this national tragedy to promote their agenda about Iraq'. The White House was not going to respond to the attacks as if they were a crime; it was not going to focus on identifying, investigating and prosecuting the culprits. Instead it was going to treat this as a 'war'. The attacks made the US look weak, forcing the administration to project an image of strength across all areas, whether linked directly to the terrorists or not. Like the Cold War, this was to be a wide-ranging campaign involving a fight for general US dominance across the military and political spectrum. As in any war, defeating the enemies meant binding together civilian populations behind the country's leadership, and bringing allies together under national leadership. Also, as in any war, victory could mean not just defeating the foe but also constructing a new settlement between the victorious national powers. Winning leadership among the victors could be as important a prize as breaking the enemy.

Hill & Knowlton's Citizens for a Free Kuwait front had done its work when the US pulled together a military coalition to expel Saddam Hussein from the country in the first Gulf War. The Kuwaiti government then employed a new PR firm, the Rendon Group, to maintain political support for its regime. The firm had been founded by Ralph Rendon, who had a history of political campaigning within the Democratic Party in the 1980s. He had, it seems, come to the attention of the CIA in Central America: the US wanted to overthrow General Noriega of Panama, who, like Saddam, was a former regional strongman and US ally who had had the audacity to turn on his former masters. Rendon was involved in offering PR advice to Noriega's opponent. An association between Rendon and the CIA appears to have started at that time.

In Kuwait the Rendon Group had a task described by the *Washington Post* as

> deflecting attention away from the controversial aspects of the country: the lack of a democratic system of government, treatment of women as second-class citizens, the flamboyant lifestyle of some members of the Kuwaiti elite and a predilection for leaving all nuts-and-bolts work to foreign guest workers.

It was in both the Kuwaiti and Saudi governments' interests that the public did not focus on the Kuwaitis' tendency to 'arrest dissidents and torture them without trial'.[14] When, for example, the press was filled with reports of exiled Kuwaitis dancing the night away in discos in Cairo, the Rendon Group organized a highly publicized mailing of 20,000 Valentine's cards to US troops. The company also got thousands of small US flags into the hands of newly liberated Kuwaitis so that they could wave them at the columns of American troops driving through their country, making a striking television picture. The Group's propaganda work was here funded by the Kuwaitis, but aimed squarely at the US population.

The Rendon Group's next Iraq contract was funded directly by the US: the company was paid to help undermine Saddam. But while Rendon's new work was ostensibly focused on Iraq, it arguably still affected a mostly US audience. It also represented a step forward for privatized psychological warfare, and helped build and shape the war on terror. While Saddam's 'mother of all battles' simply failed to materialize, his much vaunted Republican Guard melted before the overwhelming force of the allies (quite literally in some cases, as the attackers made liberal use of incendiary weapons on the Mutla ridge), and his occupation of Kuwait ended in an ignominious retreat, the dictator remained in power in his own country. In the run-up to the war, President Bush had called for 'Iraqi people to take matters into their own hands to force Saddam Hussein, the dictator, to step aside'. In the aftermath of Saddam's rout from Kuwait, they did just that. Returning soldiers sparked a Shiite rebellion around the southern city of Basra, while Kurdish forces rose up in the north. But US officials feared that the southern rebels would lean towards Iran and be guided by Islamic politics, while the northern revolt might cause problems with Turkey – an American ally with its own restive Kurdish population. The White House's preferred option of a coup and a new Saddam-lite failed to materialize, so instead the allies stood by while the Republican Guard put down the uprisings with extreme brutality, often within sight of US troop lines. In particular, the US allowed Saddam's forces to use their helicopter gunships to put down the revolts, despite absolute allied air superiority. Faced with genuinely independent revolts against Saddam's regime, the United States dithered. The American government would in later years try and build up a dependant and dependable opposition to Saddam, but they did not feel able to support the real thing when it sprang up in the streets of Iraq.

The great scale of the uprising, and the deep violence of its suppression, left Saddam further entrenched in power, and took the polish off the US victory. Consequently, the US began a long psychological war over Iraq involving the Rendon Group. This represented another major step on the road to privately run psychological warfare: the work of both Hill & Knowlton and Rendon in the first Gulf War had broken new ground in the use of PR in the cause of war. But while the campaigns were clearly carried out with the cooperation of senior US politicians, they were ultimately paid for by the Kuwaitis themselves: Rendon's new contract was directly funded by the US.

Saddam was able to stay in power after his defeat in Kuwait partly because of the fractiousness of internal opposition. His dictatorship bred many rebels who tried to build underground or exiled opposition groups.

However, these did not coalesce under one leadership. Instead the opposition fragmented on poltical lines, or by religion or nationality, or by their relation to the ruling Baath party or their sponsorship by different states bordering Iraq. The opposition was hampered by this split between Kurdish, Shiite, Sunni, Islamic, secular, Baathist, military, and other groups. The CIA set out to pressure Saddam by paying the Rendon Group to pull together the Iraqi opposition. In 1992, at a Vienna meeting organized with Rendon's help, the new 'Iraqi National Congress' (INC) made its debut before the world. Ahmed Chalabi, the group's leader, announced, 'We want to get rid of the traditional opposition under the control of people who for decades have failed to overthrow Saddam.'[15] Chalabi's boasts were backed by substantial CIA funds – around $326,000 a month – paid to the Rendon Group. Some estimates suggest that Rendon made $100 million through the INC contract up to 1997. The INC seemed to work like a classic PR front: ostensibly it represented the independent voice of Iraqi democrats; in fact it was a piece of CIA ventriloquism. Even the name was allegedly picked out by Rendon. The PR firm and the INC were so close that one of Rendon's key staff, Francis Brooke, changed hats and became a key member of the INC itself.

Judged by the standards of other liberation movements, the INC was a miserable failure; it was unable to maintain a coalition of forces against Saddam. According to British Foreign Office briefings the INC 'soon collapsed amid infighting' after its foundation. The INC suffered its worst setback in 1996, when Saddam's forces killed hundreds of INC supporters after a failed uprising attempt in the Iraqi Kurdish city of Irbil. The Foreign Office papers also make clear that Saddam was able to break up the INC because of infighting among his opponents and support for Saddam's army from one of the Kurdish parties. A 2004 briefing paper reveals that in 1995 the INC

> made a failed attempt to remove Saddam with CIA support. Following an invitation from the Kurdistan Democratic Party to retake [Irbil] in 1996, Saddam Hussein's forces and his Kurdish allies attacked INC bases in northern Iraq, killing 200 supporters and forcing thousands to flee.[16]

The Rendon Group hoped to build the INC's strength by using CIA funds, by political negotiation among the anti-Saddam groups, and by propaganda aimed into Iraq. Rendon helped with scripts calling for Iraqi army officers to defect, broadcast on two INC radio stations with transmitters in Saudi Arabia and Kuwait.[17] Rendon organized a travelling photographic exhibition of Iraqi atrocities, as well as videos and radio skits that ridiculed Saddam Hussein, and even an anti-Saddam comic book. But this 'covert PR campaign' had negligible impact on Saddam. A journalist asked Rendon, 'Do you think that the campaign was designed to bring him down or just to irritate him?' Rendon responded, 'I don't know.'[18]

It was not clear to its participants whether this private psychological warfare was anything more than an irritant to the Iraqi regime; but that is possibly the wrong way to judge the campaign. Viewed as propaganda aimed not at Iraqis, but at the US and British populations, it was entirely successful. Rendon's CIA money set up INC offices in London, Boston and Washington. His counselling apparently helped the INC – which the British Foreign Office had described as having 'little or no credibility' in Iraq – to pose in the US and UK as a serious opposition force. The INC acted like a classic PR front group, persuading western populations that Saddam was a real and present danger to the West, rather than an isolated and weakened dictator. The INC operation also used its CIA millions and PR-firm guidance to give the impression that there was a united secular Iraqi opposition that was generally warmly disposed to the West – rather than the patchwork of split, often Islamist groups that were still angry about the 1991 betrayal.

The US was able to fund propaganda that acted on its own population, circumventing the 1948 Smith–Mundt Act which banned government funded propaganda being aimed at US citizens. By privatizing the propaganda war, they were able to keep responsibility for their actions at arm's length. The support for the INC and its PR allies showed all the dangers of other elements of the privatized war on terror: the US government hired commercial operators so that it could avoid responsibility for the war; it handed over power to private firms that acted beyond the control of democratically elected legislators; it ended up with a vastly expensive and often inefficient apparatus; worst of all, it created a permanent financial lobby for more 'security' spending. After the failure of the 1995 action against Saddam, the CIA cut off funding for the INC. However, while under the Rendon Group's tutelage the INC had not developed the ability to challenge Saddam seriously, it had become skilled at lobbying Western officials. The INC simply used its lobbying skills to find a new source of funds. After persistent approaches to US politicians, the INC became, from 1998 on, the chief beneficiary of millions of dollars from the State Department under the Iraq Liberation Act. The INC could not take on Saddam, but it could outmanoeuvre the CIA in the search for public money. Most importantly, the Rendon-supported INC pumped out story after story about Saddam's supposed weapons of mass destruction and links to terrorism, creating a whole narrative based on bio-terrorism, nuclear terrorism, and support for state-sponsored terror.

From 1999 onwards, Rendon's work was augmented by that of another 'public affairs' company. BKSH, part of the international PR giant Burson-Marsteller, was paid a reported $25,000 a month to help with the INC's 'communication initiatives'. Burson-Marsteller had a typically unattractive portfolio of clients. In the mid-1990s the firm formed a 'national smokers' alliance' for Marlboro manufacturer Philip Morris, to pose as a grass roots revolt against restrictions on smoking. The company had long experience in the US of polishing the image of repressive regimes: Burson-Marsteller had represented Indonesia when the country faced heavy criticism for its bloody annexation of East Timor. The firm had at various times held Washington accounts for dictators ranging from Romania's Nicolae Ceausescu to the Saudi sheikhs. BKSH also had powerful political connections: its chairman, Charles Black, worked on the presidential campaigns of both George Bush Sr and his son. BKSH put Ira Levinson onto the INC account. She had previous experience in marketing a 'rebel' group to US conservatives: she had successfully represented Jonas Savimbi's UNITA. With her help, UNITA won US money to help fund its battles with the MPLA government of Angola, while glossing over the dismal human rights record of the warlord's African army.[19]

For its part, the Rendon Group denied any direct involvement in the INC's dissemination of tales about Saddam's links to terrorism or stocks of WMD, but there was no denying its support for and shaping of the INC itself. Moreover, the INC's focus on lobbying, publicity and propaganda about Saddam, aimed at Western populations and governments, reflected the Rendon Group's experience and strengths as a public relations firm. The Rendon–INC contract had the Anglo-American flavour of many of the private contracts that would coalesce around the war on terror.

Rendon set up its own operations and those of the INC with a London office, and the INC used it to circulate propagandistic stories about Saddam to the British newspapers, which in turn influenced the US press. The INC's London office acted like a funnel to pour disinformation back into the US, outmanoeuvring the Americans' Smith–Mundt Act and allowing US-funded propaganda to reach the domestic population.

In March 2004 the Knight-Ridder news agency got hold of a letter from the INC to the US Senate Appropriations Committee justifying the millions of dollars the group had received from the US. The letter was effectively a bill for their regular $4 million payment for an 'information collection programme', authorized by the US – but it referred not to the collection of information, but to its dissemination. The letter, headed 'Summary of ICP product cited in major English language news outlets worldwide (October 2001–May 2002)', was the clearest indication that the INC acted like a PR subcontractor – a private company billing the US for its work in the information war. The document reads like an invoice from a PR firm to its client.

The INC listed 108 articles in British and US newspapers that had been inspired by INC material. Many contained 'information' that was completely untrue. The INC was invoicing the US government for spreading stories about imaginary additions to Saddam's WMD programme and false tales about Iraq's links with al-Qaeda. By paying for a private organization to take control of this part of the information war, the US government was able to put stories into the public arena via the newspapers that were too absurd to include even in their own inflated 'dossiers'; by using a paid-for third party to tell these tall tales, the US government was also able to avoid responsibility for these particular lies after the war. The British and US publics, unsettled by failures in the post-war occupation of Iraq, became very critical of the complete lack of evidence about WMD or terror links in post-war Iraq. The Bush and Blair governments faced prolonged questioning about the information they had circulated about Iraq; but thanks to the INC they could at least avoid responsibility for some of the most absurd propaganda they had funded.[20]

Major US publications like the *New York Times* and *Washington Post* went through long and anguished inquiries into the misinformation they had circulated about Iraq before the war. By contrast, most British newspapers simply turned 180 degrees and started attacking the Blair government's absurd lies about Iraq, ignoring their own elaborate fantasies about Saddam's links to the terrorist attacks. But the British press figured very heavily in the INC's propaganda invoice.

So, for example, the stories of Iraqi civil engineer Adnan al-Haideri were used in many of the INC sponsored stories. He falsely claimed to have built underground bio-warfare labs and worked on an Iraqi nuclear programme. The INC claimed credit for a *Sunday Times* article, 'Saddam's arsenal revealed',[21] describing a 'secret underground network of laboratories' where the dictator was brewing up WMD and a fleet of seven mobile biological weapons laboratories 'disguised as milk trucks'. The newspaper said the information was 'high grade', but it was actually completely untrue. The INC also claimed credit for an article in *The Times*, the *Independent*, the *Express* and the *Daily Telegraph*, all repeating al-Haideri's stories about secret underground weapons factories without a hint of scepticism. The INC-inspired stories in the British newspapers even said the Iraqi regime was secretly building atom bombs and other terrifying weapons at sites including a factory hidden beneath Baghdad's hospitals.[22] The INC also listed a number of articles by Anglo-American journalist Christopher Hitchens, including pieces in the *Evening Standard* and *Guardian,* claiming that Saddam was 'within a measurable distance of acquiring doomsday materials', and 'certainly has nerve gas and chemical weapons'.[23]

The links between Saddam and terrorism make up many of the stories the INC say they were paid to peddle, which shows that drawing Iraq into the war on terror was one of the central functions of the INC. Claims that Saddam was behind 9/11 are prominent in the list of INC propaganda funded by the US, including a *Daily Telegraph* article claiming Saddam 'armed Bin Laden and funded Al Qaeda allies', and that 'Iraq sent conventional and perhaps biological or chemical weapons to Osama bin Laden in Afghanistan'. The INC also claimed to be behind a *Times* article saying that Iraq had a 'terror training camp' which 'teaches hijacking', suggesting that Saddam 'had a hand' in the 9/11 plot.[24] The INC's most impressive success linking Saddam and terror came in a 2,500-word 'Focus Special' in the *Observer*, claiming that Saddam was not only behind the 9/11 attacks, but also probably linked to the US 'anthrax letters'.[25] These INC-planted stories took up thousands of words in newspapers with millions of readers. They were spread out over the years between the attack on the Twin Towers and the attack on Iraq, creating a steady drum-beat on the road to war. They were funded by the US government but seemed to come from trusted third parties, making them invaluable propaganda.

The work of communications companies in helping to make Iraq a front in the war on terror was not secret, but nor was it terribly open. After Saddam's fall, the British and US governments started to use private companies in the propaganda war far more openly and aggressively, and across a wider battlefield. The allies in the war on terror had a formal information policy that looked very like the Cold War approach: the coalition of the willing mobilized men and women from the political and advertising worlds to help build confidence and fight specific campaigns. In an echo of the old Cold War Advertising Council, the US government mobilized figures from the world of marketing. Charlotte Beers, who had made her name promoting Uncle Ben's Rice, was made the under secretary of state for public diplomacy in 2001. Beers had moved from promoting commercial brands to trying to sell 'Brand America'. In 2005 Kevin Roberts, chief executive of Saatchi & Saatchi and also a 'brand expert', was invited to the Pentagon to discuss the battle of ideas with Islamic extremism. In 2001 the 'Coalition Information Centre' was built around Alastair Campbell, Tony Blair's abrasive press spokesman, and Tucker Eskew, a Republican official who had been very active in the campaign to ensure that Florida went for Bush in the hotly contested 2000 election.

The British and US governments faced serious attacks on all these PR initiatives. Charlotte Beers's efforts were widely seen as ineffectual, while Kevin Roberts was mocked as being responsible for a short-lived and unsuccessful attempt to rebrand the war on terror as a 'global struggle against violent extremism' – a catchphrase that just didn't catch on. The Coalition Information Centre's output was picked over after Saddam's WMDs were exposed as a fantasy. All coalition comments on Afghanistan and Iraq became hostages to fortune, and its PR promises were picked over by the press following each coalition reversal of fortune.

By using commercial companies to run much of the propaganda war, the coalition avoided further embarrassment. While it was held accountable for official acts of public diplomacy and propaganda, it avoided contamination by the commercially run information operations. That does not mean the corporate PR in the war on terror was completely successful: while Western media companies were effective at helping direct propaganda at Western populations, they were often ineffectual when it came to addressing a Middle Eastern audience. Like so many of the privately delivered operations in Iraq, the media work was often disastrous. Private companies helped win the propaganda war to get European and US voters behind an attack on Iraq, but they largely lost the propaganda war to get the Iraqis to welcome Western forces. Private PR 'expertise' was often exposed as amateurish and useless within Iraq. The companies were good at attracting Western cash to spend on propaganda, but their products were often dire. However, despite becoming very aware of their failings, the allies continued to throw money at the information contractors, clearly believing that the advantage of passing on direct responsibility for the propaganda war outweighed the costs incurred by the badly delivered messages.

After Saddam's fall the allies set up a new media empire in Iraq. They knew they had to compete with broadcasts from the Qatar-based al-Jazeera satellite channel and a dizzying range of new Iraqi newspapers. Sometimes the allies could deal directly with the threat of media competition – al-Jazeera's Baghdad offices were hit by a US missile just before Saddam's fall, and *Al-Hawza* – the newspaper linked to Iraq's Mahdi Army – was closed down by US troops in 2004 after publishing an article saying Paul Bremer, the US administrator in Iraq 'follow[ed] the steps of Saddam'. But the allies wanted to win the information war positively. The television studio is now as much a centre of power and a player in war as a missile battery, so the occupiers set out to win the war on terror in Iraq in the media, as well as on the ground. In the event, the private contractors given this mission failed badly.

The first contract to run the Iraqi Media Network, made up of the al-Iraqiya television station and the *Al-Sabah* newspaper, went to a US-based multinational, the Science Applications International Corp. – known as SAIC – that also had contracts to help set up Iraq's new post-Saddam prison system. The company had no previous experience of running television stations, publishing newspapers, or handling radio stations, which were also included in the contract. SAIC did, however, have plenty of government contracts and strong links to the military–industrial complex. Former UN weapons inspector David Kay – whom the president later turned to in a last fruitless search for Saddam's WMD – was a SAIC vice president from 1993 to 2002. The firm employed many staff who had formerly worked in the US security services. It had many military contracts, not all of which worked well – it paid a $500,000 fine in 2004 following allegations that it had exaggerated the efficiency of a computer system intended to keep US army bases clean. The following year SAIC paid a $2.5 million fine for overcharging on a contract to clean a Texas air force base.[26]

Failing to keep army bases clean was one thing, but failing to run the Iraqi media was altogether more serious. After eleven months, the Pentagon handed the contract to another firm, after SAIC's TV station was widely condemned as amateurish and too propagandistic to win Iraqi support. SAIC soaked up tens of millions of government dollars in the first year after Saddam's fall, but managed to broadcast only a mixture of Arabic singing and coalition announcements. Don North, a respected correspondent for the NBC television network who advised SAIC, said that its station was 'an irrelevant mouthpiece for Coalition Provisional Authority propaganda, managed news and mediocre programs'. SAIC wasted money prodigiously on the scheme. The Pentagon's inspector general, auditing the contract, noted that SAIC's costs had shot up from $15 million to $82 million. Contractors were paid while on holiday; executives demanded that 'Humvee' four-wheel-drive cars be airlifted into Iraq; but the station's output failed to seize the attention of Iraqis.

Tony Blair was widely criticized for not persuading his senior partner, George W. Bush, to handle the post-war occupation better. The occupying forces began losing control of Iraq because they imposed Western troops and companies on the region with no regard for local feelings, and it seemed that the British government was doing nothing to blunt US arrogance in this area. But the intensely media-conscious Blair government did pick up very quickly on the failures of the occupiers' information war. George Packer's incisive study of the failures of the occupation[27] reveals that Blair was personally angry about the lacklustre state of the official media in post-occupation Iraq: Packer reports 'everyone in Baghdad knew that the media project was a disaster. In London, Tony Blair knew and he was tearing his hair out trying to get it fixed.' This was confirmed by the release of a 2003 memo from John Sawers, the UK's top diplomat in the region, to Downing Street. The memo, entitled 'Iraq: What's Going Wrong?', focused quickly on the failures of the Iraqi Media Network, pointing out that street leaflets 'calling for the killing of all US forces' had greater purchase on the population than the Iraqi media. The occupiers' TV station suffered from 'tightly controlled' content and 'risk[ed] not being credible'. Sawers warned that 'the clock [was] ticking', and worried that the occupying authorities had 'no leadership, no strategy, no coordination, no structure, and [was] inaccessible to ordinary Iraqis'. He suggested that the first thing the television station should do to mask its propagandistic nature was to broadcast one British Premier League football match to the Iraqis each day. Sawers was deeply frustrated that the Americans refused to try and placate the Iraqis with video recordings of Manchester United, Chelsea and Arsenal on the pitch and complained that the US officials 'just don't get it'.

While other areas of the 'reconstruction' of Iraq continued to flounder, it seems that Blair did apply enough pressure to change the direction of television in the country. SAIC was replaced with another firm, Harris Communications, which was also a largely military company, but did have some broadcast experience. Another contractor, Albany Associates, run by former British Royal Marine Simon Haselock, was brought in by the UK to offer more advice to the Iraqi Media Network. Haselock had experience as a UN spokesman in Bosnia, and was appointed for his media savvy. Another British firm, Chiltern Broadcast Management, run by a colonel formerly with the British army's 'psychological operations' unit, was also engaged to help Iraqi TV.

The fate of official Iraqi television was improved by a populist gesture, albeit in the form of broadcasting brutality, rather than British Premier League football. In 2005 al-Iraqiya television began showing what became the country's most popular television programme. Al-Iraqiyah had found its populist spirit, and was broadcasting a reality show that brought Iraqis together around the television set. 'Terror in the Grip of Justice' did not show the cavortings of minor or wannabe celebrities, but instead featured captured terrorists confessing on camera to police interrogators. Iraqis – especially Shiites who had suffered from sectarian attacks – were gripped by a show that displayed their enemies as weak and humiliated. Captured fighters confessed to hideous murders, but also admitted that they were drunkards, criminals and homosexuals: the feared killers confessed to drunken gay orgies in mosques.[28] The programme was a powerful weapon in the propaganda war, delegitimizing one strain of the insurgency: thanks to the programme, 'mujahedin' became street slang for 'gay'.

British-funded media contractor Simon Haselock defended the programme, telling the BBC: 'We have to understand where they're coming from.' It was important, he said, 'to draw the right balance between the independent, professional public approach that we would be familiar with, and the understandable urge by people here to see retribution for things that have been done to them'. But the 'retribution' in the show was more fierce than the contractors suggested, and ultimately demonstrated a new danger in Iraq. The confessions were not part of any recognized legal process; many of the confessing terrorists had obvious bruises; some of the confessions seemed implausible, and appeared to be offered up in fear. The televised confessions were given in front of a banner reading 'wolf brigade', an elite police commando group regularly accused of sectarian killings and torture, and of running secret prisons. On one programme a former police officer from the Iraqi town of Samarra – wincing, breathing with obvious difficulty, and sporting two black eyes – confessed to sectarian murders. Within days the police officer's dead body was dropped off at his father's house.[29] Months later, allied politicians would worry that Iraq was spiralling into a vicious sectarian civil war, as the morgues filled with tortured bodies. Their surprise was odd, since the civil war had first been rehearsed on television, in broadcasts by stations put together by UK- and US-funded companies.

The allies fought other battles in the propaganda war by using private contractors; but whereas the al-Iraqiya output came to be brutal but effective, other sorties in the propaganda war were less successful. In 2005 the Pentagon announced $300 million worth of contracts for three companies – SAIC, SyColeman Inc., and the Lincoln Group – to work with the military's Joint Psychological Operations Support Element in what it referred to as 'media approach planning, prototype product development, commercial quality product development, product distribution and dissemination, and media effects analysis'.

This slick-sounding privately run propaganda operation became a major embarrassment in the US when the crude nuts and bolts of the scheme were exposed. The Lincoln Group turned out to be a small new company run by Christian Bailey, a young British Oxford graduate with no military experience. His school friends remembered a 'nerdy', 'geeky' but business-minded boy who had gone on to found a firm selling self-help tapes. In Iraq, however, Bailey reinvented himself as a propaganda expert. His firm took on an ex-US Marine and a former British army intelligence officer, but their operations were still decidedly amateurish: the company simply paid Iraqi newspapers thousands of dollars to print 'good news' stories passed to them by the US army. One of the interns passing on the stories revealed that he had been recruited straight out of Oxford University, given a submachine gun and a pile of cash, and told to hawk his stories around town.[30] The intern, Willem Marx, explained that none of the Lincoln Group 'spoke any real Arabic – nor were friendly with many Iraqi journalists', so they simply relied on ever larger sums of money to try and get Iraqi newspapers to print their stories. The propaganda was crude. As Marx recalled, 'All the stories blamed terrorists for Iraq's problems and lauded the work of the coalition troops. I had never encountered journalism like this before.' The amateurism soon backfired, as the Lincoln Group's pay-for-news scheme was exposed. While the revelation of the Lincoln Group's good news for hire added to US embarrassment over its Iraq policy, the American army showed no obvious concern. An official audit declared that, while officials had violated rules by failing to keep proper records, they had done no wrong in paying for fake news.[31] The advantages of having third-party paid-for propagandists was clearly very attractive: instead of being dropped, the Lincoln Group was awarded another $6 million contract.

The Iraq occupation had a Wizard of Oz quality: official news from inside the heavily fortified Green Zone seemed as self-deceiving as life in the Emerald City; the violence and chaos in the Red Zone – the majority of Iraq – was not reflected in the official language of the Green Zone. This good news zone was ably supported by a phalanx of PR firms. In 2004 Bell Pottinger was hired to promote Iraq's new constitution. This British firm was led by Tim Bell. Nicknamed 'Mrs Thatcher's favourite ad. man', Lord Bell had helped to mastermind Conservative election campaigns from 1979 onwards. His firm had also built up good connections with the New Labour government, hiring former top Blair aide Dave Hill. The new constitution finally gave Iraqis an election, although the US remained the Iraqi government's senior partner after the vote. Bell Pottinger had a strategy for the Red Zone involving the delivery of thousands of leaflets extolling freedom and democracy; but Coalition Provisional Authority officials soon saw this elegant PR campaign undermined by crude political assaults on the new constitution.

Before Bell Pottinger's television advertisements were aired, or their brochures delivered, leaflets denouncing the new constitution were making waves on Iraq's streets. Western reporting of the election emphasized all the points made in the Bell Pottinger campaign – the argument that the new constitution created freedom and democracy under the rule of law; local criticisms were ignored. Consequently, the way insurgency and sectarian fighting increased after the 2005 election left the US and British publics confused. The private information war seemed, again and again, able to deceive only voters in the West, rather than persuading the enemy in the war on terror to lay down its arms.

7

Mystery Train

In November 2005 a video was posted on the internet that had been filmed by British security contractors through the back window of the car they were driving along Iraq's highways. As Iraqi vehicles driving on the same road came within ten car lengths of the vehicle, the contractors sprayed their engine blocks with automatic fire, forcing the Iraqi drivers off the road. As one Iraqi driver steps out of his ruined car, a British voice can be heard on the recording saying, 'Fuckin' hell man – that is comical!' The video was distributed by men claiming to be disgruntled former employees of Aegis, a British security firm with a major contract with US authorities both to provide guards and coordinate other private soldiers in Iraq. The film showed graphically that certain qualities belonged just as much to the private security companies as to the official troops – the arrogance of occupying forces, and a readiness to threaten ordinary Iraqis with gunfire. Such behaviour had lost the occupiers much of the popular credit they had accrued from the fall of Saddam. The armed men who had made these 'trophy' videos, and were now broadcasting them to embarrass their former employers, had dubbed on a soundtrack: the footage of Iraqi cars dodging western bullets played to Elvis Presley singing 'Mystery Train'.[1] The soundtrack was appropriate: the allies had authorized and organized the widespread use of private soldiers in Iraq, but they had no idea where this new tactic was going. Presley's haunting ballad about an unknown journey – which actually refers to the journey to the grave – fitted the use of Iraq as a giant laboratory for privatized war all too well.

This experiment in the privatization of war made it much easier for the coalition to make Iraq a centrepiece of the war on terror. The existence of the private contractors substantially lowered the bar when it came to choosing military action. Military leaders complained about lack of troops and overstretch before and during the Iraq mission, but the Anglo-US political leaderships believed the contractors would supply plentiful skilled staff to supplement the military machine, all just a contract signature away. British and US politicians were convinced that the superiority of the market would mean that private forces in Iraq would offer efficient and imaginative help to its occupiers. In fact the privatization would hobble the occupation: contractors brought corruption, failure and violence. Crucially, the contractors contributed to the breakdown of the Iraqi state. Instead of feeling the benefits of 'reconstruction', Iraq's government and economy fragmented as the attempt to rebuild a country through contracts with security companies failed.

General Petraeus became the new commander of Multi-National Forces in Iraq in 2007. High hopes rested on the general; he was seen as a warrior-intellectual with a sharp mind and intelligent tactics who offered a last chance to rescue the occupation from its history of blunders and failures. Petraeus, who specialized in 'counterinsurgency', was to lead the 'surge' – an increase in US soldiers designed to crack the resistance and cement the authority of the new Iraqi government. To many, this seemed like a make-or-break strategy, a last roll of the dice in Iraq. It is a measure of how central privatized soldiers were to the Iraq occupation that Petraeus repeatedly told senators at his nomination hearing that he counted contractors among his assets. He said that the number of private soldiers in Iraq was central to his plan for victory.

Petraeus did not deny that the number of coalition troops he had to hand to battle the insurgents was either 'inadequate or the bare minimum' for the job of pacifying the country, but he remained optimistic because 'there are tens of thousands of contract security forces'. The mercenaries could free up troops for aggressive missions against insurgents by guarding facilities and securing institutions. As Petraeus's own counterinsurgency manual made plain, there were no clear battle-lines in this war. Supply convoys, any part of the economic infrastructure, and indeed any public area, were all potential war zones. The areas guarded or secured by the commercial soldiers often constituted the battlefront itself. At his Senate hearing Petraeus repeatedly told sceptical senators that, while on paper he did not have a large enough counter-insurgency force, he could supplement his soldiers with 'additional forces, these tens of thousands of contract security forces'. The general described this use of contractors as a 'modern evolution of counterinsurgency strategy'. Petraeus brought home the degree of integration of the private soldiers into the US war machine and their importance by pointing out that

> the US embassy is guarded by contract guards. My personal security on my last tour was actually contracted out to, I think it was, a British security firm so that we could free up the military police to secure my own officers who did not have security provided for them. So again, that frees up our forces, and it does that in numerous different places.

So two of the most significant US assets in Iraq – the embassy and Petraeus himself – were secured by the hands of a hired army. According to the head of the allied forces in Iraq, he could not fight the insurgency without these hired hands.

Petraeus never gave a firm figure for the number of contractors involved, because nobody was counting. A variety of estimates were available for the number of contractors, but all the figures are very approximate. In December 2005 the US Army Central Command carried out a rough survey and found that 100,000 contractors were working in Iraq, compared to 140,000 US troops. It is difficult to make a direct comparison, as many of these contractors were carrying out jobs – driving, construction, administration – that might have been carried out in previous expeditions by troops from logistics or engineering formations, but might also have belonged to local civilians.[2] In 2004 Paul Bremer estimated that there were 20,000 private security employees in Iraq.[3] This number represented the armed men in uniform, working in a purely military or paramilitary way. Other estimates put the number of these privately employed armed men closer to 30,000, or even higher. One contractor's trade group estimated that 48,000 security guards were working for around 180 different firms.[4] The number of soldiers 'replaced' by private operatives fell somewhere between the 20,000 or more armed guards and the 100,000 contractors. The proportion of private employees was unprecedented, as was the absolute number of privately employed men on the shifting battlefield. The armed contractors were a private military force of a size not seen for over a century. These commercial legions had grown without any obvious central plan or authority. No elected legislature – either in the US, Britain or Iraq – had been consulted or even forewarned about the raising of this mighty armed posse in the war on terror. Leaving aside the political or social costs, the financial costs were colossal.

By 2005, spending on security represented the 'largest single component' of the total £3.6 billion spent on reconstruction in Iraq.[5] In the early days after the fall of Saddam, some of the leading security firms could charge £650 a day for a single security guard. A former British SAS man who was on the 'circuit' of private military work could command as much as £500 a day. Three years later, market pressures had forced down pay rates, but a former SAS soldier could still look at a day-rate of between £325 and £400. A former British infantry NCO in a team leader position could expect around £250 a day, and a former British soldier around £175. 'Third-country' nationals like Gurkhas or Fijians could expect much more modest sums – £30 to £40 a day – which were still at least three times as much as an Iraqi security guard would earn. The market drove down initially high pay rates, and pushed more work towards guards from the developing world or Iraq itself. But companies charging for their services still had to pay for kit, weapons, equipment, armoured vehicles, premises, and of course their profits and bank interest. Security costs ran at up to 20 or 30 per cent of the $18 billion spent by the US on reconstruction.[6] The British government spent £165 million on security – a quarter of its entire aid budget for Iraq – in the first four years after the invasion.[7]

The biggest cost incurred by the private military contractors was political. Their presence and influence distorted strategy, and helped to push the war on terror towards even greater military action. There was never any public debate about the use of private soldiers in Iraq before war began: the British and US governments simply imposed the private armies on Iraq after the invasion without any announcement, let alone discussion about whether this was an acceptable approach to the occupation. As neither British nor US politicians have ever sought to justify or discuss the largest use of private soldiers for a century, there are only a few clues to the rationale for the policy. But public statements made in the approach to the invasion suggest that the availability and enthusiasm of the private contractors encouraged the drive to war; their prominent presence in the allied train that rolled into Iraq had helped policymakers decide that the journey would be possible in the first place.

Before the attack, some of the most senior military men in the US had warned that large numbers of troops would be needed to occupy Iraq after the invasion. In 2002 Chief of Staff General Shinseki earned a public rebuke from US Defense Secretary Donald Rumsfeld with his suggestion that only a force of 200,000 troops could stabilize the country after Saddam's fall. In the same year, former Middle East military commander General Zinni expressed deep 'worry about the commitment and cost of the aftermath'. The possible need to commit such large numbers of troops and resources was a powerful disincentive to launching a war on Iraq. Even after 9/11 changed US politics so radically – allowing for a newer, more aggressive foreign policy – the Bush administration still showed some nervousness about international engagement: it only committed relatively small numbers of ground troops to the latter part of the 2001 Afghan intervention, for example. Building political courage for and consensus behind the massive Iraq mobilization was no easy task.

The private contractors helped to calm queasy stomachs, however. The private sector could promise to provide plenty of support in security, reconstruction and military supplies. Rumsfeld was able to propose an acceptable 'invasion lite', with plans for far fewer troops than Zinni or Shinseki had suggested were necessary. The privatization of the occupation meant – by the magic of the market – that the difficult part of the war could be carried out by the use of an off-the-shelf kit, bought by a carefree government. This new product washed away anxieties about costs, because officials believed it would fund itself: Iraq's oil would pay for the companies to rebuild the country in the image of US capitalism. Far from being faced with an onerous imperial stretch, the US merely had to take on the role of a light-touch regulator, enabling Iraq's business-led reconstruction into a friendly, prosperous state. At any rate, this was the theory. Before the war began, Deputy Defense Secretary Paul Wolfowitz told Congress, 'We're dealing with a country that can really finance its own reconstruction, and relatively soon', while White House Press Secretary Ari Fleischer argued that Iraqis could 'shoulder much of the burden for their own reconstruction'. This meant that Iraqis could shoulder the burden of costs, while Western firms enjoyed the benefits of lucrative contracts.

The commercialized occupation actually proved defective and difficult, but the political leadership, already predisposed to believe that corporations were more effective than the public sector, clearly accepted the salesman's patter from the military contractors. Because they were touting for business, the military contractors had an interest in putting a positive spin on their capabilities. For military leaders, proposed wars represented a danger to their forces; for private companies, war represented new business and new profits. A few years later, in 2005, I got a small flavour of the private military companies' 'can-do' attitude, and the way they exaggerated their powers. The Foreign Policy Centre, a Labour-oriented think tank, had arranged a fringe meeting on Iraq. The Centre has strong links to the Labour leadership – Tony Blair is a patron, and the organization is regularly addressed by cabinet ministers. The meeting was addressed by Sir Jeremy Greenstock, Blair's former special envoy to Iraq. He was joined by Eric Westropp, a former brigadier who had swapped his uniform for a suit to become a director of a firm called Control Risks Group. Westropp's firm supplied the armed men guarding Foreign Office staff in Baghdad. Control Risks also funds the Foreign Policy Centre. Greenstock gave a realistically gloomy analysis of the security situation in Iraq, admitting that the 'situation [was] bad on the ground'. He added that, like the insurgents, 'the Iraqi security forces and the coalition forces also only hold the strategic ground which they happen to be present on at any one moment' – effectively, coalition troops only controlled the ground under their feet. Where Greenstock was glum, Westropp was upbeat. His private guards had, he claimed, entirely won over the Iraqis by what he called 'a smiley-wavy policy': by smiling and waving at Baghdad's friendly newspaper-sellers, Westropp claimed that Control Risks had won the hearts and minds of Iraqis, who then helped them to defeat the bombers. As subsequent events have shown, Greenstock was right, and Westropp hopelessly wrong about the state of play in Iraq. But Westropp had two powerful weapons: money and an upbeat message. His firm was able to buy its way into political debate, and his absurd optimism about the possibilities of winning ground in Iraq were obviously music to the government's ears. This security firm clearly made the government believe it could win more easily in Iraq, although the only winners in the end were its managers and shareholders.[8]

Having made the war easier to start, however, the private companies went on to make it harder to win. They failed to live up to the claims of their advertising. The incursions of private industry into security operations had built up slowly over the preceding decade – sometimes making an advance, sometimes retreating behind a scandal. Then, in post-war Iraq, the security industry made a massive leap forward. Every element of the allied occupation and 'reconstruction' of Iraq used – and often relied exclusively upon – private contractors. Every element of the failure of Operation Iraqi Freedom can be traced partly to the involvement of the private security industry. The private firms added much both to the confrontation with Iraqis after the war and their disillusionment with the occupiers, as well as to the fragmentation of the Iraqi state and society that still threatens to tip the country into civil war.

The initial invasion of Iraq was a military success. 'Shock and awe' tactics and the weakness of Saddam's forces meant that the allies were able to dominate the battlefield. The first 'thunder runs' of armoured convoys into Baghdad took place within a fortnight of the start of the 2003 invasion, and within a month the US announced that it had occupied the capital city. Overwhelming force, closely timed heavy bombing and shelling, and fast movement by a mechanized military all made for an overwhelming victory – although they also caused serious destruction of the country's already weakened infrastructure. Light losses among the allies were matched by a heavy burden falling on Iraqis, who suffered large numbers of casualties and widespread destruction.

The success of the invasion was soon more than matched by failures of the occupation. Promises to the Iraqis about establishing democracy were put on ice when, on 23 May 2003, the allies declared themselves 'occupying powers'. Just as the war demonstrated US military power, so the peace was set to demonstrate US economic might. The war was used to show the US's ability to dominate the Middle East by force of arms; the initial plans for the peace seemed designed to demonstrate the ability of the US to dominate Iraqi society both economically and politically. A US proconsul was established to run the 'Coalition Provisional Authority' (CPA), with a small group of appointed Iraqi exiles acting as a 'consultative' decoration. All Iraqi ministries, the Baath Party, and the Iraqi army were dissolved, leaving the occupiers to refashion Iraqi governance as they saw fit. Great swathes of the economy were handed over to Western corporations, while US administrators governed politics. Prime Minister Blair and his advisers found a justification after the event for the occupation: the prime minister's envoy, John Sawers, declared that Iraqi 'attitude problems' meant that they could not cope with self-rule. Proper democracy would not work because the 'radicals' would 'detect' weakness, 'exposing the moderates to pressures they are not able to deal with'. Blair's envoy worried about 'an instinctive resistance to the idea of occupation', but believed this was a minor issue 'compared to the overwhelming support for getting rid of Saddam'. The opposite was the case.[9] Iraqi 'gratitude' for their bloody liberation was in any case limited; but even the contents of these shallow wells of good will were evaporated by an arrogant, violent and incompetent occupation. Instead of handing over sovereignty to Iraqis, the occupiers either kept hold of the levers of power or passed power on to Western companies. A fragmented resistance grew into an insurgency that was divided along sectarian lines: Sunni and Shiite militia fought both with the occupiers and with each other. The allies were unable to rule, but the disunited insurgents were unable to force them to leave. The resulting impasse led to a slow, grinding drive to civil war.

To justify the war, George Bush declared in his pre-invasion State of the Union address that 'Saddam Hussein aids and protects terrorists, including members of al-Qaeda.' With only a little more caution and qualification, Tony Blair also told British MPs that he did 'know of links between al-Qaeda and Iraq'. The possibility that Saddam might give his chemical, biological or nuclear weapons to al-Qaeda was a central justification of the war. In the end none of the dots joined: Saddam had neither the weapons nor the links with al-Qaeda. But the disasters of the occupation meant that Iraq moved from being an imaginary front in the war on terrorism to a real one: the war in fact summoned up the al-Qaeda presence in Iraq that had not previously existed. Dick Cheney claimed that a Jordanian terrorist, Abu Musab al-Zarqawi, was the proof of Saddam's links to al-Qaeda. In fact Iraqi officials had formed a committee to chase down Zarqawi, whom they loathed; and Zarqawi was not affiliated to al-Qaeda at the time. After the invasion all this changed, as Zarqawi used the post-war chaos to launch attacks in Iraq. He also now announced that he was the regional representative of al-Qaeda: the Iraq adventure was proposed as a central battle in the war on terror, but in fact increased the influence of the main terrorist enemy.

The invasion of Iraq put the country at the heart of the war on terror, which in turn put the private security industry at the forefront of that war. The contractors then became intimately involved with the full range of the occupation's failures. Allied confidence in the private security industry encouraged the dissolution of the Iraqi army: the contractors seemed to offer a way of taking up the security slack after the Iraqi army was dissolved, although this proved to be a false promise. The private soldiers were able to get into armed conflict with Iraqis, but could not build security. The contractors given the work of training and rebuilding the Iraqi security forces botched the job. The presence of a patchwork of foreign armed contractors encouraged the growth of a patchwork of Iraqi militias. Contractors were given the job of rebuilding Iraq's economy – a task they spectacularly failed in, leaving Iraqis angry, resentful and unemployed. Contractors who created Iraq's official post-war media facilitated the drive towards sectarian conflict. Contractors were even involved in one of the occupiers' biggest political scandals – at Abu Ghraib.

The commercialization of Bush's intervention began before the fighting. In March, before a shot was fired, the US Agency for International Development (USAID) began preparing for war by calling in five companies to bid for Iraqi 'reconstruction' contracts. They were offered a set of contracts worth £580 million to fix things that were not yet broken. The companies offered work in this strange piece of military Keynesianism were also politically connected players in the military-industrial complex. Halliburton subsidiary Kellogg Brown & Root grabbed the largest slice of the rebuilding work, with contracts covering oilfields. They were at the same time going to be in Iraq building bases for the US soldiers who had destroyed the oil installations they were now to repair. The firms' links to Vice President Cheney and their past military work (see Chapter 2) gave them a distinct advantage bidding for these contracts. Bechtel, a firm with equally solid political links – most notably in the person of George Shultz, who had shuttled between posts in the Nixon and Reagan administrations and a seat on the Bechtel board. Bechtel joined Halliburton in the contract bonanza. The company already had plenty of experience in Iraq. Bechtel, like the US government, had previously had a rapport with Saddam Hussein's regime, and had worked on a number of engineering projects in the country. The close relations between all parties notably came into play in 1983, when Secretary of State Shultz sent future Secretary of Defense Donald Rumsfeld to Iraq to discuss with Saddam an oil pipeline in which Bechtel had an interest.[10]

Parcelling out the 'reconstruction' of Iraq to US companies had disastrous consequences. The decision confirmed many Iraqis' suspicion that the US wanted to control their country's resources. But the firms then failed to carry out the work, leaving Iraqis without electricity, water, sanitation or jobs. While Iraqi engineers had restored utilities soon after the destruction of the first Gulf War in 1991, US contractors struggled to get the lights on and taps running after the war of 2003. In 2006 America's official auditor of post-war US plans, the special inspector general for Iraqi reconstruction, commented that 'most of the projects planned in sewerage, irrigation and drainage, major irrigation, and dams have been cancelled'.[11] Electricity in Baghdad was 'less available than before the 2003 conflict'.[12] The inspector general told Congress that 'in many places throughout the country, they hope for things people of many other nations take for granted: reliable electrical power, clean water, functioning sanitation systems, jobs, incomes'.[13]

Handing over swathes of the economy to US contractors created a focus for nationalist opposition to the occupation. The failure of those companies to do anything like the job in hand raised the temperature by many degrees. By making Iraqis unemployed while failing to restore their basic services, they acted as a recruiting sergeant for the fighting groups, militias and insurgent cells. Contractors typically blamed insurgent attacks and the lack of a 'permissive environment' for spiralling costs and incomplete work. There was certainly some truth in this, although the appointment of the foreign contractors had created a focus for insurgent attacks in the first place. The inspector general calculated that security added as much as 26 per cent to the costs of rebuilding work. There was a real alternative, however: give the job of Iraqi reconstruction to the Iraqis. Immediately after the invasion, Britain's top military official in the Gulf, Air Marshal Brian Burridge, said that the Iraqis should run the key port of Um Qasr, in the British area of control in the south of Iraq. Tony Blair blocked the move, meekly handing the port over to a US firm. US Air Force Colonel Sam Gardiner, who ran a study on the effect of aerial bombardment on Iraq's electricity grid before the war, said that the important thing was to keep Iraqi engineers on the job: 'If we had just given the Iraqis some baling wire and a little bit of space to keep things running, it would have been better. But instead we've let big US companies go in with plans for major overhauls.'[14] Official reports showed that rebuilding failures were due to much more than security. The US auditor found that overhead costs for design–build contractors on the largest projects 'were high in 2004 because of delays between the mobilization of these contractors and the actual start of construction work'. Companies 'rebuilding' Iraq won 'no bid' contracts: they were appointed without competition, apparently relying on their strong political connections. Working in a captive market, they appeared to 'feather-bed' their work, running up big bills by retaining expensive Western staff and having engineering plant sit idle before the jobs had started – while Iraqis themselves also sat idle, and became increasingly angry.

The combination of high costs and low achievement in the privatized 'reconstruction' of Iraq was demonstrated by the high-profile Basra Children's Hospital. Costs on this nationally important medical centre (it had received particular attention from former presidential wife Barbara Bush and from soon-to-be Secretary of State Condoleezza Rice) were projected at $50 million. Two years into the job, however, Bechtel said that it would need another $98 million, and the work was far from done. The scheme was effectively nationalized, as Bechtel willingly passed the project on to the US Army Corps of Engineers: the military, it seems, were better equipped to build a hospital than one of the world's largest engineering firms. This picture was repeated in hospitals, clinics, schools, highways, and a host of other civil engineering contracts across Iraq.

The US corporate invasion of Iraq's economy was supposed to represent the 'soft' power in the war on terror. Instead, the failures of the reconstruction fed the insurgent enemy in two ways. Firstly, the failure to get basic services running alienated Iraq's population. Not only were Iraqis left with dirtier water, less electricity coverage, and poorer hospitals and schools than they had had under Saddam; Iraqi employers and employees were also last in the queue for the economic benefits of reconstruction spending. Money trickled down through US companies to Gulf state contractors before it reached Iraqi hands, the chain of cash having been worn and damaged by favouritism, bribery and corruption. This left a pool of angry, unemployed and poorly served people open to the call to insurgency. Secondly, the presence of the private contractors led to the greater involvement of uncontrolled private soldiers. The reconstruction firms were expected to provide their own security, so they turned to private military companies. The presence of such large numbers of unregulated soldiers-for-hire contributed to the fragmentation of Iraq's security services. The private soldiers became just one more militia in Iraq, as society slid into warlordism.

While the reconstruction companies' need for private security fed the demand for mercenaries in Iraq, they were not the only consumer in the military market: the first agency to hire privateers was the state itself. The British army could look back at its performance in the war against Iraq with satisfaction. As the principal ally of the US it had played its part in an overwhelming military victory, routing Saddam Hussein's troops while taking few casualties. Apparently unimpressed by its own soldiers' success, the British government decided that its army was not good enough to provide security in the new occupied Iraq. Thanks to current military thinking, the CPA southern headquarters – the Basra-based centre of the British wing of the occupation – was protected by private armed guards from Group 4. Only months before, this company had been described as 'a laughing stock' in a British court (see Chapter 1); but now they were being hired to provide the front line in military security. At the same time, the Department for International Development, sharing this apparent lack of confidence in British troops, hired former members of South African Special Forces, working for a company called Tactical Meteoric Solutions, to provide 'close security' for its staff. The Foreign Office believed that two more private firms – Control Risks and the Armor Group Ltd – provided the best protection to its diplomats. These contracts were the first sign that an unregulated, untested, and unknown band of 'security firms' would become the country's third largest armed force. Within a year the British enthusiasm for mercenary firms would link the government to a tawdry coup plot in Africa, to some of the more vicious assassins of apartheid-era South Africa, and to the new corruption in Iraq. At the same time, despite the supposed superiority of free market methods, the use of private soldiers did nothing to add to post-war Iraq's stability.

The decision to use armies-for-hire to secure Iraq soon contributed to the failure of post-Saddam Iraq. The Coalition encountered great difficulty in disarming the many Iraqi militias and armed groups that challenged central authority in the post-war state, while simultaneously inviting in foreign soldiers of fortune. When international mercenaries stood guard outside key economic targets, it was also difficult to persuade suspicious Iraqis that the war was intended to liberate them from Saddam – rather than to liberate their oil and industry for foreign exploitation. The use of private foreign-owned security companies diminished already weakened Iraqis' involvement in their own security. This proved disastrous, because in the end only Iraqis had the knowledge of their own land and commitment to their own future necessary to protect the country's oil, power, and other essential services. The insurrectionists in Muqtada al-Sadr's Mahdi army might have been demobilized by the availability of real jobs. One Mahdi soldier told a reporter from the *Guardian* newspaper, 'There are three kinds of job you can get now: a guard, a janitor, or making sandbags for the American camps.' Like many Iraqis, he found fighting the occupying forces a more attractive offer.

The coalition defeated its enemy in Iraq, but found that it had few friends. Opinion polls showed that Iraqi relief at the end of Saddam's regime soon turned to resentment towards the occupiers. The failure to provide jobs, electricity, and water, or to properly re-equip schools and hospitals, and the abuses by the troops, only served to lose hearts and minds. Even immediately after Saddam's fall, Iraqi attitudes to the invaders were at best equivocal: the US army later admitted that the famous toppling of Saddam's statue in Firdos Square, which had attracted an enthusiastic but small crowd, had in fact been initiated by a US army commander supported by a 'psyops' team, for the benefit of journalists in the nearby Palestine Hotel.[15] US Vice President Cheney had said before the war, 'I really do believe that we will be greeted as liberators'; but such warm feelings as did exist for the invading armies soon evaporated in the heat of the occupation.

Many corporate executives, finding themselves lonely and friendless in a foreign city, hired companions for the evening; the Coalition and its business friends did the same, although the escort companies serving Iraq's new visitors supplied men carrying guns, rather than women in high heels. The tenders for private security guards were a substitute for the rebuilding of Iraq's security forces – a substitute that proved counterproductive.

The decision by CPA chief Paul Bremer to disband the Iraqi army in May 2003 meant that there was no effective security apparatus in Iraq outside the US and British armies. It also meant that the Iraqi army's arsenals were unguarded, and that the 700,000 men trained to use these weapons were now unemployed. Together, these furnished the materiel and manpower for the country's militias. Many political parties and religious groups already had their own militias, and others were able to build them. Groups that cooperated with the CPA, including the Islamist Da'awa party and the Supreme Council for the Islamic Revolution in Iraq (SCIRI), also had their own militias. Some, like SCIRI's 'Badr Brigade', or the Kurdish Peshmerga guerrillas, had been built up in the long years of opposition to Saddam, but were augmented after his fall. Some, like al-Sadr's Mahdi army, were mostly built in reaction to the occupying forces. The militias inspired loyalty by providing basic security in the lawless days after Saddam's fall, by occupying frustrated young men, and by taking up the banner of national dignity and autonomy. They presented a serious challenge to the CPA's status merely by existing: when the Mahdi army launched an insurrection against the CPA at the same time as the armed groups in Fallujah fought against US Marines, the CPA was thrown into its most serious crisis. Its reaction was different from that of previous imperial occupations: Britain's centuries-long occupation of India was built by the East India Company, a private business with its own army. But the 1857 mutiny, when Indian soldiers launched a rebellion against the British, led to a disbandment of the Company: after the mutiny had been suppressed, the government took direct responsibility for the rule of India. They did not trust the future of the empire to a privately run army. The uprising by the Mahdi army sent the occupiers of Iraq in the opposite direction – handing more security to private firms. The British and US governments' commitment to privatizing security was so great that new firms rose up to meet the demand: security companies that previously had one or two consultancies training businessmen in how to deal with kidnap, or providing safety advice and occasionally guarding journalists in the world's trouble spots, or possibly advised shipping firms on how to deal with the threat of piracy, were transformed into the managers of significant paramilitary forces in Iraq.

Disbanding the Iraqi militias was a top priority for the CPA. The Authority addressed the issue in its third law, passed in May 2003. This regulation made it illegal to carry weapons in public, and the occupying powers announced that they would use the regulation to outlaw Iraq's irregular armed groups. But an amendment to the same law, added in December 2003, legalized the new mercenaries. The new law said that private military firms 'may be licensed by the Ministry of the Interior to possess and use licensed firearms and military weapons'. But the rules governing the private companies' 'use' of the arms – including when they were allowed to shoot and kill Iraqis – remained completely unclear. Incredibly, the CPA gave immunity to any foreign contractor who did kill Iraqis. Paul Bremer issued CPA order 17 on 27 June 2004 – an extraordinary law declaring that contractors 'shall not be subject to Iraqi laws or regulations in matters relating to the terms and conditions of their contracts'. All private businesses working in any way for the US and British governments were free from Iraqi legal control – the private soldiers could only be prosecuted by their 'sending states'. Bremer issued this proclamation as a gift to the supposedly sovereign Iraqi government that took power the next day – so the new, theoretically independent Iraqi government had no powers over either the foreign soldiers or the mercenaries on its soil. Bremer's diktat, issued before he left the country in a secret helicopter flight, was to remain in force until the last member of the Multi-National Force (the American and British soldiers) had left Iraq. The regulation left in force existing 'regulations governing the existence and activities of Private Security Companies in Iraq, including registration and licensing of weapons and firearms'. But that is all the law said: Bremer's rules allowed for the issuing of licences to commercial groups to bear arms. They were silent about when the private soldiers could discharge their weapons. Unsurprisingly, Iraqis refused to disarm their militias, leaving a country with many armed groups perilously close to rule by warlords, and increasing Iraq's resemblance to the other frontier in the war on terror: Afghanistan.

The connection between the private security firms, the militias, and the fragmentation of Iraq's armed forces was most obvious in the story of the Facilities Protection Service. After dissolving the Iraqi army, and crippling the Iraqi police force by dissolving the Baath Party, the CPA struggled to rebuild Iraq's uniformed services; but one organization grew well beyond expectations. In August 2003 the CPA announced the formation of the new Facilities Protection Service (FPS). This organization would be charged with the static guarding of ministries, hospitals and other public buildings.[16] The Coalition said that the force would eventually have around 11,000 guards. By 2006 the FPS was a sprawling monster, with around 150,000 armed guards. It was also one of the principal conduits through which militias, death squads, and criminals infiltrated the Iraqi state. The FPS had no meaningful centralized command; Iraqi interior minister Bayn Jabr commented that it was 'not under our control'. Jabr specifically compared the organization to the private security companies in Iraq, as examples of armed groups beyond the government's control. This comparison was made because the FPS not only mimicked the lack of central authority in the private security business: many of its guards had actually been drawn from the Iraqi employees of the security firms.[17]

After the Iraq war the drive towards commercialization in the war on terror became so strong that substantial new companies were conjured out of the air, based on just a few ingredients – some military experience there, some connections here, and a new 'security company' came into being. So, for example, Harry Legg-Bourke, formerly aide-de-camp to British Chief of Defence Sir Charles Guthrie, pulled Olive Security together. Legg-Bourke also gave the firm a royal flavour, as he was a skiing partner of Prince William, while his sister was nanny to the British royal family. His business partner, Jonathan Allum, was the son of Tony Allum, a company director of British engineering firm Halcrow. Allum senior was sent by the British government to win contracts for the UK in the reconstruction of Iraq, as the British government worried it would not get its share of the spoils of war. Following this trip, both Halcrow and Olive were subcontracted by Bechtel, supplying engineers and armed guards respectively.

Olive hired Andy Bearpark, formerly the director of operations and infrastructure for the CPA, and hence one of the top officials within the occupying forces. In the 1980s Bearpark had been a private secretary to Margaret Thatcher. After leaving Thatcher's office, Bearpark became a British official specializing in reconstruction after the Balkan wars: he served in Bosnia and Kosovo, administering Thatcherite medicine. As head of the European Union mission in Kosovo, Bearpark argued for the closure of factories, leaving thousands unemployed, because '[i]t's a question of moving the economy forward to attract private investors'. Bearpark oversaw a similar privatization regime in Iraq, which left angry, unemployed men with little more to do than join the various armed groups fighting the CPA. He did not face joblessness himself, however, moving easily from the CPA to the burgeoning private security business.[18]

Another British firm that blossomed on Iraq's bloody ground, Global Risks, also had royal connections: its press officer, Natalie Hicks-Lobbecke, was a friend of Prince William. Prince Charles also made a morale-boosting visit to the firm's guards in Basra in February 2004. Global was a bigger player than Olive, with perhaps 1,000 men under arms in Iraq. By 2004, according to the US inspector general, Global had £35 million worth of contracts from the CPA. Global won the contract to protect the British headquarters in Basra. They replaced Group 4, whose guards were at least Iraqis: Group 4's spokesman explained to me that anti-Saddam

Iraqi officers had carefully identified his Iraqi guards. They were given numbered weapons when they went on duty, and relieved of these weapons when they finished their shift. The Iraqi guards were treated with caution because they were viewed as a security risk. Global Risks found an easy way to avoid these complex procedures: they recruited Fijians and Nepalese Gurkhas instead. The firm had military connections, having been founded by ex-Marine Damien Perl and former Scots Guard Charlie Andrews. Most importantly, they hired Colonel Sakiusa Raivoce – a Fijian who had previously recruited his fellow countrymen for the British army. Colonel Raivoce now hired Fijians to work for Global In Iraq. These men and the Gurkhas they worked alongside had many advantages: they had military experience, they were a great deal cheaper than British ex-soldiers, and they did not present the same security dangers as Iraqis. A CPA spokesman told me that Global's guards lived 'above the shop' in the allied compound, unlike their Iraqi predecessors from Group 4.[19]

Global's contracts illustrated the way in which the private security companies undermined Iraq's cohesion. One of the firm's most high-profile contracts involved escorting Iraq's new currency around the country. The Coalition saw replacing Iraq's currency as a high priority: the old banknotes bore Saddam's face, and remnants of the regime were believed to have large bundles of the old cash to fund terrorist activity. Iraqis could not fail to notice, however, that while the old notes were printed in Baghdad's mint, the new notes were made in Basingstoke, England,[20] and delivered by Fijians working for a British firm. Global was paid £17 million for this work from the Development Fund for Iraq. This fund, handed over to the CPA by the UN, came from oil receipts. So Iraqi oil money was used to pay Fijians working for a British firm to distribute Iraq's new money – itself printed in Basingstoke. Iraqis' control over their own currency looked minimal. In the end these security measures were ineffective against an inside job. While Global Risks kept the banknotes safe from bandits, $22 million worth of dinars went missing when the old currency was exchanged for the new notes. The pervasive corruption of the new regime saw the Iraqi money spirited away despite Global Risks' efforts. First, twelve lowly female bank tellers were imprisoned for the theft; then the minister who had them imprisoned was arrested himself. The banknotes were never recovered.[21]

Global's other high-profile contract, Operation Skylink, further illustrated the effect of private security companies on post-war Iraq's fragile cohesion. Under Skylink, Global guarded Baghdad International Airport – a strategic link between the capital and the outside world. The Iraqi government elected in 2005 immediately began trying to negotiate a reduction in the $4 million-a-month contract, withholding payment as part of the negotiations. In June and September 2005, Global responded by going 'on strike', cutting off the capital. Iraq's transport minister said that he would send troops to reopen the airport after the second Global 'strike' in September 2005: 'This issue is related to Iraq's sovereignty. Nobody is authorized to close the airport', he insisted.[22] US forces quickly mobilized to deal with the crisis: as Iraqi troops approached, they set up roadblocks – apparently to defend the contractors and back the shutdown. The Iraqi transport minister was forced to admit that he had 'ordered the [Iraqi] forces to pull back after American forces were deployed at the first checkpoint on the road', because he 'did not want to create a confrontation'. American politicians repeatedly lectured Iraq's new government, saying that they should be ready to take over security from the US army. But when they tried to stand up against Western private soldiers, they were quickly undermined and humiliated by the occupiers and their contractors.

Another key security contract showed how the privatization of military forces desperately weakened the government of Iraq. Iyad Allawi, a member of the US-backed interim Iraqi Governing Council, accused Ahmad Chalabi's INC of having dubious links to one security firm – Erinys – which had an extensive contract to guard Iraq's key oil pipelines. Allawi was the leader of another anti-Saddam group of former exiles called the Iraqi National Accord, and a long-time rival of Chalabi's. Allawi found that there were business links between Chalabi's group and Erinys,[23] and the firm also included members of the 'Free Iraqi Forces' among its armed guards. This was a small INC militia that was flown into the country with Chalabi by the Pentagon. Allawi feared that Chalabi was linked to a small private army with the contract to guard Iraq's oil. Allawi told the *Financial Times*, 'If such security companies are not under central government control there will be anarchy.' He said they should be under the control of the Iraqi government, not that of a private army. Chalabi fell out of favour with the occupiers, and Allawi became the US choice as Iraq's interim president. On his accession to power, however, Allawi found that he was entirely dependent on the US and British armed forces: the new Iraqi army was by itself no match for the rebellions and insurgencies throughout the country. Reliant on the allies for his security, Allawi also had to comply with their privatization plans, so Erinys' contract to guard the oil wells was extended. The fledgling Iraqi government was less powerful and less important than a private security company, and was not even able to control the security of Iraq's most significant resource, oil. Instead of trying to build influence with Iraq's population, the isolated Iraqi politicians inside the Green Zone were reduced to fighting for influence with security companies. In these circumstances it is no surprise the fragmented, privatized Iraqi state was unable to conquer the insurgency.

An off-duty and possibly drunk Blackwater guard from a US military company called Blackwater violently expressed the subservience of Iraq's government to the private security industry when he shot dead the personal bodyguard of the country's vice president, Adil Abdul-Mahdi, on Christmas Eve 2006. The shooting took place in the Green Zone, representing a rare breach of security. However, because of the legal immunity of contractors, the shooter was whisked out of the country without charge. Documents uncovered using the Freedom of Information Act revealed that the Iraqi vice president was pleading with US Secretary of State Condoleezza Rice, because 'Iraqis would not understand how a foreigner could kill an Iraqi and return a free man to his own country'. However, while the Iraqi vice president knew his countrymen would be outraged, he also knew that persuading the Americans to prosecute a contractor would be hard, and so was reduced to covering the incident up. The US ambassador to Iraq said that Abdul-Mahdi 'had tried to keep the issue from the public eye and had not disclosed to the press the nationality of the suspect'.[24]

As well as adding to the fragmentation of Iraq's fledgling administration, the private security contractors were involved in some of the most direct confrontations with the country's increasingly restless population. While contractors cost far more than regular soldiers, they did have the advantage of keeping down the body count – Olive Security, Global, Control Risks and many other firms lost men to bullets and bombs in Iraq, but none appeared on the headline body counts, so their deaths did not add to the political pressure on the occupiers. But as well as taking casualties, the contractors also inflicted them. All but one of the firms I spoke to would not discuss their 'rules of engagement', although most of the major security firms did have their own rules about when they could use lethal force. Olive Security's spokesman said they were using the British army's 'yellow card' rules as a model; other firms shied away from questions about how, when and why they would kill Iraqis to earn their fees. Global staff told the *Telegraph* newspaper about using overwhelming force to defend government buildings in Hilla, killing insurgents, and fighting their way into towns by taking out half a dozen Iraqis.[25]

These armed confrontations had a political cost. Security contractors were involved in one of the key turning points in the occupation of Iraq. Obvious signs of friction between occupier and occupied began in April 2003, when US troops opened fire on residents of Fallujah, who were protesting against the soldiers' presence in the town. In June of that year, US soldiers opened fire on demobbed Iraqi soldiers demonstrating about their unemployment in Baghdad. A month later, an Iraqi mob killed six British military policemen shortly after British soldiers had fired plastic bullets − a novelty in Iraq − at a crowd demonstrating against intrusive weapons searches. But none of these events turned the politics of the occupation as much as the killing in March 2004 of four private soldiers working for US firm Blackwater. The US guards were attacked and killed outside Fallujah while working for a British catering giant, Compass, that was supplying the food for workers in the international reconstruction programme. They took a wrong turn into a hostile zone and were killed by local gunmen. After their deaths, the guards' charred bodies were dragged behind cars, beaten in the street and hung from a bridge outside the city. The grisly images strongly resembled a similar display of the corpses of US soldiers in Mogadishu, Somalia in 1993 − an event that had helped to persuade President Clinton to end the US intervention on Somalia. President Bush was determined that this echo would not undermine US power in Iraq.

Paul Bremer, the US viceroy in Iraq, vowed that their deaths would not go unpunished. The fact that Blackwater had a $23 million contract to provide his own personal escorts may have added to Bremer's fury. US troops responded with an unsuccessful attempt to capture the city, followed by a siege, and finally a successful, overwhelming attack on Fallujah − all prompted by the killing of the Blackwater contractors. This was a turning point in the occupation; an announcement that the battle with the insurgency was as intense as any war. While the Sunnis of

Fallujah fought US troops, the Shiites linked to the Mahdi army in Baghdad and the south launched their own uprising. Facing a battle on two fronts, the US in effect attacked the Sunnis while trying to co-opt the Shiites, splitting the insurgency but setting a sectarian template for the future of the occupation. So one of the key battles of the 'war on terror' in Iraq was spurred by the involvement of private contractors on what rapidly became a new battlefield. The Blackwater men were victims of a gruesome murder in 2004, but they were also capable of killing. A video surfaced in 2006, which had been filmed in 2004, showing Blackwater men firing from a rooftop on what they identify as 'Mahdi army' fighters below. They were in fact facing the southern insurrection in Najaf. They exchanged round upon round with the fighters below, apparently hitting targets, and leading one Blackwater rifleman to exclaim, 'It's a fucking turkey shoot', while his 'spotter' says, 'You really cleaned them out.'[26]

Blackwater was another example of a small firm transformed by the war on terror into a financial and military giant. It was founded by Erik Prince, who inherited a fortune from his father's car parts business. The Princes were a family of politically connected Republican millionaires with a long history of supporting the organizations of America's religious right. Prince's father, Edgar, had helped found and fund the Family Research Council, a Christian conservative group that campaigns against gay marriage laws, in favour of 'creationism' being taught in schools, and so on. Prince served in the US navy as a 'SEAL' Special Forces officer. He set up Blackwater in 1997 as a paramilitary training outfit, and in effect it began as a large shooting range in Virginia. Prince eagerly examined disasters to see if they held clues to expanding his business: after the Columbine high school massacre in 1999, Blackwater built a schoolhouse on their campus, called the 'R U Ready High School', to allow police to train for similar sieges. Within days of the 9/11 hijacks the firm was touting for business training 'sky marshals', the armed officers appointed to police aeroplanes in the wake of the suicide hijackings. Blackwater's president, another former US navy SEAL called Robert Jackson, said that the firm's business was far from secure in 1998, and that creating the company was a risky business. Jackson said of the venture: 'This was a roulette, a crapshoot.'[27] In 2000 the value of Blackwater's central government contracts stood at no more than a quarter of a million dollars; by 2006 Blackwater had received over $300 million from just one State Department deal – the Worldwide Personal Protective Service contract under which the company supplied armed guards in many hazardous international locations. The firm already had strong political contacts, which it strengthened in 2005 by hiring Cofer Black, formerly the Department of State's coordinator for counterterrorism. Two months after its guards were killed in Fallujah, Blackwater published guidance for its staff on dealing with the people of the Middle East. The firm's 'Tactical Weekly' newsletter included an article written by retired Colonel Ed Badolato.[28] He advised the Blackwater guards that the essential problems they would face in Iraq lay in the Arab psyche, not the nature of the occupation. He wrote that the dangers they faced were created by the childhood and culture of all Arabic people rather than by their own behaviour . According to the paper, titled 'Learning to think like an Arab', the style of Arab parenting was responsible for many behavioural traits the mercenaries would face. According to his analysis, young people in the Arabic world were caught between 'a loving mother and stern disciplinarian father'. The resulting 'fluctuation' between 'love and discipline . . . fosters schizoid personality traits'. In adults this led to a 'roller coaster type of behavior . . . often demonstrated by cool self-control followed by uncontrolled public outbursts of emotion'. The apparently 'schizoid' Arabs presented many threats to Blackwater's private army. 'An Arab crowd is high strung emotionally, and violent crowds are a frequent occurrence during periods of stress and crisis', he warned. 'In the Arab world', he added,

> there is little stigma placed on the loss of self control and what westerners would consider hysterical public outbursts of emotion. This is a particularly frequent factor in group dynamics, and it is often demonstrated by the way in which a crowd can suddenly give way to outbursts of anger and violence.

All in all, Badolato said that 'conflict appears to be such a normal behavioral characteristic in Arab group dynamics at the individual, group or even international levels'.[29]

The weird musing of Blackwater's 'expert' on Arabia suggested that the privatization of military force did not bring commercial expertise into the Iraqi battlefields. Instead, the private companies seemed to be putting the military equivalent of the snake-oil salesman into the volatile mix of post-invasion Iraq. The lucrative Iraqi market dragged in other companies with a similar mix of Republican politics, military experience, and entrepreneurial recklessness. Some mixed in extra doses of both unfocused violence and economic corruption. The invading governments expected slick, businesslike assistance from the private military contractors, who they hoped would act like armed management consultants. Instead, some of the contractors behaved like cowboys and outlaws in Iraq's new wild east.

In 1978, sardonic rocker Warren Zevon recorded a song declaring that what a desperate man needed, when caught in the crossfire in the darker corners of the world, was an immediate shipment of 'lawyers, guns and money'. One contractor, Custer Battles, seems to have taken this as its guide. The firm's rocketing growth showed how desperate the Coalition was to throw money at military start-ups. It was founded in 2001 by two former soldiers. Former special forces officers Scott Custer and Michael Battles first teamed up in an attempt to win a seat in Congress on the back of the 9/11 attacks. Battles tried to win the Republican nomination with a marathon walk across the Rhode Island constituency. His army buddy Scott Custer coordinated supplies of suntan lotion and clean shirts for the march. One of Battles' assistants held a sign declaring that his campaign was 'the walk for democracy'.[30] Battles claimed that a military background was essential for politicians after 9/11, but his opponents did not possess 'a very good understanding of what it takes to fight and win a war'.[31] The voters disagreed, and Battles was knocked out of the race.

Custer and Battles tried another means of advancing themselves through the war on terror. In early 2003 they flew into the Middle East and caught a taxi from Jordan to Baghdad, arriving in the Iraqi capital with a satellite phone and a fistful of dollars. They founded Custer Battles using the British and US former soldiers they could pull together. Such was the Coalition's hunger for private security to augment their forces that, by 2004, the firm were awarded contracts worth tens of millions of dollars to guard part of Baghdad's airport and to deliver the new Saddam-free currency. The firm swelled to perhaps 2,000 armed men, making it one of the largest private security firms in Iraq. Battles said that Iraq was 'the greatest investment climate since New York City at the turn of the century', and he was the man to exploit it thanks to his unique combination of military and business elan: 'It takes a certain skill set and mentality, which is that of a green beret with an MBA', he noted. He said that he needed to look beyond 'venture capital' to build his business, thus calling his new business 'adventure capital'.[32] Battles was the perfect soldier for the privatized war on terror – armed with a business degree, a bullet-proof vest, an assault rifle, and a 'can do' attitude.

It is easy to understand Battles' upbeat, 'booster' attitude to the new military business in Iraq. Millions of dollars were flowing into a company that only a year ago had comprised two men crossing into a war zone by taxi. But it is harder to understand the most powerful military machine in the world handing over any responsibility to these small-time opportunists. Two years later, not surprisingly, things turned sour. After the guns and money came the lawyers: two members of Custer Battles' staff – including a former FBI agent – claimed that the firm was ripping off the US government by over-billing, double-charging, and failing to supply the properly trained security guards as promised. The army also became restive, as many of the trucks the firm had supplied to transport the new currency across Iraq broke down, making them easy targets for insurgents or bandits. Some former staff also alleged that Custer Battles was at fault when one of its guards, a Welsh former paratrooper, was shot dead in the Iraqi town of Hit. The 'undermanned' and 'under-equipped' firm sent a convoy through the town, foolishly ignorant of an anti-occupation demonstration, which turned ugly and killed the Welshman after assaulting the convoy.[33]

Custer Battles defended itself against the whistleblowers in a series of court cases. In one case the firm was able to escape a guilty verdict because the judge ruled that the legal status of its employer, the CPA, was insufficiently clear; but the judge did find that there was ample evidence that the company had submitted 'false and fraudulently inflated invoices' in the case. The whistleblowers claim that they were identified by the firm's management, disarmed, held at gunpoint, then evicted to fend for themselves outside the secure Green Zone in the streets of Baghdad. The jury in the case agreed that they had been unfairly victimized.[34] Because of the privatization of military force in Iraq, the management of one of the leading armed units guarding some of the most strategic sites were focusing firstly on paying themselves multi-million-dollar bonuses, and secondly on defending those bonuses in court. Custer Battles scraped through the court cases, but was banned from further work for the military, and left Iraq. The two principals took their money and settled in Florida.

All of Custer Battles' Iraq contracts passed to a mysterious new firm called Danubia, which was based in Romania – though it was ultimately

owned by another body in the British Virgin Islands. This opaque
structure led many to suggest that the new firm was in fact still connected
to the banned Custer Battles, or was linked to former officials in the CPA.
Danubia certainly inherited many of its predecessor's staff, as well as its
contracts. The new firm also drove immediately into new troubles.
Danubia's business strategy was to undercut its rivals. For example, it
charged $7,500 to send a convoy through the dangerous badlands of
Western Anbar, instead of the going rate of $15,000. Danubia hoped to
cut costs by using cheaper former soldiers, from Eastern Europe and
Pakistan. In 2006 a convoy of these cut-rate soldiers guarding supply
trucks on their way past Fallujah was hit by roadside bombs, snipers, and
machine-gun fire in three separate incidents on the journey, losing both
men and vehicles as a result. The Iraqi National Guard claimed that, in
retaliation, Danubia men had opened fire on their troops, killing an Iraqi
colonel and three of his men.[35] The new company was then barred from
convoy work in the area by the US military, and reduced to a much
smaller presence in Iraq. The increasing danger in the country seemed to
be placing the standards and status of some private security companies on
a downward spiral.

   The killing of Iraqi security forces by private security guards was one of
the worse recorded incidents of friction between commercial and traditional soldiers, but such tensions had surfaced earlier in the Iraq intervention. In 2005, US Marines arrested nineteen contractors from a US
company called Zapata Engineering. Zapata was a small industrial
company that had won a contract to help destroy ageing shells and
other munitions in Iraq. However, because of the way security was
managed during the occupation, the firm also had to field its own armed
guards: the engineering company was transformed into an armed force,
though apparently not a very effective one. Marines near Fallujah said that
Zapata's staff had fired repeatedly on them from their armoured lorries
and pick-up trucks. Zapata staff claimed that they had merely been firing
warning shots at an Iraqi builders' lorry to make the local construction
workers drive well away from the American engineers. The arrested
Zapata staff claim that the Marines had stripped and abused them,
squashing their testicles, pushing them, and raging at the contractors'
high salaries. The Marines, who eventually decided not to charge the
Zapata men, denied the claims, and insisted that the contractors had acted
recklessly.[36]

A privateer from another firm, Triple Canopy, faced similar allegations. Triple Canopy, like Custer Battles, was brought into existence by
the Iraq adventure. The firm was founded in September 2003 by a
group of ex-US Special Forces officers. Despite being late entrants into
the market, the firm expanded from nothing to win contracts worth
over a $100 million within a few years. Triple Canopy won security
contracts, in Iraq and beyond, protecting US officials and businessmen.
Three of its staff alleged that a frightening gung-ho attitude existed
within the firm. The Triple Canopy staff claimed that their supervisor
had shot wildly at Iraqis in the summer of 2006. They testified in court
that their team leader – a 6ft 3in former army ranger with a shaved head
and goatee, nicknamed 'Shrek' for his resemblance to the cartoon
character – had gone on a 'shooting rampage' over a few days. The
guards said that he had announced that he was 'going to kill someone
today' because he was leaving Iraq for a holiday in 24 hours. They said
that he had fired rifle rounds at an Iraqi vehicle without reason or
provocation, and that he had squeezed off rounds from his handgun at a
passing Iraqi taxi, apparently hitting the driver, after announcing that he
had never killed anyone with a pistol before. Triple Canopy spokesmen
denied the claims, insisting that they were motivated by staff who had
themselves been sacked for failing to report the shootings, and now
wanted to go to court for revenge or financial gain. A third guard – a
Fijian who resigned voluntarily because of discontent with the firm, and
was not pursuing any court case – supported the story of the unprovoked shootings to the *Washington Post*. The Fijian left Iraq because,
he said, 'I couldn't stand what was happening. It seemed like every day
they were covering something.'[37] He also told reporters that Triple
Canopy staff were hard-drinking, with their own very well-used bar in
their headquarters, and that they claimed to police themselves through
their own self-administered set of 'big boys' rules', rather than following
any official orders.[38]

The presence of contractors had the power to distort and corrupt the
direction of the occupation. Hundreds of millions of dollars of Iraqi and
US money simply disappeared from the books in the years after the
2003 invasion. Few officials were charged with corruption, but investigators did catch up with Robert J. Stein, the comptroller and
funding officer for the CPA in the south central region in 2005. He was
tried and sentenced for running a network of theft and bribery in Iraq.

He had passed contracts on to a US businessman called Philip Bloom. In return, Bloom had given Stein and other officials $1 million in cash, sports cars, a motorcycle, jewellery, liquor, and other trinkets. Bloom had also laundered millions of dollars' of worth of the 'bricks' of dollars that Stein had stolen from the office. Stein and Bloom had also stolen assault rifles and grenade launchers. Bloom had wanted to use the weapons and money to set up his own private security firm in Iraq, to be called Anaconda. He emailed one of his co-conspirators that 'objectives of the company are making money while allowing us to look cool and have cool stuff. That ought to be easy to do.' So while the security plan for Iraq, based heavily on the use of contractors, allowed the country to slide into chaos, the officials administering the country were ready to steal to become like the 'cool-looking' private security firms.[39]

THE SOUTH AFRICAN CONNECTION

The corruption and incompetence of some of the military contractors in Iraq only became apparent over the years of the occupation. But the strong links between many of the contractors and the old apartheid regime in South Africa gave an early sign that the privatization of the Iraqi battlefield could have bad results. Some of the managers of the leading military firms had been deeply involved in the counter-insurgency programme of the racist South African state. Some of their footsoldiers had taken part in vicious and brutal killings during the last bloody battles of the apartheid regime. In his pre-Iraq white paper proposing the use of private military companies, British Foreign Secretary Jack Straw predicted that the new mercenaries were 'respectable organizations', not the 'disreputable thugs' who built up a 'bad reputation' in the bad old days. The record of some of the South African fighters in Iraq showed that Straw's hopes were at best naive.

The end of apartheid was one of the most positive international developments of the previous decade. The South African government had fought a long and bloody campaign in the wars in the frontline states, and within South Africa itself, to preserve racial rule. The decades-long conflict was marked by massacres, assassinations, attacks on civilian populations, the use of undercover and proxy fighters, and other brutal- ities. Remarkably, the final end of apartheid was, after the long years of violence, relatively peaceful. Apartheid's vicious fighters were successfully demobilized in a 'Truth and Reconciliation' process. Many members of the Blair government had been closely involved in supporting the anti-apartheid movement, yet they remained silent when the private military companies in Iraq were soon found re-mobilizing some of apartheid's more vicious fighters.

It was very quickly clear that one of the largest groups of mercenaries operating in Iraq came from South Africa. The apartheid regime had fought most fiercely in its last decades, attacking its real and perceived enemies in proxy wars in neighbouring countries, and fighting a dirty war inside its own borders. Shadowy government-backed groups, sometimes blurring into precisely the private 'security' firms now being hired in Iraq, had fought a grim and bloody war against real and potential enemies. With apartheid's fall, the men who had fought this war were looking for work. Their 'counter-insurgency' skills landed them work in Iraq. Erinys – named after the Greek snake-headed goddess of retribution – became the largest private military contractor in Iraq. Founded in 2001, in 2003 they went on to win the contract to guard Iraq's oil infrastructure. By 2004 the private security companies began hiring Iraqis in greater numbers. Erinys's British and South African officers commanded a huge force of 14,000 Iraqis armed with AK-47s. The fact that a 3-year-old private company was running a military force the size of seven regiments in a contract worth $39 million showed vividly how Iraq was driving the private military business boom, putting fortunes into the pockets of the ex-army men running the new mercenary firms.

The British officers in Basra who first drew my attention to Erinys thought the firm was South African. In fact, Erinys had links to older British private military companies. Alastair Morrison, a former SAS officer, had been an Erinys director when the firm began touting for trade in Iraq. Morrison, who was awarded an OBE for helping West German special forces to free hostages on a Lufthansa jet hijacked to Mogadishu, was a founder director, in the 1980s, of the British military firm Defence Services Ltd (DSL), which was later renamed the Armor Group. Other DSL veterans also worked for Erinys. Morrison was later replaced by another British officer, Major General John Homes – a former commander of the 22 Special Air Service Brigade who became the British army's Director of Special Forces. He joined the Erinys board in 2004.

But the firm had equally strong African links. Erinys brought so many veterans of the South African Defence Force to Iraq that it was widely perceived as an African operation: the firm's directors were also connected to the apartheid regime, and the company's founders had included one Sean Cleary. Cleary had been second in command to South Africa's 'administrator general', who ruled Namibia in the 1980s when illegally occupied by South Africa, exporting apartheid laws to its African neighbour. While Cleary had helped to run Namibia as director of the administrator general's office, the UN recognized the South West African Peoples Organisation (SWAPO) as the country's rightful rulers. In 1985 Cleary went private, founding the 'Transcontinental Consultancy' in Namibia, as well as a public relations firm, 'Strategy Network International' (SNI), with London offices. His new private PR firm received £1.5 million from the South African government, and began vigorously representing Pretoria's interests. A South African army officer, Nico Basson, later said that Cleary's contract in Namibia was linked to 'Operation Agree'. This was the codename for an undercover, multi-million-pound scheme to discredit SWAPO in the 1989 UN-sponsored elections. Operation Agree activities included smear pamphlets, false rumours, and the planting of informers within both SWAPO and the UN peacekeeping force, not to mention channelling money, aeroplanes and cars to SWAPO's pro-South African opponents through a variety of front organizations.

Cleary also became an adviser to Jonas Savimbi's National Union for the Total Independence of Angola (UNITA), a guerrilla group supported by South Africa in its battle with the Popular Movement for the Liberation of Angola (MPLA) in the struggle for power in Angola, another of South Africa's neighbours. UNITA was known for gross abuses of human rights, including massacres, murder, torture, mutilation, and sexual slavery in their losing battle for power with the MPLA – which was guilty of some similar abuses. Newspaper reports said that Cleary was still advising Savimbi in 1993, after UNITA refused to recognize the MPLA's election victory and relaunched a bloody civil war, including a siege at the city of Huamba that killed some 10,000 people.

Cleary's pro-apartheid strategies included the recruitment of sympathetic British members of parliament through his London office. His lobbying outfit arranged UNITA-funded MPs' visits to Angola, and trips to South Africa funded by the South African Chamber of Mines. Tory lobbyist Derek Laud, who worked in the SNI office, recruited Conservative MP Neil Hamilton for African visits. Hamilton then worked as a consultant for the firm. Failure to declare his consultancy for Cleary's SNI was a small part of the torrent of sleaze that was finally to engulf Hamilton. Cleary's work also brought him into ex-army circles. He co-founded SNI in London with former Black Watch captain Patrick Watson. Cleary also worked with UNITA at the when it was linked to South African mercenaries: UNITA hired armed men from Eben Barlow's firm Executive Outcomes, although then as now it was claimed that these were not mercenaries, but 'security guards' looking after oil installations.

In 2003, as Erinys began to attract press attention, Sean Cleary quit the firm, although its spokesman told me that while the two parties had 'totally split' relations, this was an 'amicable' arrangement. Erinys Director Jonathan Garratt told me that the firm was British because 'we are all Brits. We are registered in the British Virgin Isles and we have a small subsidiary in South Africa.' According to South African company records, Garratt – a former British army officer – lived at the time in the Dainfern Housing Estate, a gated community with high security and excellent golfing facilities between Johannesburg and Pretoria. He also had two homes in Cape Town.

The British government was keen to back Erinys as a British success story. Tony Blair's personal envoy to Iraq, Brian Wilson, spoke in 2004 at an 'Iraq Reconstruction' conference in London, sponsored by Erinys and a number of oil companies, including Chevron, Shell and Exxon. Labour trade and industry secretary, Patricia Hewitt, told parliament that Erinys was one example of a UK firm successfully winning contracts in the reconstruction. Erinys runs its business from a secretive offshore registration in the British Virgin Islands, and does not even have a subsidiary listed at Companies House in the UK. But a spokesman for Hewitt insisted to me that the firm was still British because '[i]t's got British management and British staff, so it is benefiting the UK by employing British people. These days, with globalisation, you can't pin down what country a firm is from to the extent that you could years ago.' Erinys's international contacts include Bill Elder, a former security adviser for US engineering giant Bechtel with twenty-six years' experience in the US army – including work with the secret service. Elder also held a post as advisor to the board of Erinys. But it was Erinys's South African connection that was most alarming.

The character of the firm's apartheid veterans was exposed in January 2004, when two men working for Erinys became victims of a bomb attack at their hotel. The naming of the men rang alarm bells about the apartheid-era records of the firm's staff. Deon Gouws, who was injured, was a former member of Valkplaas, a notorious hit squad implicated in many murders. South Africa's Truth and Reconciliation Commission granted Gouws amnesty after he admitted involvement in over forty petrol-bombings of political activists' houses. Gouws also confessed to involvement in the fatal 1986 car-bombing of ANC activist Piet Ntuli, and an arson attack on anti-apartheid activist Fabian Ribero in the same year (Ribero was shot dead later in 1986). Also in 1986, an undercover South African agent rounded up nine youths in Vlakfontein, South Africa. The young men – some only 14 – thought they were being recruited to join the ANC. Instead, a squad led by Deon Guows machine-gunned them to death. Gouws then burned their bodies. Francois Styrdom, who died in the Iraq blast, was a former member of Koevoet (Afrikaans for 'crowbar'), a South African counter-insurgency unit in Namibia with a reputation for murder and torture. Erinys told me that it 'could not confirm or deny the records of these men', who were hired through a subcontractor. While the firm felt that it could guard Iraq's oil industry from saboteurs, it seemed to have only the weakest defences against employing staff with ugly histories. Garratt told me, 'We do as much as we possibly can to check the records of our men and ask them to sign an affidavit stating they have not been convicted of any crime or belonged to an illegal paramilitary group' – though he accepted that the system might have failed in this case.

Erinys firmly rejected the label 'private military contractor', insisting, 'We are a security firm, involved in guarding. We are not into creating military solutions.' As there was no fixed front line in the battle for Iraq, this is a fine distinction: with a many-headed insurgency throwing itself against targets throughout the country, there was no real distinction between security work and military operations. Erinys argued that it was simply providing security against 'rogue and terrorist attacks'; but it could equally be seen as fielding troops against a guerrilla war launched by Iraqi insurgents to end an occupation or overthrow a foreign-imposed government.

In January 2004 Erinys demonstrated the conflicts produced by rebuilding Iraq's security while employing an international pool of private armed guards. Who is more important in the new Iraq – the struggling, reconstituted police or the private contractors? Guards for Erinys in Kirkuk, in the north of the country, shot and killed a serving Iraqi police major. Erinys's armed guards working for the Northern Oil Company killed the major as he was passing a checkpoint. The nine Iraqi guards were arrested. Erinys boss Jonathan Garratt told me that Major Mohamed Shaban Al-Nassari was 'part of a large crowd of job seekers who had gathered at a gate to the Northern Oil Company. This crowd turned aggressive when they were told there were no jobs available and in the ensuing disturbance a member of the crowd, subsequently identified as Major Al-Nassari, who was not in uniform, produced a firearm which was discharged. At which point a member of the Oil Protection Force fired on the Major.'

Another British-led security firm, the Hart Group, also offered employment to apartheid killers. In 2004, the company employed 2,500 Iraqis, led by 170 foreign officers, to protect power plants and transmission lines in southern Iraq. The Bermuda-registered firm was run by former SAS and Scots Guard officer Richard Bethell, son of Lord Westbury. Like Erinys, it is linked to the Armor Group: Bethell was a founder director of DSL, although he fell out with the firm in an argument that ended up in court.

In April 2004, Shia militia in Kut killed Gray Branfield, a Hart Group officer. His death led to a front-page story in the *Guardian* suggesting that mercenaries needed more powerful weapons to defend themselves, as Coalition soldiers had not responded to his requests for aid. Following Branfield's death, author Peter Stiff, who writes extensively about South Africa's covert wars, came forward with a description of Branfield's history. He had been a detective inspector in the Rhodesian police, specializing in counter-insurgency. Branfield left for South Africa when the battle for white supremacy in Rhodesia was finally lost, going on to join the South African Defence Force's 'project barnacle', fighting a secret war against the ANC. He planned the 1982 raid on Maseru in Lesotho. This attempt to assassinate ANC leader Chris Hani claimed forty-two lives, including those of five women and two children. Branfield also helped plan a 1985 raid on 'ANC targets' in Gabarone, Botswana. South African commandos killed thirteen people, including three women and a

6-year-old child. According to Stiff, Branfield had reservations about this raid. In 1998 Branfield led a raid on Zimbabwe's Chikurubi prison to free five South African agents who had car-bombed an ANC office in that country. The would-be assassins duped an unemployed man into driving the rigged car to the ANC offices. The driver, killed by the remote-controlled bomb, was the only fatality. Branfield's raid to free the car-bombers was aborted, and the men remained in prison. Branfield was undoubtedly brave: in 1986 he had been captured undercover in Zambia, and was tortured, but he escaped. He died outnumbered in an extensive gun battle in Iraq, but his five fellow guards were saved.

The Hart Group's Simon Faulkner told me that Branfield's background 'is complete news to me', adding: 'If I knew the person I interviewed had a background of any illegality or assassinations I would not have hired him.' Faulkner told me that his firm has a 'sort of vetting procedure. We interview all the people who come to us. It is a very difficult thing to do. There are some things you have to take on face value; there is not very much you can do.' Despite these failings, Faulkner said that company rules would stop abuses by individual staff: 'We have a command structure, as it were; we have people who are leaders. We're not going round shooting people.' In fact, Branfield was the company's leader in Kut. Faulkner emphasized that Branfield's death was 'not because he was trigger happy or going out for a fight. To think that would be completely crazy. Let me tell you that what happened that night was not in any sense offensive. There were five men in a hut attacked by 60-odd crazed militia. What he did was purely defensive.'

The Department for International Development's choice of contractor to supply armed guards was also linked to the apartheid past; but it was its links to the African present that posed problems. Tactical Meteoric, the firm hired by DfID, was based in the Valhalla district of Pretoria. The firm's directors and most of its staff were veterans of the South African Police Special Task Force – a highly trained paramilitary police group used to break sieges, rescue hostages, and guard dignitaries. Festus Van Ruyen, one of Tactical Meteoric's three founding partners, said that the police task force was 'like your own Police's SO19 unit or the SAS tactical hostage group'. The Task Force was founded to deal with the student uprising in Soweto in 1976, and was closely involved in riot control training and counter-insurgency techniques, but had not been linked to apartheid's excesses for some years. Van Ruyen was keen to reassure me that his staff had no skeletons in their cupboards. He told me, 'All my people have been in the police [during the apartheid years] but all of my staff served the old regime and the new regime [in South Africa], and had the pleasure of protecting Nelson Mandela, Thabo Mbeki, France's Mitterand, Yasser Arafat, Tony Blair, and your own Queen.' He said that some of his staff were ex-soldiers, but that more were former police officers like himself. As well as working for DfID, the firm was employed by Switzerland's small diplomatic mission in Iraq, and had a contract with the CPA to train the new Iraqi police in 'SWAT'-style tactics.

Despite these comparatively respectable beginnings, the company's two other founding partners took time out of their work in Iraq to become embroiled in an African coup plot. In March 2004, two of the firm's three owners were arrested in Zimbabwe, alongside infamous mercenary Simon Mann, accused of plotting a coup in Equatorial Guinea. Lourens 'Louwtjie' Horn and Hermanus 'Harry' Carlse were arrested along with other mercenaries, and incarcerated in Zimbabwe's Chikurubi prison. They were accused of forming an advance party for the coup with Simon Mann, arriving in Harare to purchase weapons for use in a plot to overthrow the government of Equatorial Guinea by armed force. The three men tried to buy weapons, including sixty-one AK47 rifles, 45,000 rounds of rifle ammunition, 1,000 rounds of anti-tank ammunition, and 160 grenades. The weapons were allegedly to be used by some seventy mercenaries who were to fly into Harare later in March. The mercenaries – veterans of South Africa's wars in Namibia and Angola – where planning an assault in Malabo, the capital of Equatorial Guinea, where they would kidnap or kill President Obiang, the tyrannical ruler of the small oil-rich African state. The arrested men claim that they were had merely been hired as security staff for diamond mines in the Democratic Republic of Congo.

The coup plot harked back to the bad old days of African soldiers of fortune. Mann, part of the Watney's brewing dynasty, was a veteran of Executive Outcomes. He asked his associates for help in getting out of prison, saying that he might need a 'large splodge of wonga' [cash] to escape jail. Various versions of a 'wonga' list circulated, purporting to show that investors in the scheme included other names from the past, including that of Sir Mark Thatcher, son of the former British prime minister, who was ultimately fined for his part in the plot. Van Ruyen was furious with his former partner's actions. He told me, 'We completely disassociate ourselves from that kind of activity. When I heard the news I contacted the company lawyer to break all formal and financial links with them.' Van Ruyen said that his fellow directors had been on leave when they were arrested in Zimbabwe, adding, 'I was shocked when I heard the news of their arrest. Activity like that is totally against company policy.' Van Ruyen said that Lourens Horn was in charge of the company in Iraq, including the contract with the DfID, until February 2004, when he returned to South Africa to 'chill out on a hunting farm'. Hermanus Carlse left Iraq some time before then. Together, the three men set up Meteoric Tactical Solutions. But Van Ruyen no longer had time for his former partners, saying, 'they made up their beds and must now lie in them.' His former partners were beaten and badly treated in Zimbabwe, but were released because the country's authorities decided that they had not actually handled the weapons at the time of their arrest.

On their return to South Africa they surrendered to the police. In a reaction to South Africa's long, bloody history of mercenarism, the ANC government had passed this strict law against its citizens acting as guns for hire. While the ANC government had accepted the allies' use of South Africans in their military companies in Iraq, they acted swiftly once the same people became involved in military business on the African continent. This was too close to home, and too reminiscent of the past, to be ignored. The South African police also closed down Tactical Meteoric itself, apparently not taking at face value the way in which Van Ruyen had disassociated his company from the plot. The Swiss, like the South Africans, took the plot seriously. Swiss MP Barbara Haering, who served on the country's parliamentary security commission, called for the South African mercenaries to be replaced with real soldiers, because '[w]e would then have assurances that they are under democratic control and are trained to respect human rights'. While she was unsuccessful – the Swiss authorities preferred to use the mercenaries rather than send their own soldiers to Iraq – the issue was at least raised in parliament.

In Britain, however, ministers and MPs greeted the issue with an embarrassed silence. Two soldiers for hire who had worked for DfID, and had personally guarded development minister Hilary Benn in Iraq, were now caught up in a sleazy, abortive coup. However unwittingly, DfID had encouraged the plot. There is a good chance that the men from Tactical Meteoric used money they had raised working for the British government to invest, albeit in a small way, in the coup plot. The mercenaries could have been encouraged in other ways as well: Equatorial Guinea was, like Iraq, an oil-rich country ruled by an unpopular and vicious dictator. If President Obiang had fallen, to be replaced by a more friendly ruler, as the result of a mercenary-led assault on Malabo, would the West have objected? Opposition leader Sevoro Moto was accused of involvement in the scheme, although he denied it. The involvement of mercenaries might have been embarrassing, but why would Britain or the US have objected to mercenaries ousting an African dictator when they had relied on the same men to shore up their occupation of Iraq? Had the coup plot worked, it seems that its investors would have won valuable oil concessions. This was a classic illustration of the danger of using mercenaries: motivated by money rather than politics or patriotism, they could easily have slipped from performing a simple military function into a conducting a form of piracy or protection racket.

THE RETURN OF TIM SPICER

While the British government warmed to the idea of private military companies after the 'arms to Africa' scandal (see Chapter 5), they did seem to make a specific effort to keep Tim Spicer and his companies at a distance. British officials only met Spicer in secret or in confidence, and signed no contracts with his companies. The UK government seemed happy to deal with firms they felt were respectable, like the Armor Group or Control Risks, but treated Spicer as if he was beyond the pale. The government found it difficult to forget its condemnation of Spicer during the Sandline affair, or to forgive Spicer for the embarrassment he had caused them. Unfortunately, the British government was not in charge, but was both at the whim of both its US senior partner in Iraq and at the mercy of the new security market. Neither would rule out Spicer's involvement.

One of the largest security contracts awarded in Iraq showed how Britain led the market for private armies. It also showed that the new market for armed men was drawing in some familiar old faces. UK-based Aegis Security was awarded a contract to 'co-ordinate security for the

Project Management Office and ensure security of Project Management Office staff'. This bland-sounding specification in fact put Aegis in charge of most other private security firms in Iraq, while simultaneously demanding that they directly form a small praetorian guard for the staff of the occupying forces, in return for the payment of some $293 million. Aegis Security was run by Tim Spicer, who had run his former firm, Sandline, with Simon Mann as his deputy. Mann was not able to assist Spicer in Iraq because he was in detention in Zimbabwe following the botched coup in Equatorial Guinea. Spicer's Sandline had embarrassed the Labour government when it was found importing arms into war-torn Sierra Leone, in breach of a UN arms embargo (see Chapter 5). While the British government carried out a *volte-face* and encouraged the use of private military companies after the arms-to-Africa affair, they never seem to have forgiven Spicer. The Foreign Office studiously kept his name out of its consultation paper on legitimizing mercenaries. Neither did the British government ever openly hire or even talk to Spicer, although they kept in contact with him behind the scenes. Unfortunately the US government was impressed by Spicer, and British officials swallowed their embarrassment and accepted his new role.

After Spicer's reputation had been damaged by the arms-to-Africa affair, he put together his new company with some unlikely help. Frederick Forsyth – author of many thrillers, including mercenary tale *The Dogs of War* – was a founder investor in Spicer's firm, possibly hoping that it would furnish him with new plots. Spicer rebuilt his mercenary firm with the help of Sara Pearson, a marketing executive who had cut her teeth selling 'Fresh Breath' toothpaste – but she was unable to wash Spicer's past whiter than white.

While British ministers responded to Spicer's appointment with an embarrassed silence, his role did cause controversy in the US. A lively campaign in America objected to Spicer because of his soldiering past in Northern Ireland. This was probably the one issue about Spicer that did not cause waves in Britain. The UK government was cagey about Spicer, but unfazed about issues around Northern Ireland. For example, when the Armor Group sent a former Royal Marine, who had a prison record for helping loyalist terrorists in Northern Ireland, to work as a guard for Bechtel in Iraq, there was no sign of British official concern. Armor's private soldier had gone to prison for four years in 1995 on ten counts of soliciting murder after he passed army intelligence files to Johnny 'Mad

Dog' Adair's Ulster Freedom Fighters, to help them target their attacks. Serving British soldiers who spotted the ex jailbird were outraged, but the Government were unmoved. Britain happily gave contracts to the Armor Group, who also travelled in respectable circles through their funding of the Foreign Policy Centre, a think tank linked to Labour's leadership.

However, the Northern Ireland conflict was viewed very differently in America, with its large Irish population, and Spicer's record caused outrage. Before founding Sandline, Spicer had been an officer in the Royal Green Jackets, and had fought in the Falklands. Spicer had also commanded two Scots Guards who were convicted of murdering an unarmed man, Peter McBride, who had no Republican connections but was shot in the back while moving away from an army checkpoint in 1992. Spicer successfully campaigned for the release of his two former soldiers. A noisy but ultimately unsuccessful campaign was launched by Irish-Americans to cancel the Aegis contract in Iraq because of Spicer's attitude to McBride's murder. Aegis also had other opponents in the US. When it won the contract, rival mercenary firm DynCorp persuaded the US authorities to suspend the deal and investigate Spicer's past – although ultimately DynCorp's challenge was unsuccessful. DynCorp's arguments about Spicer's colourful past were somewhat weakened by its own employees' involvement in crime (see Chapter 4).

THE BALANCE SHEET IN IRAQ

Iraq was made into the most massive experiment in the privatization of the battlefield and the contracting out of military occupation. The results seem unequivocal: the new mercenaries added to the failure in Iraq. The British government's pre-war consultation paper on private military companies suggested that there was 'a valid and defensible use for private military companies', and suggested they could be useful 'for a state under threat from armed insurgents or from criminal gangs with a military capability' for 're-establishing security'. Iraq was precisely that state, and yet the widespread use of private soldiers added to the fragmentation of the country. British Foreign Secretary Jack Straw thought that using armed corporations would be 'cheaper and [certainly] quicker than attempting to train national forces'. The new mercenaries and other contractors in the occupation were not cheap. They exploited their market power, and in some cases used simple corruption, to squeeze money out of Iraq, until security costs effectively brought a halt to the reconstruction of basic services. Any apparent advantage of using the security companies instead of building Iraq's own forces soon proved to be illusory.

By 2005 it was clear that trying to substitute private companies for Iraq's own armed forces had failed to check the insurgency, and seemed instead only to have added to the break-up of the state into the fiefdoms of competing armed gangs. A dispassionate and rational government would surely have looked at the Iraq experiment and decided to abandon such extensive use of battlefield contractors. But that would have meant admitting that one of the central strategies for the Iraq occupation was simply wrong – a move that Whitehall and Washington would resist with all their political might. Now that the British and US governments were relying so heavily on private companies to launch military action, they appeared to have decided to stick with the policy, whatever the consequences.

8

Spies for Hire

Intelligence agencies have a long history of subcontracting. In Joseph Conrad's novel, *The Secret Agent*, the titular spy is a Russian anarchist, M. Verloc, who regularly takes money from a foreign embassy in London. In return he passes information from the world of the subversive émigrés to the embassy, and even promotes a bomb plot to help his paymasters discredit anarchism. Verloc is a subcontractor. This basic structure existed in real life, as well as on the page. The glamorous James Bond-type secret agent – a full-time employee of the state working undercover in a variety of disguises – has a bigger role in the cinema; but the seedy Verloc figure, who is independent of the state but works secretly as their agent, is probably more important. Major Western intelligence services have had an extraordinarily broad range of Verlocs working as subcontractors. During the Cold War, for example, *Encounter* magazine specialized in publishing articles by European authors who were well to the left of the US mainstream, but who were also militantly anti-Soviet. The magazine was secretly funded by the CIA, and so can be seen as a US intelligence agency subcontractor, hired to divert the European left away from Communist sympathizers and act as an intellectual bulwark against the Soviet bloc.

Encounter's funding was just a small part of a major political and financial drive by the CIA, organized around the Congress for Cultural Freedom. The myriad anti-Soviet groups on the US payroll were effectively US secret service subcontractors. The Cuban exiles who launched the unsuccessful assault on Castro's government at the Bay of Pigs in 1960 were also a CIA-funded operation. Despite their humiliating failure in the Bay of Pigs – the Cuban army overpowered the invaders, then traded them for millions of dollars' worth of medical aid

– the CIA was enthusiastic about using this particular 'firm'. Cuban fighters were also hired by the CIA to try and track Che Guevara in Bolivia and put down a rebellion in the Congo in the early 1960s. All of these forms of covert action can be seen to represent a kind of privatization.[1]

But this use of private agents is essentially driven by a need to maintain secrecy and 'deniability' – to make actions by the security services look like actions by some other party. By the time the war on terror started, a new kind of subcontractor to the intelligence agencies had developed: un-secret agents, forming a marketplace of firms openly doing the state's spying for cash. The CIA's network of secret subcontractors included many political and military organizations, but also some with a distinctly commercial structure: from the 1960s onwards, the CIA established enough 'cut out' companies to fill an undercover *Yellow Pages*. These companies were known in the Agency as 'proprietaries'. Some of these firms might simply provide cover employment for CIA agents; but some carried out extensive services for the agency, especially in transport.

The CIA's best-known 'proprietary', Air America, appeared to be a private airline, formed by veteran pilots from the US air force's daredevil 'Flying Tigers'. But it was wholly owned by the CIA. A major airline, with 165 planes and 5,000 employees, its CIA missions included parachuting guerrillas, mercenaries, money and arms into the Agency's 'secret' wars in Vietnam and Southast Asia – the wars were secret from the US population, but not from their Southeast Asian victims. Air America and other CIA 'proprietary' firms used surplus US bombers to fight in Indonesia, the Congo, and Vietnam, as well as in the Bay of Pigs fiasco. Air America looked like a private airline, but was CIA-owned, and acted as a secret cargo courier in Southeast Asia. While Air America was related to the firms that would later make up War on Terror, Inc., the commercial structure was essentially a cover for the CIA, rather than a financial reality. Indeed, CIA agents were instructed to avoid attracting attention by running their companies with only middling business panache, to make sure they avoided commercial success – much to the annoyance of their agents. One complained that, though business failure might keep an agent under the radar, 'you look like a horse's ass' and 'even your kids think you're a loser'.[2]

In the mid-1970s the US secret services faced sustained political difficulties. Failure in Vietnam and the Watergate scandal led many

Americans to question the role of the intelligence services. In 1975 a committee of Senators led by Frank Church began a wide-ranging set of inquiries into misbehaviour by the country's secret services. The Senate's 'Church Committee' picked over and exposed covert actions by the whole range of national, international, military, and police units, and issued fourteen reports into the conduct of both the FBI and the CIA, cataloguing spying on US citizens, the actions of agents provocateurs, assassination plots, the promotion of secret wars, coups, and other shocking behaviour. The Committee followed in the wake of political campaigners and investigative journalists who had exposed the US intelligence services' darker corners. The services retreated in the face of this political crisis, and many of the proprietaries were wound down as a result – though some were sold off instead, and the commercial relation established in the process formed the basis for some of the companies that would grow into the new style of secret contractors.

But the immediate effect of the running down of the proprietaries was to make the blurring of boundaries between commercial companies and the security services somewhat unfashionable. In the 1980s, US administrations, in emulation of Thatcher's experiment in the UK, started a wave of privatizations. Thatcherite contracting out in the security services held the potential to establish genuinely independent firms that could sell their services to the CIA, FBI, and Defence Department, rather than generating commercial subsidiaries of the CIA. But the first publicly declared plans to privatize the CIA barely got off the ground. In 1982, the US government tried to privatize the 700 guards stationed outside federal buildings, but the CIA, the State Department and National Security Agency prevented their cops from becoming rent-a-cops, more or less killing the proposal.[3] In 1983 the government tried again, this time aiming to privatize the CIA's office cleaners,[4] but the policy withered. In 1984 Reagan's contracting-out drive finally hit the CIA, when the agency contracted 2,000 private custodial agents and electricians;[5] but this was pretty small beer.

Other attempts to privatize security services also ran into the ground during this period. A private firm, the Intertect Group, was given a $2 million contract to carry out security clearances for the Office of Personnel Management (OPM). The OPM vetted staff for security jobs outside the CIA. They were behind with clearances for over 1,000 staff waiting for jobs in the nuclear weapons industry and elsewhere, and passed the work on to the private detectives. But the contract ended in acrimonious argument, as officials accused the company of 'creative writing' in relation to the vetting reports, while the company claimed that officials were obstructive, and wondered 'whether the project was ever meant to work'.[6] In 1996 the whole vetting function of the Office of Personnel Management was privatized, forming a firm called USIS, which was partly owned by the politically connected Carlyle Group. The new private company became intimately involved in the war on terror when it started hiring and vetting officers for the anti-terrorist training programme in Iraq.[7]

The Reagan administration breathed new life into US covert action. Reagan's election signalled a revival in US confidence – specifically, the confidence to interfere militarily in other nations. His enthusiastic supporters saw the new presidency as a way to end the soul-searching and self-criticism characterizing the rule of his Democratic predecessor, Jimmy Carter. Some of the Reaganauts were disgusted by the way in which the Watergate crisis and the Vietnam war had led to the exposure to criticism of the country's secret missions, accompanied by cutbacks. In the words of a subsequently disillusioned participant in one of the era's secret wars,

> Reagan's California mafia came to power with what it believed was a mandate from the American people to show the world that the United States was back and ready to kick ass after its sobering surrender in Vietnam and years of post-war self-flagellation.[8]

A combination of circumstances meant that the revival in undercover US wars took on a distinctly more commercial character. Firstly, some defence and intelligence agents were still affected by the revelations of the Church Committee, and were reluctant to become involved in new undercover adventures. This meant that Reagan staff like Colonel Oliver North sought to bypass official channels for their missions in the Middle East and Latin America. But avoiding official channels also meant avoiding official cash, so North had to find his own source of funds. He had what he described as the 'neat idea'[9] of selling arms to Iran in order to gain influence in the region, and using the cash to fund the Contras, who were fighting against Nicaragua's left-wing Sandinista regime. North's operation – raising its own funds, avoiding official control, and relying on a few political 'entrepreneurs' allied to a shady Iranian arms dealer – was in itself seen by many commentators as a 'privatization' of foreign policy.[10]

The Iran–Contra affair also involved commercial companies related to the old CIA 'proprietaries'. But these formerly CIA-owned firms had been sold off, and were now profit-making concerns. The 'horse's ass' instructions to do badly in business were gone. The new semi-CIA companies seemed to have mixed motives: were they there to make money for their owners, or to make military mischief for the intelligence service? In 1986 the Nicaraguan Sandinista government shot down a Hercules aeroplane carrying arms to the Contras. The captured pilot, Eugene Hasenfus, revealed the plane belonged to Southern Air Transport. The company had been a CIA 'proprietary' until it was sold in 1976. Now a genuine profit-making company, it continued to carry out undercover military missions. Records showed that Southern Air also shipped US weapons to the Middle East for sale to Iran. The company's planes also seemed to be flying material to Jonas Savimbi's UNITA rebels in Angola. It was like Air America all over again – only this time the firm really was a money-making venture.

Southern Air acted as a private air force in the secret war against the Sandinistas. An organization called Civil Military Assistance (CMA), based in Alabama, organized the army. CMA sent a motley crew of mercenaries into Nicaragua – a role that became famous when Sandinista fighters shot down one of its helicopters. The organization received funds from various right-wing US groups, but the bulk of the cash came from Oliver North's operation. Indeed Jack Terrell, one of its co-founders, was the first to reveal North's role, when he became disillusioned with the incompetence and money-grubbing character of the firm.[11] While CMA and Southern Air received funds for North's operation, they were apparently founded independently of the state: the CIA's wide-ranging counter-insurgency operations had been cut back following the crises of the Nixon administration. The Reagan administration was only partly able to rebuild the political will to launch new secret attacks. But Oliver North was able to circumvent the reluctance of the defence and intelligence establishment to get back into the undercover shooting match by using private funds and private companies.

The Iran–Contra affair ended in embarrassment: Colonel North ended up on trial, although charges against him were finally overturned; Tom

Posey, who founded Civilian Military Assistance, faced a number of lawsuits and finally ended up in prison for stealing night-vision goggles from the US army.[12] Many of the Civilian Military Assistance men had trained at a mercenary school run by Frank Camper in Dolomite, Alabama. Camper's biography showed the transition from official to unofficial counter-insurgency and covert operations. He was a Special Forces officer in Vietnam, and then became an undercover FBI operative, infiltrating the Alabama branch of the Communist Party, then posing as a 'military adviser' to groups like the Black Liberation Front in order to investigate them for the security services. But by the 1980s he went private, and offered any buyers military training at his mercenary school. Camper was also involved in arms dealing for the Contras. Shortly after the Iran–Contra affair he was jailed for two years for a bomb plot. He had been hired by two businesswomen to blow up the cars of disgruntled employees, but was jailed before the conspiracy reached fruition.[13] These small and seedy adventures in low-level warfare might be seen just as a sordid coda to the CIA's post-war escapades, were in not for the fact that they set a model for undercover activity in the 'war on terror'. Camper's escapades should have faded into history, but instead the use of independent profit-making businesses to work for the security services was revived after 9/11.

One of the principal stimuli to the use of private companies to support the Contras was a desire to circumvent issues of political responsibility. The US Democrats were able to hobble Reagan's legal attempts to back the Contras by means of the Boland Amendment – a piece of legislation forbidding direct funding of the Nicaraguan fighters. But the back-door, private routes ran around and under the Boland Amendment. Support for the Contras avoided official channels, but as a result ran straight into a mass of conflicts of interest, corruption and bad behaviour. As Jack Terrell, a disenchanted participant in the operation, recalled: 'The Boland Amendment meant the administration had to privatize the pressure on the Sandinistas.' However, 'That privatization . . . meant a lot of people turned their heads from immoral and illegal activities that were taking place in the name of democracy'.[14]

When George W. Bush became president, looking back on the support to the Contras, he and his staff seemed to have much more vivid memories of the joyful freedom that privatization allowed than of the scandal that had been precipitated. The Bush administration not only used privatization to avoid political scrutiny, but also used private companies to get around what they saw as the too prissy attitudes of the State Department and the CIA. In the war on terror, private companies provided a way of shifting power in intelligence operations into the hands of the more aggressive officials in the Defence Department. But the use of private companies also, of course, shifted power to the companies themselves: substitute the Middle East for Central America, and Terrell's description of the Contra affair sounds like a prediction of events in the war on terror. He wrote:

> There was no Congressional oversight and no executive control of the operation. Ineptitude, corruption and criminal activity were endemic. The foreign policy goals of the Untied States were of secondary concern to many of those involved. The Contra war had become a money-making scheme designed to pad the pockets of a few individuals. Americans paid with their tax dollars while the Nicaraguan *campesinos* paid with their lives. In some instances, pecuniary interests took precedence over patriotism. There was a lot of money to be made in this war.[15]

Admiral Stansfield Turner, who had been the director of the CIA under President Reagan's predecessor, President Carter, pointed out the danger of the use of the commercial sector in undercover operations in the Iran–Contra scandals. Turner had himself used the 'proprietary' companies as cover for secret operations. But in 1987, as the Iran–Contra scandal became public, Turner highlighted the danger of using businesses with a real profit motive for undercover work. He contrasted the idea of using fake firms to give undercover agents convincing alter egos with the use of real firms with their own commercial imperatives to carry out intelligence work. According to Turner, 'The proprietaries have been one of the sources of the problems the agency has run into over the years.' He argued that there was a risk that businessmen brought into an operation would convince the intelligence agents to act for profit, not politics, which he referred to as 'the tail wagging the dog'.[16] Turner's analysis was of Iran–Contra, but is even more apt today: the commercialization of the war on terror means that private companies are much more extensively involved in covert operations than during the Reagan years. The business tail is in a much stronger position to wag the intelligence dog. However, after the Iran–Contra scandal died down, Turner's critique was forgotten, and a new Republican administration has enthusiastically returned to the policy of covert-action-by-contract begun on a smaller scale by the Reagan administration.

The final exposure of the Iran–Contra affair held back the privatization of this kind of clandestine operation for a time; but the model was put on ice rather than into the dustbin. The 9/11 attacks unfroze that ice, and President Bush's administration returned to the idea, only on a much larger scale. Instead of remaining a sordid piece of the country's past – a cut-rate echo of the undercover excesses of the Cold War carried out by seedy small traders – Contragate became the model for much more widespread business-led covert action in the war on terror. Bush's presidency signalled its attitude to Reagan's Central American scandal by rehabilitating a number of figures from the Iran–Contra affair. Bush placed Elliott Abrams – an Assistant Secretary of State who had sought to raise millions in private money to fund the Contras, and had pleaded guilty to misleading Congress over Iran–Contra on the National Security Council, in charge of 'democracy promotion'. This echoed the fact that Oliver North's plan to use mercenaries paid for by arms sales to attack the Sandinistas had itself been dubbed 'operation democracy'. John Negroponte, who had overseen support for the Contras as US ambassador to Nicaragua's neighbour, Honduras, became ambassador to Iraq. US Colonel James Steele, a senior military adviser in El Salvador (where the government worked closely with death squads), had monitored supplies for the Contras, then reappeared as an adviser to the new Iraqi police's most feared squad after the fall of Saddam.[17] As well as re-hiring Iran–Contra politicians, the Bush presidency built heavily on Oliver North's 'neat idea' of using private companies and non-US funds to run a counter-insurgency operation.

As with the war on terror, the private companies involved in the Iran–Contra operation were an Anglo-American affair. The US had the political will, muscle, and money to intervene, but the British still had some useful expertise left over from the Empire, and a political closeness to the US elite. A joint UK–US team of mercenaries was arrested in Costa Rica in 1985 on its way to fight with the Contras. It included a former Green Jacket and an officer in the British Territorial Army, who had travelled to Latin America from Solihull, near Birmingham.[18] As well as the Alabama private soldiers, Oliver North contracted an ex-SAS man,

David Walker – a former British colonel who had set up two private military companies. Papers showed that North had hired the British firms, Saladin and Keeny Meeny Services (a name derived from SAS slang), to 'perform military actions' in Nicaragua. North would not reveal what actions, but press speculation included attacks on Sandinista arms dumps, the flying of arms to the Contras, and their training in sabotage.[19] Walker's companies were moving towards respectability, with recent contracts to provide security for British embassies; the exposure of his role in the Nicaraguan affair was a setback on the rehabilitation of his kind of mercenary firm. Walker would have to wait seven years, until 1994, before he could appear easily in polite society again, by which time he had hired former Conservative Party defence minister Archie Hamilton as a non-executive director of Saladin. Hamilton then approached British embassies to try and win contracts for the private military company.[20] When the Iran–Contra politicians welcomed back into Bush's government launched the second Iraq War, Saladin was able to generate new business from the war on terror. By 2006, Saladin claimed to have a force of 2,000 guards working in Afghanistan.

Though the exposure of Contragate set back commercial covert action for a time, another strand of corporate undercover work, with a domestic focus, remained unaffected, and acted as a nurturing ground for the private companies that would blossom during the war on terror. While the retail end of the private investigation industry concentrates on divorce, the serving of summonses, missing persons, and so on, the corporate side has traditionally been involved in much more complex and contentious work. The US, in particular, has a strong tradition of private investigators acting as spies, *agents provocateurs*, and militias – and indeed across the whole range of covert activities. Allan Pinkerton founded the US's first detective agency in the 1850s. His company's logo – a large eye, and the motto 'We never sleep' – is one possible origin of the term 'private eye'. During the Civil War, Pinkerton used his undercover skills in the Union Intelligence Service, and foiled an assassination attempt on Abraham Lincoln.

Born in Scotland, Pinkerton had been a member of the Chartists, the nineteenth-century workers movement, before leaving for the US. But Pinkerton and his sons built the family firm into a massive national force by hiring out agents to beat the country's infant workers movement. As the US industrialized, unions formed and fought strikes in the new mining, steel and railroad industries. The Pinkerton agency found a fantastic business opportunity among the strife. Hired by railroad and coal-mining magnate Franklin B. Gowen, Pinkerton sent an undercover operative to infiltrate the mineworkers' union in Pennsylvania. Pinkerton's agent spent years pretending to be a militant, before claiming at a trial that the miners had formed a secret society dedicated to violence, called the 'Molly Maguires'. Pinkerton's agent was, and still is, accused of being a liar and *agent provocateur*, but in 1877 ten men were hanged on his evidence. On the back of this success, the Pinkerton agency wrote to large employers, arguing that

> there is so much dissatisfaction among the labouring classes and secret labour societies are organizing throughout the United States. We suggest whether it would not be well for railroad companies and other corporations, as well as individuals who are extensive employers of labour, to keep a close watch for designing men among their own employees, who, in the interest of secret labour societies, are inducing their employees to join these organizations and eventually to cause a strike.

The agency said that it could provide 'a detective suitable to associate with their employees and obtain this information', and a 'private police patrol' to deal with matters when strikes broke out. The Pinkerton agency then both ran undercover agents among trade unions and fielded thousands of armed men to break strikes – with a larger force than the US standing army of the time. But when, in 1892, a corps of 300 of Pinkerton's men fought a gun battle with strikers at a Carnegie Steel Mill at Homestead, near Pittsburgh, ten strikers and seven of the agents were killed. The scandal – plus the fact that the Pinkertons lost the battle, and had to be rescued by state militia – led to a closing down of their armed operations. A Congressional investigation, followed by a series of state laws against the Pinkerton patrols, meant that the agency retreated away from the use of armed men as strike-breakers. But the company kept up its undercover work within trade unions, and continued to attract accusations that its employees were acting as *agents provocateurs*. In the 1930s a new wave of trade union growth and strikes in the US led to a new settlement. The combined force of new labour-friendly laws and exposure by a Senatorial commission – the La Folette Commission –

pushed the Pinkertons and other agencies away from this full-blown labour espionage.

The history of the Pinkertons showed that, while private companies ran the initial conflict with labour, when the latter became more powerful the state would step in. Just as the Indian Mutiny hastened the nationalization of the East India Company, so the labour mutinies of the late nineteenth century and the 1930s led the state to take over and regulate the relation between boss and worker. Something of the Pinkertons' spirit lived on in the Wackenhut Corporation,[21] although on a smaller scale. Wackenhut kept blacklists of 'subversives' to help employers screen out unwanted staff. Wackenhut was able to make money out of an ongoing 'red scare', until a Congressional investigation in 1975 exposed and embarrassed the company.[22]

By the 1990s the commercial corporate investigation scene was a much more conservative affair, neatly illustrated by the activities of two companies – Kroll and Control Risks. Kroll Associates, founded in 1972 by former district attorney Jules Kroll, specialized in corporate investigations – picking up business especially from takeovers and acquisitions. 'Wall Street's private eye' helped look for skeletons in the closet when one company tried to buy another.[23] Kroll tried to cash in on the post-war Iraq boom by setting up the ill-fated Kroll Security International, which supplied armed guards to Iraq. The firm hired people like former head of British Special Forces Jeremy Phipps, and Alastair Morrison, the ex-SAS man who had founded one of the world's largest private military companies. Kroll also hired Lady Olga Maitland, a cartoonish Tory activist who had done battle with the Campaign for Nuclear Disarmament (CND) in the 1980s. Maitland founded a campaign group in support of nuclear weapons, called Families for Defence, to hold counter-demonstrations against CND. Maitland's group was derisively nicknamed 'Mummies for Missiles'. Kroll, however, took Maitland very seriously. Maitland tried to use her diplomatic skills to sell a Kroll plan in Nigeria to use private security staff as guards for frequently sabotaged oil platforms. Kroll failed to retain its security contracts, and its foray into private military work was wound down in 2006.

Control Risk Group began as a subsidiary of an insurance company advising on the dangers of kidnap, especially in Latin America. There was a mini-furore when top UK policeman, Sir Kenneth Newman, joined the firm in 1987. The firm already had on its board Sir Robert Mark, another Commissioner of the Metropolitan Police, and former Northern

Ireland Army commander General Frank King. But the company kept a low profile as it branched out into other kinds of corporate investigation. After the fall of Saddam Hussein, the firm supplied – and lost – armed guards in Iraq, but throughout the 1980s and 1990s the company had quietly operated in business circles.[24]

In the 1990s, however, two related tendencies led to changes in the corporate private investigation scene. Firstly, after the collapse of Communism, the establishment found a new threat in the shape of what finally developed into the 'anti-globalization movement'. Radical protest movements based on environmental, peace and other causes began to grow and coalesce. Activism on such diverse issues as road-building, exploitation of the developing world, the fate of indigenous peoples, and even the outlawing of spontaneous 'acid house' parties, brought a new generation into political activity. By the end of the decade, these movements came together under a broad anti-globalization banner after a massive turnout of protestors outside the 1999 meeting of the World Trade Organisation in Seattle. The 1999 demonstration represented a high point for these new political currents, but they had been growing for years. While both traditional social democracy and socialism had waned, protestors developed new causes, often targeting specific companies. In Britain, protestors against road-building saw their primary enemies as being the construction companies and their retinue of lobbyists and security firms, rather than the politicians sponsoring the schemes themselves. Similarly, protestors against the arms trade focused directly on the arms manufacturers. These developments excited many on the left, but the direct focus on named corporations alarmed those in the boardroom.

Fear of environmental protestors, no matter how rowdy or undisciplined, now seems touchingly precious, given the more serious dangers of international terrorism. But before 9/11, 'violent anarchists' were the newspapers' demon of the day. The corporate security industry quickly saw a sales opportunity. A new private undercover industry, reminiscent of the Pinkerton agency, built businesses offering companies a paid-for response to the supposed 'threat' of the new protests. The commercial nature of these intelligence operations was stimulated by some larger privatization trends. The boards who hired these new security companies were obviously influenced by the general trend for the state to retreat and the private sector to take over formerly public services. There were also more direct stimuli for privatized intelligence. Firstly, the British govern-

ment handed over road-building and arms programmes to the private
sector. The Conservative government balanced the running down of the
public rail network with the expansion of privately built roads, and
increased the size of the private arms industry by handing state-owned
arms maker Royal Ordnance over to the private military company British
Aerospace. The private security industry built its business servicing these
newly privatized areas. The companies that hired the new private
intelligence operatives had themselves benefited from the shrinking of
the state sector, and so presumably found it natural to look to a private
solution to new security 'threats'.

Secondly, the new Thatcherite spirit, now riding triumphant following
the same collapse of Communism, meant that the pull of private
enterprise began to be felt in the British security services. For some time
the most high-profile money-making scheme a former employee of MI5
or MI6 could launch had been to release a book with some embarrassing
revelations; but a new generation of companies using former undercover
agents was now established to compete with Kroll and Control Risks. It
seems that some of the companies broke into the market by offering some
of the older, less constrained activities reminiscent of the Pinkertons or
Wackenhut, and perhaps reflecting the arrogance of recently discharged
government agents.

In 1995 the Hakluyt Foundation, a private company, set up shop
offering risk analysis and investigation services for multinationals; it
employed many former MI6 agents. According to the *Financial Times*,
the security services were giving tacit approval, or even encouragement,
to the foundation of consultancies like Hakluyt, based around former
intelligence officers – such companies could fill a gap left by shrinking
MI6 budgets.[25] The company was named after a Tudor traveller and
adventurer, and promised to give companies information about difficult
foreign territories, guiding investors through the choppy seas of the
former Soviet Union, or the developing world. But it became embroiled
in a scandal closer to home. Hired by BP and Shell to investigate their
critics, Hakluyt paid an undercover agent to spy on green groups in
London, Munich and Zurich.

Manfred Schlickenreider had worked for German intelligence since
the 1980s. In the 1990s he went private. Manfred had a well developed
cover identity as a left-wing documentary maker; using his camera, he
could gain access to many campaigners. But a Swiss left-wing group,

Revolutionaire Aufbau, became suspicious, and acquired papers proving that Schlickenreider was not who he claimed to be. The papers included invoices to Hakluyt for 'Greenpeace research'. They looked through the documents and found that he had been spying on Friends of the Earth, Body Shop, and Greenpeace for Hakluyt on behalf of Shell and BP. The oil companies were shaken by campaigns relating to the killing of Nigerian activist Ken Saro-Wiwa, and to pollution. The information from Hakluyt helped the oil companies launch opposing propaganda campaigns and lawsuits against campaigners. Shell and BP said they were not aware of Hakluyt's methods. Some of the fake documentary maker's papers showed that Manfred Schlickenreider was also producing material for minerals giant Rio Tinto Zinc.[26]

This was not an isolated event. Evelyn Le Chêne has powerful connections in the security services. She is a member of the Special Forces Club, a London club whose membership is restricted to members of the Anglo-American military and intelligence elite. In the 1990s she founded a company called Threat Response International. Barry Gane, a former deputy head of MI6, who joined the board of private security firm Group 4 in 1993, also had a place on the Threat Response board, as did Bob Hodges, a former British army major general. Le Chêne's son, Adrian, ran a Threat Response subsidiary firm called Risk Crisis Analysis.

Evelyn Le Chêne also had experience in other fields where the private security industry had a foothold. She was reportedly very friendly with Jonas Savimbi of UNITA. Savimbi's group fought with US backing to keep a slice of Angola out of the hands of the 'Marxist' MPLA, and both used mercenaries and had mercenaries used against them. Le Chêne was also reportedly involved in 'Project Lock' with Sir David Stirling, who founded the SAS during World War Two before setting up his own mercenary company. Project Lock was a 1980s scheme launched by the World Wildlife Fund to stop poaching in southern Africa. However, the mercenaries from Stirling's KAS Enterprises soon moved from infiltrating and fighting poachers to taking on ANC fighters: they conspired with South African intelligence to use 'Project Lock' as a cover for taking on anti-apartheid activists who used the same routes as the poachers.

Le Chêne's companies focused closely on the new radical movements. Firstly, they set out to persuade oil, arms and other companies that their critics were dangerous – often by exaggerating the protestors' strength, and drawing alarmist pictures of the activists. Secondly, they promised to provide the most detailed and intimate information about the protestors, and even set about disrupting and disorganizing them by the use of undercover operators. From his home near Bolougne, Adrian Le Chêne targeted a Dutch anti-arms industry group called AMOK and an environmentalist organization named Aseed. It appears that he also focused on radical environmentalist group Earth First. Both he and his mother seemed to believe that Earth First was the most important group behind the new protest threat.

His work was uncovered in 1988 by a radical research group called Buro Jansen & Janssen (BJJ), which had grown out of Amsterdam's squatting movement. It was tipped off in a letter from one of its supporters:

> Until recently I was working as an assistant to the head of security for a multinational oil corporation. During this time my boss was approached by a person who offered to sell him information about extremist groups that were planning to attack the company. He said that senior staff and their families were in danger from these people and they were violent and very dangerous.[27]

BJJ identified this 'security consultant' as Adrian Le Chêne. He joined a number of environmental and political groups in Europe, and also invented a number of front organizations, establishing phoney campaign groups. The informant made clear that his method involved exaggerating the threat from activists in order to win contracts from corporations. He was exposed in Europe in 1998, but the slim resources of the protest movement meant that he and his mother were able to continue working undercover in Britain until 2003. Papers obtained by BJJ suggest that he was working for mining conglomerate Rio Tinto Zinc, and arms manufacturer British Aerospace, as well as for a major French arms company. His security firm also showed interest in protests about Shell Oil's record in Nigeria.

From at least 1995, Le Chêne worked for British Aerospace. She offered it and other firms a database of 148,900 of what she called 'known names within CND, trades unionists, activists and environmentalists etc.', some with full biographies. In one of her reports for BAE she explained: 'putting together profiles is not an overnight job. It takes time to get to know people, their nick names, habits etc.' Her firm placed agents inside the protest group Campaign Against Arms Trade (CAAT), including Adrian Le Chêne. Threat Response operatives downloaded the entire contents of a central computer at CAAT's headquarters, including membership lists and bank account records. Agents collected letters to MPs, and legal advice in cases where the group had challenged arms exports in the courts. The agents passed on details for demonstrations and press campaigns by the anti-war campaigners. Threat Response had one agent inside the CAAT headquarters and one agent almost running the group's local association near a major British Aerospace factory in Humberside. More slick than her son, Le Chêne arranged to have her agent arrested and manhandled at a protest outside the arms firm's annual general meeting, in order to build his credibility.

More than 14,000 pages of Le Chêne's reports to British Aerospace were leaked to the *Sunday Times*, so Threat Response's operations in this area are well documented; but Le Chêne's spies worked elsewhere. Papers and recorded calls show that she targeted British environmental groups like the protest camp against the Newbury bypass. A long-running encampment of demonstrators tried to stop this road being built through what they felt was a valuable piece of countryside. Group 4 securities was hired to deal with the protestors, and Le Chêne claimed to have agents at Newbury, and to be regularly passing information on the activists' tactics to Group 4. Threat Response also focused on Reclaim The Streets, an imaginative anarchist protest group.

Papers from Threat Response show that the firm tried to talk up the relationship between anti-road and anti-arms protestors. It told companies that it needed people 'who had a good knowledge of the background to both BAE's problems and the anti-road protest movement', as there was 'networking' and a 'quid pro quo' between these activists. The firm claimed that anti-war activists were pushing the most militant tactics at the anti-road protests. This analysis reflected the imagination of the company directors more than reality: the fact that legitimate protest could be spun into a terrible danger justifying dubious business behaviour suggested that when a real, violent threat came along, the financial rewards could be massive. Hakluyt and Threat Response were able to build private security businesses, staffed by people closely linked to the security forces, on the basis of opposition to the 'anti-globalization left', and to convince companies to fund their activities by persuading them that this new left was a real threat to their business.

The belief that the new protestors represented an anarchist threat to society was widespread in the press at the time, but can be viewed almost nostalgically in light of the much more deadly threat of terrorism. But if the new security industries could build business based on the low-level risk posed by protestors, imagine what they could do with the very real threat posed by global terrorism. Having built steady business by promising to battle the anarchist bogeyman, the private intelligence companies soon found themselves in a boom, thanks to al-Qaeda, and new companies came into existence as a result.

Diligence LLC, a company founded by former CIA officer Jim Roth and former MI5 man Nick Day, illustrates some of the avenues followed by the new security industry. The company reflected the Anglo-American domination of the private security business. It also owed its existence to the cashing in of political chips by members of the transatlantic political elite. Former British Home Secretary and Conservative leader Michael Howard became the chairman of Diligence in 2006. His appointment was a demonstration of the growing respectability of the private intelligence world. Diligence was founded with financial help from another company, New Bridge Strategies, which had been widely criticized as an influence-peddling operation. New Bridge Strategies promised to help clients win massive contracts in the 'reconstruction' of Iraq. Its board included two men who were advisers to George Bush Sr.[28] The company's chairman, Joseph Albaugh, seemed to have more expertise in how to build political influence than in how to rebuild in disaster areas. Albaugh had been George W. Bush's campaign manager in the 2000 presidential race, so he knew how to reach the president. He had also been head of the Federal Emergency Management Agency (FEMA). In that role he had been in charge of a large organization supposedly expert in reconstruction. Shortly after Albaugh left FEMA, however, his legacy at the organization was tested and found badly wanting: FEMA's response to the New Orleans hurricane disaster was generally viewed as woeful, in no small part because Albaugh had not left FEMA in a strong position to deal with real disasters. Its political connections to Bush seemed more important to investors and clients of New Bridge Strategies, however, did than Albaugh's management abilities: the firm's website placed more emphasis on Albaugh's Bush and Cheney connections than on his experience in dealing with emergency management.[29]

New Bridge Strategies in turn funded and became an affiliate of Diligence LLC. Diligence promised to use its former secret agents' skills in 'intelligence gathering and risk management' to help businesses prosper. The actual diligence of some of its top staff was open to question. Politically connected firms live in a small world. Diligence's chairman, Richard Burt, had been a US ambassador. He had also served, like Richard Perle, on the board of Hollinger, publisher of the *Telegraph* newspaper. Burt was on the audit committee, which checked expenditure by the company's chairman, Lord Black. In this role Burt had simply failed to spot the fact that Black was involved in what was called 'corporate looting' – running the firm as his personal fiefdom at the expense of the shareholders.

However, it seems that this apparent failure by the firm's top management did not put off clients. Again, the fact that Burt and his former staff were former political and security insiders seemed more important than Burt's failure to spot a serious financial crime from inside the boardroom of Hollinger.[30] Diligence was soon accused of using its intelligence skills in a questionable way: accountants KPMG launched a lawsuit claiming that Diligence's agents had acquired papers 'through wrongful means that include fraud and bribery'. Diligence was working for a finance house, and wanted access to papers from an official Bermudan investigation into a business battle over mobile phone contracts. KPMG was carrying out the investigation for the Bermudan authorities, and alleges that Diligence staff claimed to be acting MI5 staff to get the accountants to hand over confidential documents. Diligence denies the charges, but the suggestion that its staff claimed to be government agents fighting crime to get hold of secret papers is serious. Not only would such activity be fraudulent; it would also endanger real security service investigations. Accountants would be less likely to cooperate in future with real intelligence agents if fake spies are also on the scene.[31] Diligence settled the case by paying KPMG $1.7 million, whilst denying any responsibility.

As well as being involved in adventures in the Caribbean, Diligence was drawn, like the whole of the private security industry, to the 'wild west'-like business scene in Iraq. Diligence owed its financial birth to funding from New Bridge Strategies, a company founded to exploit post war business opportunities in Iraq. Unsurprisingly, Diligence was soon providing armed security and intelligence for companies and governments in Iraq.

So a small clique of firms created a market for private intelligence by exaggerating the threat of anti-globalization protestors. This market expanded massively under the 'war on terror', with companies able to sell the skills of former intelligence agencies to the corporate sector – either specifically for work on the frontlines of the new conflicts like Iraq and Afghanistan, or to provide more general risk assessment and security advice to combat terrorism. This meant that there was a large, economically strong and politically well connected business lobby with a financial interest in talking up the terror threat, which had rehabilitated the idea of private intelligence work that had been tarnished in the Iran–Contra years. But these firms largely built their business by selling their services to the private sector. The Afghan and Iraq conflicts brought forward the next step in the privatization of intelligence work: the use of private spies by the state itself.

The US army found itself overwhelmed with prisoners from both the Iraq and Afghanistan conflicts. Detainees rounded up in Iraq, Pakistan and nearby areas were incarcerated in the new US camp at Guantánamo Bay, Cuba. Iraqis who were captured by or blundered into the hands of allied forces in Iraq were imprisoned in Saddam's old prison of Abu Ghraib, or held in other temporary camps dotted around the occupied country. According to the US version of the war, these were the 'bad guys' whose aggressive war against the free world had caused the two military interventions. They were the enemy – not simply locals caught up in a wider war – and they held the secret of the vast conspiracy against the West. Much of this war talk did not hold together for long: after years of imprisonment, few Guantánamo inmates faced convincing charges. The link between Iraqis and al-Qaeda, so loudly proclaimed before the war, seemed insubstantial and elusive in the first years after Saddam's fall. But the official analysis of the war on terror meant that these numerous captives needed to be interrogated to prise out terrorist secrets. The US found itself facing a major interrogator shortage, and turned to the private sector for help. Some firms that already supplied the intelligence services with technical support or computer consultancy were pressed to hire intelligence specialists, while a number of new companies sprung up to service the need.

The story of the Phoenix Consulting Group shows the recent historic development of private intelligence work. The firm was founded in 1990 by former intelligence officer John A Nolan III. Nolan called his firm Phoenix because he and his co-founders had been involved in Operation Phoenix in Vietnam,[32] in which the CIA had tried to disrupt the Viet Minh by means of widespread assassinations and vicious interrogation methods. But life in the private sector initially tamed Nolan's Phoenix.

His firm was apparently chiefly involved in commercial undercover work. Shampoo firm Proctor & Gamble hired the Vietnam intelligence veterans to spy on their rival, Unilever. The top management of Proctor & Gamble became uncomfortable with the operation, which involved agents 'dumpster diving' – searching the dustbins of the target firm for intelligence – and cancelled Phoenix's contract.[33] But the war on terror washed away this embarrassing stain on the firm's reputation, and brought the Vietnam veterans back into the military fold. The firm now advertised itself as a major supplier of intelligence staff to the government, saying that it 'will provide the Government customer the opportunity to gain access to the most dedicated and competent intelligence professionals at the most competitive price possible'. Phoenix's staff included a former Guantánamo Bay interrogator, Jeannette Arocho-Burkart. She had been disciplined for her interrogations at Guantánamo: she had dressed in skimpy clothing, sexually touched and taunted inmates, and at one point smeared an inmate's face with red ink that she produced from inside her underwear, making him believe it was menstrual blood. These imaginative tactics produced no confessions, but did lead to her eventual admonishment.[34] She then went to work for Phoenix, who sent her back to the US army intelligence school in Arizona to teach interrogation tactics to new students.

The Phoenix story illustrates the fact that some of the private intelligence firms grew out of the most controversial parts of the state sector. Tens of thousands of Vietnamese were assassinated after being identified as 'Viet Cong sympathisers' in Operation Phoenix. The Phoenix programme even began to cast its shadow on Iraq: evidence that death squads were operating within the security forces of the new Iraqi government – in a state that relied on US patronage – led many commentators to fear that the US was sponsoring a new Phoenix Programme in a desperate effort to head off growing insurgency. Vincent Cannistraro, a former chief of CIA counter-terrorism, was among those worrying that 'Phoenix-like' undercover killings were on the cards in Baghdad and beyond.[35] Officials denied that the US was involved in any such sordid business, but at the same time the government was happy to hire a company named after operation Phoenix. Private intelligence agents had been reduced to hiring out their skills in shampoo wars until a combination of staff shortages and an enthusiasm for private enterprise brought them right back in to the secret services – but this time in the form of a profit-making business.

Other ghosts from the past reappeared as contractors in the new private intelligence business. United Placements came into business in 2003 with the intention of 'transitioning military retirees, veterans and clearance-holding government contractors with secure careers in the U.S. defence and homeland security industry'.[36] In 2004 this mission included placing advertisements for thirty 'interrogators' to work in Iraq. The would-be interrogators needed to demonstrate 'five years of humint [human intelligence] collection'. Some hint of the rough conditions of inter-rogation centres in Iraq appeared in the job descriptions, which described locations 'in a field environment with minimum medical facilities'.[37] United Placements proudly announced they had hired a leading figure they described as their 'Industry Associate'. United Placement's important adviser was none other than Colonel Oliver North. Since his 'neat idea' of linking up private businesses, arms sales and unauthorized undercover operations to fight the Sandinistas had been uncovered, North had been making a living through the media, with a show on Rupert Murdoch's Fox network. Now, thanks to the privatization of intelligence, he was able to be more than just a media warrior, and to join battle in the war on terror.[38]

Staff from a number of private companies contracted to the govern-ment were subsequently involved in the interrogation scandals in both Guantánamo and Iraq. Prisoner abuse in Guantánamo involved techni-ques euphemistically called 'sleep management', 'stress positions', 'dietary manipulation', 'environmental manipulation' and 'yelling/loud music'. It also seemed to focus heavily on underwear: in an effort to disorientate and humiliate inmates, they were regularly forced to wear thong underwear and bras while being interrogated. Thongs seemed to loom large in the mind of the US interrogator; one former Guantánamo sergeant, Eric Saar, revealed that 'there hung a short skirt and thong underwear on the hook on the back of the door' of an interrogator's office in the Cuban camp. Saar commented that he had subsequently 'learned that this outfit was used for interrogations by one of the female civilian contractors . . . on a team which conducted interrogations in the middle of the night on Saudi men who were refusing to talk'.[39]

Contractors were involved in a much more serious scandal in Iraq's Abu Ghraib detention centre. In April 2004, US television revealed that American troops were abusing and humiliating Iraqi prisoners at a prison fort. The Americans had commandeered the Abu Ghraib complex, which had been notorious as a site of torture under Saddam Hussein. Photographs apparently taken as trophies by US camp guards showed staff forcing their prisoners to pose naked in strange piles, as well as simulated sex acts. Army investigations prompted by the images showed that the guards had acted in 'sadistic, blatant, and wanton criminal abuses', beating prisoners, attacking them with dogs, and humiliating them with odd sexual practices. The images of naked Iraqis forced to masturbate for their grinning guards, or cowering before dogs, slashed away at US legitimacy in Iraq.

Supporters of the Iraq war hoped this behaviour indicated only a loss of control on the part of some of the lower ranks, but official inquiries and press investigations revealed a different picture. In 2003, Major General Miller, the official in charge of the Guantánamo Bay camp, was sent to Iraq to advise on toughening up the interrogation regime. Little useful intelligence had come from the swathes of Iraqis swept up into Abu Ghraib – in fact, little useful intelligence had come from those snatched from Afghanistan, Pakistan and elsewhere into Guantánamo bay – but the US government did not recognize the failures at its high-profile fort in the crusade against the Islamic threat. Guantánamo Bay was abbreviated to 'Gitmo' by most US troops, and General Miller set out to 'Gitmo-ise' Abu Ghraib. His recommendations included that 'the guard force be actively engaged in setting the conditions for successful exploitation of the internees'. In layman's language, the wardens were expected to soften up the prisoners. It also seems that specific inter-rogation techniques were brought in from Gitmo, including the use of dogs and sexual humiliation. Underwear again emerged as one of the foremost weapons used by US interrogators.[40] The report into the abuse scandal by Major General Taguba showed that male prisoners had been forced to wear women's underwear, as well as being sodomized with chemical light sticks[41] and possibly broom handles, stripped, left in very small cells for days without water or a toilet, and routinely beaten with chairs and broom handles.[42] The report suggested that the ordinary prison guards who had photographed themselves debasing the inmates were following orders from their superiors and from interrogation staff. Not only were top brass implicated in this abuse scandal – the report also made clear that contractors had been involved in the abuse, and that a private firm had been the military's tool for bringing torture to Abu Ghraib.

CACI International[43] was founded in 1962 as an information technology company. It grew with large defence and other public contracts, offering computing and management consultancy work. Other firms involved in the world of privatized intelligence were small businesses set up by former agents, whereas CACI was a large, well established multinational firm. It is an indication of the political and economic pull of the new privatized security trade that CACI came to be drawn into this world. In 2003, CACI responded to a 'request by the US Army, which did not have sufficient, available personnel for assignment to the Iraqi theatre at the onset of the war'. CACI set about 'identifying and hiring qualified individuals with previous experience in information gathering and analysis'. In short, a staff shortage in the war on terror led the army to seek out CACI, and to transform it into a private intelligence contractor.[44] CACI's contract for supplying private interrogators went unreported until the Abu Ghraib scandal broke. Oddly, the contract was initially with the US Department of the Interior, which makes it seem if the US government was using some creative accounting to keep the contract relatively obscure.

CACI's interrogators became central to the process of 'Gitmo-isation'. Two sergeants defended themselves in a trial over their use of dogs to terrify Abu Ghraib prisoners by suggesting that they had been acting on commands from both their senior officer and CACI contractors. Their witnesses told the court that the use of dogs to terrify prisoners – sometimes causing them to soil themselves – had been ordered by General Miller, the Guantánamo commander. They also said that a CACI interrogator, Steven Stefanowicz, had also given the order to use unmuzzled dogs.[45] Stefanowicz, a 6ft 5in former naval intelligence officer, nicknamed 'Big Steve', was identified in the two official investigative reports into the abuse scandal – the Taguba and Fay reports. Charles Graner, one of the low-level guards successfully prosecuted for the abuse, said that 'Big Steve' had encouraged him to hurt and humiliate inmates for interrogation purposes.[46]

The Fay report describes how several other CACI interrogators increased pressure on the inmates.[47] According to the report, one CACI interrogator 'bragged and laughed about shaving a detainee and forcing him to wear red women's underwear'. Another CACI interrogator 'encouraged' a soldier 'to abuse Iraqi police [officers]' who had been detained by the army. The contractor threatened Iraqis with beatings and dogs, and put them in 'unauthorized stress positions'. A third CACI interrogator

> grabbed a detainee (who was handcuffed) off a vehicle and dropped him to the ground. He then dragged him into an interrogation booth and as the detainee tried to get up . . . would yank the detainee very hard and make him fall again.

This same CACI interrogator had other failings. He 'drank alcohol' at Abu Ghraib, and had to be 'placed in a remedial report writing class because of his poor writing, he did not pay attention to the trainer and sat in the back of the room facing away from the trainer'. Not only did he ignore attempts to get him to write better intelligence reports, he also 'refused to take instructions from military trainers'. When confronted about his inadequate interrogation techniques, he replied, 'I have been doing this for 20 years and I do not need a 20-year-old telling me how to do my job.'

CACI denied that their interrogators helped to push Abu Ghraib along the road of violence and sexual humiliation, pointing out that none of their staff had been prosecuted for their behaviour in Iraq. Other contractors faced worse charges. Another firm, Titan, supplied translators for the US army. With around 4,000 translators in the field, it was in charge of a large operation; with over 100 translators killed in the first three years of the Iraq war, it was a dangerous one. But US troops were concerned about the quality of Titan's translators: many appeared to be Arabic-speaking taxi drivers and shopkeepers, not trained translators.[48] Titan, like CACI, was a high-tech firm supplying computing and electronic services to the Department of Defense. One post-9/11 contract changed them into a private intelligence company. In 2002 they won a deal to supply translators at Guantánamo bay, and this was soon expanded to cover the supply of translators in Iraq. Titan found its translators partly by looking up Arabic-sounding names in Californian phone books.[49] In Abu Ghraib these untrained staff were drawn into the abuse of prisoners. The Fay report says that one Titan employee in particular had been present during the making of grotesque and bizarre photographs of the prisoners, and had hit a detainee so hard he needed stitches.

Titan staff caused other problems in Iraq. One translator, who was using an assumed identity, took classified military documents. Investigators feared that he might have acted as an agent for the Iraqi insurgents, and the army suspected that this translator with no name had passed on military secrets to Iraqi fighters.[50] Another translator was prosecuted for trying to bribe a senior Iraqi police officer into buying thousands of bulletproof vests.[51] He could fairly have claimed to be acting in the spirit of his company. Shortly afterwards, Titan paid a $28.5 million fine after admitting to paying a $2 million bribe to the president of Benin, in West Africa. The firm's senior executives had been party to paying the bribe in return for a massive telecommunications contract in Benin, making the bulletproof vest scam look like vary small beer.

None of this discouraged the US army from using either CACI or Titan. The contractors played an important role for the military. Firstly, they apparently helped the US army to introduce new and bizarre interrogation techniques into Iraq. The companies were able to effect 'change management' in the treatment of prisoners by quick contractual orders, without the need to deal with the army's bureaucratic structures of command. Secondly, when the scandal broke, the contractors were able to melt away. They lived in a legal netherworld: while some low-ranking soldiers were prosecuted for the abuse at Abu Ghraib, the contractors – exempt from military discipline and largely beyond the reach of ordinary law – removed their staff, sacked a few, and continued with their business. While US soldiers were sent to prison for abusing Iraqis at Abu Ghraib, CACI and Titan were given new or extended contracts worth hundreds of millions of dollars.[52] Titan, in particular, brushed aside the Abu Ghraib scandal as bigger companies lined up to acquire it, excited by the growth of military contracting. Titan was finally bought by a company called L-3 – a specialist in providing commercial services to the defence and intelligence sector.

In December 2002 the *Washington Post* introduced a new phrase from the war on terror to their readers: 'extraordinary rendition'. The newspaper revealed that, since 9/11, the CIA had found 'a way round restrictions' on the outright torture of suspects. Dissatisfied with the levels of abuse they could commit themselves, US agents were 'rendering' suspects over to foreign intelligence services – often in Jordan, Egypt and Morocco – with a list of questions to be answered. As one US Congressman from Massachusetts noted, this was effectively the 'outsourcing of torture'. So, for example, Binyam Mohammed, an Ethiopian who had grown up in west London, was arrested in Pakistan on his way out of Afghanistan, and eventually found himself in Guantánamo Bay. US authorities said that he had been involved in terror plots – a charge that he denied. Mohammed was not flown directly to the Cuban prison camp; instead he spent a year and a half in Morocco, where interrogators beat him and cut his genitals with a scalpel.[53] In 2002 Canadian Maher Arar was flying home from Tunisia, a journey involving a stopover in New York. Arar did not make it back to Canada because American officials detained him in New York. US authorities accused Maher Arar of terrorist involvement. He was bundled into another aircraft and flown to Jordan. From there he was driven to Syria and tortured for a year, after which he was finally released.

This 'outsourcing of torture' involved a great deal of international cooperation. Not only were the actual torturing nations involved, but so were various intelligence services and countries offering stopovers. The testimony of those who were 'rendered', along with other evidence,[54] shows that British agents helped to interrogate and identify some of the prisoners, and that German agents were aware of secret bases in Europe used for transit or for the abuse itself. Canada's 'Mounties' were implicated in the rendition of their own citizens. The programme also involved a shadow system of aircraft. The Gulf Stream and 747 jets carrying the prisoners in shackles, blindfolds and nappies were owned and leased by a series of CIA-linked airlines reminiscent of Air America and its offspring.

But there is one crucial difference between the involvement of other countries and that of private companies. While a nation's complicity may be deeper, the involvement of other countries also led to greater exposure of the 'spider's web' of official kidnapping and abuse. As the story began to leak or to be squeezed from official sources, many nations set up their own investigations. The Council of Europe and the European Parliament launched investigations that threw a spotlight on the rendition programme. Canada held a judicial inquiry into the Maher Arar case. While nations were as capable as were private companies of involvement in abuse, they also had political systems that allowed for inquiries and made some level of democratic inspection possible. The political backwash of the rendition programme also put limits on future national involvement. Indeed, even when the programme was secret, some state agents expressed their dissent from the programme. Weeks after 9/11, German intelligence agents were invited by the US to visit the secret 'Eagle Base' in Bosnia. They found that US interrogators had beaten a 70-year-old terrorist suspect rendered to the base with rifle butts, until his head wound needed twenty stitches. The Americans offered the Germans documents that were 'smeared in blood'. The German agents refused to help the interrogation, and informed German federal prosecutors, remarking that the Serbs had 'ended up in the International Court in the Hague for this kind of thing'.[55] While German officials appear to have hushed up the event, the immediate reaction of their agents was at least unhelpful to the abusers.

By contrast, the private companies involved lacked such instincts, traditions or systems of dissent. One former pilot who had worked for Aero Contractors – one of the more prominent rendition charter services – told investigative journalist Steven Grey that the airmen considered themselves 'bus drivers in the war on terror', adding, 'You would just notice someone not too happy was in the back.'[56] This was a rare voice from inside the private rendition industry, and revealed no disquiet with the system. Aero Contractors was founded by a former CIA pilot, and is now owned by Air America. But the rendition system also seemed to involve more straightforwardly commercial companies. A subsidiary of Boeing with the cheery title of Jeppesen International Trip Planning advertises itself using the slogan, 'Making Every Mission Possible', and promises to 'offer everything needed for efficient, hassle-free, international flight operations'. One of its employees told the *New Yorker* magazine that this included making hassle-free rendition missions possible. The informant said that the company's managing director had commented, 'We do all of the extraordinary rendition flights – you know, the torture flights. Let's face it, some of these flights end up that way.' The employee added, 'It certainly pays well. They spare no expense. They have absolutely no worry about costs. What they have to get done, they get done.' The company would not respond to enquiries on the subject, although documents suggest they assisted in one of the more notable renditions – in which a German car salesman called Khaled al-Masri, in an apparent case of mistake identify, had been seized in Macedonia and flown to Iraq and Afghanistan for harsh interrogation, until Condoleezza Rice authorized his release.[57] This story suggests that the commercial subcontractors in the rendition programme were as aware of the potential for abuse as were foreign government agents. While the international intelligence community worried about the ethics, however, the subcontractors seemed to worry only about the cash. Official international cooperation in the suspect flights opened the door to inquiries, while commercial involvement kept the scheme behind an opaque screen of business confidentiality and 'deniability'. The rendition programme put the relation between the US and its international allies under strain, but made commercial subcontracting in the war on terror look more attractive.

'Intelligence' became one of the most contested terrains in the war on terror. George Bush pledged to use 'every tool of intelligence' in September 2001 to defeat the new enemy. Tony Blair began his self-appointed task of building international support for George Bush's strategy by emphasizing the president's careful use of intelligence, rather than blind force, to defeat the terrorists. In the same month that Bush highlighted his use of intelligence, Blair had an article published in a British Asian newspaper, declaring that

> despite the scale of the tragedy there has been no rush to retaliate by the US. Instead the US deserves credit, at a time of tremendous national emotion, for patience and care as it has gathered, with help from intelligence sources round the world, the evidence which reveals the people and groups behind last week's attacks.[58]

A few years later the image of the intelligence services was mired in scandal: phoney stories of Saddam's nonexistent WMD; secretive kidnapping and shuffling of prisoners around the world in the 'extraordinary rendition' programme; and the abusive interrogation of prisoners in Abu Ghraib, Guantánamo, Afghanistan's Bagram airbase, and other unknown jails and 'hard sites' – all hung over the allied intelligence agencies. The political crisis for the intelligence agencies was as great as that which faced the CIA in the wake of revelations of misbehaviour during the Vietnam War.

While intelligence agencies wrestled with a crisis of public confidence, the private contractors who had been intimately involved in these failures and scandals remained mostly unscathed. Like the tailors who made the emperor's new clothes, the private contractors scuttled away with their bags of loot while officials were left naked – no caches of Iraqi biological weapons to cover their shame, their moral cover stripped away by the lies and torture. Real life was worse than a fairytale in one respect: not only did the emperor's tailors get away unpunished, they were even invited back to cut some more dubious garments from their extraordinary cloth. The intimate involvement of private companies in these intelligence scandals did not act as a bar to any further privatization of the secret services: the market remained buoyant.

The historic balance sheet shows that business for private intelligence companies, which was growing slowly before the 9/11 attack, has expanded massively during the war on terror. In the wake of Thatcher's privatization drive, a number of companies began offering the services of former intelligence officers to private industry, putting the sometimes questionable tactics of the spying game at the service of the free market. These firms looked set to be curiosities, acting on the fringes of business, and hit by the occasional scandal. But as the war on terror gathered pace, the private intelligence firms offered their services back to the state, to run the battle against the nation's enemies in return for profit. Far from being fringe outfits, they became central actors in the most important events of the decade.

These contracting companies contributed to the crimes and misdemeanours of the war on terror in a variety of interlocking ways. Firstly, they created a 'permissive environment'. Unsurprisingly, the US government responded to the threat of terrorism by hurling vast resources at the problem; but the scale of the operation did not guarantee its effectiveness. Like Bush and Blair, US Vice President Dick Cheney also emphasized the role of undercover agents in the war on terror in 2001. With a certain honesty, Cheney promised that the US would be prepared to 'work the dark side', and operate 'a mean, nasty and dangerous business' in the undercover war. He stressed that US work 'in the shadows' would 'penetrate these organizations' using 'some very unsavoury characters on the payroll'.[59] But while subsequent events suggested US forces did indeed have some unsavoury people on the payroll, few were informers or agents who could work undercover in the Islamic terror cells. Instead, the contractors supplied the US with large numbers of reconditioned former CIA operatives. As many as three-quarters of the staff at the CIA's Islamabad station – one of the crucial sites for chasing bin Laden – were contractors from US firms. In the Baghdad CIA station, contractors outnumbered employed staff.[60] The contractors allowed the US government to get many more officers onto the intelligence beat, but increasing numbers did not obviously increase their penetration of terrorist groups. It seems that, instead of acquiring the services of Arab or Asian double agents, the US just got back a stream of recently retired US officers. The privatization drive made the numbers look good, but did not change the quality of the intelligence operation.

By turning to private intelligence contractors, the US helped to build a permanent commercial lobby that would try to persuade officials and legislators to take on more contractors. Federal records show that the companies supplying private intelligence staff spent some of the funds raised from their businesses on lobbying Congress and supporting particular candidates. Current officials could look to post-retirement jobs working for the private intelligence companies. None of this increased the accuracy of Western intelligence – it just created more business for the companies involved.

As well as allowing, and even encouraging, the authorities simply to expand their less than perfect intelligence services (rather than trying to find a better way to deal with the terrorists), the private companies also made responsibility for intelligence failures unhelpfully vague. A series of British parliamentary and US Congressional inquiries took place into the false official data behind the claims of Iraqi WMD. None has yet satisfactorily pinned responsibility for the widespread disinformation in the war on terror, but they have at least brought some important facts into the public arena. But the private firms apparently linked to the WMD stories – particularly those that serviced the Iraqi National Congress (see Chapter 7) – have not been officially examined. These private operators worked beyond the scope of official inspection: the participation of private companies in making the case for war has not provided a subject for official inquiry.

The involvement of two companies in making the phoney case against Saddam was alluded to in official inquiries. Before the invasion of Iraq, the CIA examined a set of aluminium tubes that Iraq was trying to import, to discover whether they were the special type of tubes used in centrifuges for purifying uranium for bombs. A CIA analyst thought they were, but experts from the Department of Energy and other agencies disagreed – they believed the tubes were actually components for conventional rockets, and would be useless in making nuclear weapons. The CIA then appointed a contractor to investigate the tubes and break the deadlock. In 2002 the contractor was paid and briefed by the CIA, and did not speak to officials from the dissenting departments. Within a day the analysts-for-hire agreed that the tubes were evidence of Saddam's nuclear ambitions. Contractors were again hired in 2003 to carry out tests on the tubes. Initially they found that the tubes were not the right kind for producing nuclear weapons. The CIA complained, so the contractor changed its mind and issued a 'correction', showing that they were after all nuclear tubes. On two occasions, intelligence contractors came up with the answer they were paid to give; the problem was, it was the wrong answer. The tubes were for conventional missiles – Saddam had no nuclear programme. The contractors' findings became central in the case for war. Condoleezza Rice's famous remark – that it was wrong to waste too much time looking for a 'smoking gun' to link Saddam with 9/11, lest the next 'smoking gun is a mushroom cloud' – was based on these phoney, paid-for results.

The contractors are identified in two of the official US reports that examined the American intelligence failures on Iraq: the report of the 'Robb-Silverman' commission ordered by President Bush, and the report of the United States Select Committee on Intelligence.[61] Because of commercial confidentiality, however, the names of the contractors are blacked out: private companies were central to the fake intelligence that led to the war on Iraq, but they walked away without punishment. In the same way, there have been inquiries and trials, and even some successful prosecutions, relating to prisoner abuse in the war on terror; but the private companies involved have walked away without blame. Far from being punished, in fact, they have been awarded new contracts. In the case of both phoney intelligence and prisoner abuse, the US government was able to pass responsibility for its own crimes and errors on to an opaque, commercial netherworld. With no one taking responsibility when privatization is involved, it is not surprising that the arrangement was attractive to both the state and its commercial servants.

9

Database State

In June 2002 the US public began hearing about an innovative technological programme from their Department of Defense directed at the
new terror threat. The military was developing a computer system
codenamed 'Total Information Awareness'. The system aimed to dig
through the electronic records of millions of personal transactions, 'data
mining' for nuggets of terrorist behaviour. The Total Information
Awareness project aimed to sift through existing electronic traces of
personal behaviour – credit card purchases, phone calls, travel itineraries,
internet use, banking records – for evidence of potential terrorist activity.
Officials wanted to use algorithms that supposedly predict the way
terrorists shop, travel, browse the internet, and so on, to find future
threats. The US military leadership argued that inspecting the electronic
footprints of private citizens with these formulae was the best way of
dealing with the new public danger. The programme seemed to bring the
Department of Defense dangerously into conflict with civil freedoms at
home in the US. Worse still, Total Information Awareness was under the
jurisdiction of Admiral Poindexter, a former assistant to Ronald Reagan
who in 1990 had been convicted of lying to Congress, destroying
documents, and obstructing legal inquiries. The *Washington Post* re-
marked that the programme seemed to have been invented 'with the
specific aim of terrifying the Orwell-reading public'. Congressional
disquiet killed the programme in 2003.[1]

While the Total Information Awareness programme died, its short life
signalled that the US and British governments would repeatedly reach for
information technology as a weapon in the war on terror. In particular,
computing systems, surveillance programmes, and identity checks would
be turned on home populations in the search for a terrorist 'fifth column'

within the Western nations. These technological weapons had the potential to undermine civil liberties and foster the creation of a new database state standing over the citizenry. Politicians on both sides of the Atlantic had already hyped up the potential of digital technology to transform their societies, so it was no surprise that they would also see it as a major weapon in their new war. The Anglo-US leadership also seemed to delight in the opportunity to grasp new authoritarian powers to combat the danger on their shores, but they were also encouraged down this technological route by a powerful commercial lobby. After 9/11 the British and US governments suspected that the greatest threats were likely to lurk within their own civilian populations: the new weapons systems developed for the war on terror included massive, commercially provided databases designed to track potentially dangerous people.

These technical fixes to the terror threat presented a tremendous opportunity to private contractors, who could see vast riches to be made supplying these new databases. The companies and their lobbyists pushed hard to persuade governments to ignore criticisms and take the techno-logical route. The silicon snake-oil salesmen became an important part of the new security–industrial complex, wooing the holders of state power and taking over large slices of government itself. Left to their own devices, politicians in the UK and US probably would have tried to build up the database state in response to the terrorist threat. But they were not left to their own devices: they were joined by an influential swathe of industry that used lobbying lessons learned over decades to build up a new, expensive and authoritarian private digital police apparatus – an apparatus that would drive their profits up as much as it would push individual freedom down.

Some of the leading firms offering computerized weapons in the war on terror had also been major defence contractors that had enjoyed enormous influence during the Cold War: they were thoroughly in-tegrated into the political, military and bureaucratic elites of the West. Generals and politicians moved between their boards and high offices of the state, taking advantage of a revolving door between the political, military, and commercial spheres. Sometimes these companies pushed their influence too far, and were caught in major bribery scandals that briefly exposed the mechanics of the 'iron triangle' between politicians, officers and executives. Then, in 1989, the companies faced their worst possible threat: peace. Former military contractors sought refuge in giant public welfare contracts. Having retreated from the battlefield into the welfare state, the contractors were then able to use their new territory in government contracting as a bridgehead from which to launch their bids for bureaucratic and technical contracts in the new battle for 'homeland security'. The arms contractors had been accused of forming a 'military–industrial complex' by President Eisenhower in 1961, with their need to sell products determining national policy, rather than the other way round. In fact it is clear that the contractors formed an 'iron triangle' of influence not only in military contracting but also in later welfare bids – and finally in the war on terror. In each case the contractors influenced the political process both by effective lobbying and by using their industrial might to delineate the bounds of the possible for politicians. The corporations had larger research departments and a greater industrial base than the military or civil service. They were able to design new weapons systems or databases, and simply present them to politicians in the same way that a supermarket lays out goods before its customers. Their marketing departments and lobbyists offered tempting one-stop solutions to complex political problems. Legislators certainly took the bait – even when the contractors repeatedly offered expensive, malfunctioning systems. So the contractors enticed politicians to take ever more authoritarian steps in order to shift their products.

The end of the Cold War sent a shiver of fear through the boardrooms of the big defence contractors: weapons makers really believed that arms sales would fall as peace broke out. Many arms companies sought to diversify away from the killing business. US giant Lockheed took the peace protestors' slogan literally, and moved from warfare to welfare: it began running computerized benefit systems in the US in an attempt to compensate for the expected loss of weapons sales. DynCorp, a military contractor that would later triumph as a private sheriff for the world's policeman, hedged against fears that the world would become more peaceful and less profitable by winning a $27 million contract to run occupational health tests on welfare applicants in three US states.[2] In Britain, warship builder Vosper Thorneycroft won contracts to run careers advice services for local education authorities. It was so enthusiastic about this business that they hired Baroness Blackstone, a former Labour education minister, to join its board and help build its educational profile.

By 2006, the arms industry's fears of the death of its Cold War cash cow looked foolish. The largest surge in arms spending came in the last days of the rivalry between the Soviet Union and the West, with military shopaholics spending £547 billion worldwide in 1987/88. By 2006, however, arms spending, which had been declining until the late 1990s, soared beyond Cold War levels to an estimated £561 billion a year.[3] The war on terror restored traditional arms sales to their former glory – but they could not foresee the way Osama bin Laden would refresh their markets when the Soviet Union became the enemy that failed. They were forced to seek new business in the 1990s in civil contracting. Happily for the defence contractors, their non-military work provided a platform from which to win new security business in the war on terror.

Bureaucracy is one of the chief weapons of the state. The growth of bureaucracy defined the formation of modern nation-states: legions of officials gave governments the power to understand and regulate their societies. But in Britain and the US the coincidence of computerization and the first wave of privatization meant that the extension of state bureaucracies failed to keep pace with advances in information technology. Instead, the British and US governments often used the arrival of computerized systems to hand slices of their bureaucratic apparatus over to the private sector. This process was notable in welfare systems on both sides of the Atlantic. Both civil and military contractors took control of IT-based welfare systems and other government functions. When they launched the war on terror, governments looked to bureaucratic powers to deal with the new danger. They searched for administrative means to increase the general power of the state in response to the perceived threats. But governments followed the practice developed in other areas by subcontracting the new authoritarian systems to private enterprise. The companies who had flourished by delivering computerized government services had a distinct advantage when it came to developing the new database state.

So Lockheed, one of the world's biggest arms companies, transformed itself into a welfare specialist in the mid-1990s. The company retained some of its hard edge, however, by emphasizing the tight control, and even punitive nature, of its welfare work: Lockheed's F-16 'fighting Falcon' jet sought and destroyed enemies in the Middle East and beyond from its first flights in the 1980s onwards. It then moved into non-military contracts, first by creating electronic systems to help seek and collect parking fines; it then used the relationships it had thereby created with state officials to branch into the caring services. It announced that it would seek out the 'deadbeat dads' failing to support their families. Lockheed set out to build a presence in the US welfare state by administering payments to families with dependent children. But it promised a mix of authoritarian, business-minded and cost-cutting methods – a promise that fitted well with President Clinton's approach to welfare reforms. Clinton wanted to cut benefit rolls, allow individual states to experiment with the system, and emphasized the 'personal responsibility' of claimants. Lockheed pitched its business to chime perfectly with political trends, but its ability to deliver was much less sure-footed. In 1997, after $111 million of expenditure, California dropped its 'deadbeat dads' contract with Lockheed because its system had failed. Auditors found that the company had 'failed to provide the project team that was promised, developed a flawed system design and failed to test systems components adequately'.[4] California and Lockheed battled it out in lawsuits for the next five years, until total penalties and court losses meant that the authorities lost nearly $0.5 billion that might otherwise have been spent on the poorer residents of the 'Golden State'. Losses to welfare recipients, who faced delays and confusion, were also substantial, although the travails of the poor were less well reported than the extra costs borne by the authorities. Meanwhile, in Florida, a Lockheed Martin system to hunt 'deadbeat dads' managed to spend £5.4 million collecting just $162,000 in child support payments from the errant fathers – in effect spending $25 for each three cents collected.[5]

These failures did not impede Lockheed's political ambitions. During the California crisis, its lobbyist told senators that it had now 'become the premier provider of child-support services', offering 'technology and management techniques' that could transform delivery.[6] Even though Lockheed's failures became well known, state and national officials had become reliant on private contractors, and no longer had the capacity to administer their own systems. Instead legislators were reduced to rotating work between Lockheed and the other half-dozen or so big systems firms. Lockheed's adventures in welfare were far from unique. Computing giant UNISYS specialized in government contracts, including big military systems. UNISYS was formed in 1986 through the merger of companies including the Burroughs Corporation – a firm founded by the grandfather of experimental author William Burroughs, whose novels are peppered with sinister authority figures. Given the company's later activities, this was unhappily appropriate.

UNISYS hardware and software powered early warning systems, naval computers, and so on. UNISYS was big in the defence sector, and was also apparently corrupt. An FBI investigation called 'Operation Ill Wind' gave a picture of the scale of the company's defence work. The federal investigators scrutinized UNISYS contracts for three years from 1986, and what they found was far from pretty. UNISYS had been engaged in systematic fraud and bribery to win military work. In one part of the scam, a top UNISYS manager set up dummy companies in the Caribbean and in Guernsey using company money. These front companies then bought a holiday home, at a wildly inflated price, from a naval official in charge of contracting.[7] The fake companies were used to pay money to other Pentagon managers. In return, UNISYS received confidential documents, details of competitors' bids, and favourable contract decisions. Faced with this and other evidence of bribery, UNISYS agreed in 1991 to pay a record $190 million fine.[8]

In common with other US military contractors, the firms that made up UNISYS had had a relationship with Saddam Hussein in the 1980s and 1990s. They had worked in line with US foreign policy of the time, which tilted towards Iraq as a counterbalance to the Islamic Republic of Iran. UNISYS companies had sold Iraq computers that were likely to have been used on the country's nuclear programme. In a sinister turn, UNISYS also sold the Iraqi Interior Ministry a personnel database. As arms trade campaigner Gary Milhollin revealed, this $8 million computer system was certainly capable of being used to keep track of dissidents, and was sold to the Iraqi government department in charge of the country's brutal internal security forces.[9]

Despite its military success, UNISYS began worrying about its massive defence division in the 1990s. With the end of the Cold War, was this cash cow turning into a dead – or at least ailing – duck? In 1991 UNISYS prepared for the sale of its defence division, but gave up when no buyers could be found: the combination of their enthusiasm for a sale and the unwillingness of any serious contender to buy it demonstrated the tough judgement of the markets on the future of the defence industries, now that the old Cold War enemy had gone.[10] In 1995 the market picked up a little. In 1989, US philosopher Francis Fukuyama proclaimed the 'End of History',[11] suggesting that the end of the Cold War would mean the end of old conflicts and the triumph of Western liberal democracy. By the mid 1990s, however, it looked as if the engine of history was sputtering back into life with some vicious regional conflicts. Defence budgets did drop substantially after the collapse of the Soviet bloc,[12] but there was soon enough war in the uncertain new world order to rekindle some interest in defence companies. The slight revival in the military economy did not persuade UNISYS to retain its defence arm, but it did help the firm sell off the division in 1995 for $800 million.

Having freed itself from the business of warfare, UNISYS decided to make money from welfare. Taking over the state social security bureaucracies and other arms of government looked like a sure thing. The firm made great financial headway in these fields, although it did not always deliver impressive final products. In 1990, Washington State's Department of Health And Social Services wrote off $19 million given to UNISYS for a 'Community Services Management and Operations System' – known as COSMOS. Despite the grandiose name, this welfare scheme delivered less than modest benefits: the UNISYS system for distributing local welfare payments simply did not work, and had to be abandoned.[13] In 1993 the state of Michigan signed a $53 million deal with UNISYS to provide a computerized system to distribute food stamps and other welfare payments to the state's poor. The system came on line in 1998 – two years late and over $60 million over budget. While UNISYS got its cash, claimants had to wait for their benefits: administrators reported that the system was slow and inefficient. Welfare workers said that there were 'people unable to get food stamps when they're desperate for food'.[14]

Like Lockheed, UNISYS emphasized an authoritarian and restrictive approach to the welfare state. The firm focused on claimants' identities, and the security of welfare rolls. UNISYS had made money patriotically, helping to fend off the Russians, who had wanted to overthrow the western system. Now it would find a new patriotic business: fighting off the welfare frauds who tried to cheat the system. It approached this new role apparently unembarrassed by its own history of defrauding the taxpayer. In 1995 UNISYS unveiled a 'total suite of personal I.D. solutions to fight fraud in large-scale government operations'. It showcased its new identity systems to the American Public Welfare Association – the conference of officials working in what Americans call 'Human Services Organisations' at state and federal level. As it turned out, the firm was not always that good at fighting fraud. In fact, it even introduced fraud into the system.

In 1996, UNISYS was removed from a contract to register voters in Massachusetts after state officials called its work 'shoddy and inferior'. In 1995 the company paid Wisconsin $2.2 million in fines for its poor work in running medical benefits. In 1998 thirteen UNISYS employees were jailed after a gang stole nearly $0.5 million from Florida's health insurance system. A grand jury panel found that, while UNISYS officials 'did not direct such offences to occur, we find that there existed a corporate culture which tolerated the employees' misdeeds'. UNISYS called these charges unfair, but the firm left its $86 million a year contract two years early, as complaints about poor service built up.

Identification and surveillance were the key areas helping defence contractors like UNISYS to break into the welfare state. They also provided opportunities for the same firms to move back into the new areas of security expenditure after 9/11. The political leadership in the US were shaken by the terrorist attacks, so UNISYS offered a solution. Thanks to its military and civil contracting history, the company was well practised at appealing to administrators and politicians. Among the lobbyists UNISYS hired to build its profile was one Jack Abramoff. In 2006 Abramoff was sentenced to five years in prison, and ordered to pay $26 million in fines, for crimes committed during his lobbying operations. Abramoff had access to President Bush and his top aide, Karl Rove, but he was finally brought down when his complex influence-peddling activities were found to involve bribery and corruption. UNISYS paid Abramoff's lobbying firm around half a million dollars at around the same time they began winning contracts in the war on terror, although the company was not involved in the court case against Abramoff or any of the related corruption charges.

UNISYS won some contracts from its familiar customer, the Department of Defense. The firm won a $345 million contract to help construct a new anti-terrorist agency, the oddly named Counterintelligence Field Activity, or CIFA. CIFA was set up in 2002 as an intelligence agency to help guard military bases in the US. Slowly, the agency grew into something much larger, absorbing a programme called 'Eagle Eyes', which channelled informal tips from US Air Force staff about suspicious activity around their bases into a central office. This was expanded into a larger programme, called Threat and Local Observation Notice, or TALON. By 2005 it became clear that the TALON database was filled with reports about harmless activity by US citizens: legitimate protests, demonstrations, letters of complaint, political meetings, and other 'anomalous activities' were all recorded in a military database supposedly designed to deal with al-Qaeda, and then shared with other law enforcement agencies. The UNISYS contract showed that the bureaucratic drift into authoritarian systems was supported by commercial expansion.

In 2003 UNISYS showed that it could also win security contracts outside the Defense Department, when it won a $1 billion contract to help the Transport Security Administration to get off the ground. This organization was the most direct response to the new terrorism. The agency says that it was 'formed immediately following the tragedies of - Sept. 11' and 'is responsible for security of the nation's transportation systems'. The terrorist hijackers were able to board their planes partly because airport security was a ramshackle business run on a shoestring by a patchwork of private security firms. The foundation of the Transport Security Administration included, on paper at least, the nationalization of airport security. Here, apparently, was one case where the war on terror led to less, not more privatization – except that the new agency promptly began handing its new national responsibilities back to private firms. UNISYS received the biggest slice of this rich new security pie. Realizing the terrible dangers the US faced, UNISYS got down to work, and immediately started over-billing the government. UNISYS won a $1 billion contract to supply and install computers, pagers, cell phones, radios, telephones, and a high-speed network to keep the new Transport Security Administration in contact with itself. However, a 2006 audit by the Inspector General of Homeland Security found that the whole budget – which was supposed to last until 2009 – was already gone. Airport security directors were struggling with cheap phones and dial-up internet connections, rather than the high-tech communications network they expected. Apparently profiteering from the war on terror, UNISYS 'proposed too many hours and higher labor categories than necessary', according to the auditors.[15] The Transport Security Adminstration introduced itself to the public with the slogan 'I Am TSA. I am the frontline of defence, drawing on my imagination to creatively protect America from harm.' An unkind observer might believe that UNISYS was drawing on its imagination to creatively boost its books.

For Lockheed, the war on terror was a bonus on many fronts: the company had the traditional arms manufacturer's enthusiasm for war. In

2002 its former vice president, Bruce Jackson, set up the 'Committee for the Liberation of Iraq' – a Republican-leaning pressure group pushing for war with Saddam. When that war came, Lockheed supplied many of the weapons involved. The firm also had big-ticket espionage contracts, like the $9.5 billion 'Misty' satellite programme. Senators declared that this scheme was 'stunningly expensive', 'totally unjustified' and 'very very wasteful'[16] – but because of the high level of secrecy involved, they could not say why. Reports suggested that the satellites, which were eating up a quarter of the total intelligence budget, duplicated existing eyes-in-the-sky, and could not see the ground at night or on cloudy days. For Lockheed, homeland security opened up whole new markets, not based in the sky or in faraway countries, but focused on US citizens themselves. Thanks to the war on terror, the military firm was able to work on more US contracts. The same new market opened up for UNISYS and other contractors. The big military systems firms that had hedged their bets at the end of the Cold War by moving into welfare work and public bureaucracies now found that these welfare programmes now gave them a ticket into the new market in homeland security.

So, for example Lockheed became front runners to win the Transport Workers Identification Card, or TWIC, from the US Transport Security Administration – the same organization that had struggled with UNISYS. Looking for unexpected vulnerabilities after 9/11, security experts had summoned up a series of transport-related nightmares: a petrol lorry could be transformed into a giant improvised explosive device by a determined, suicidal terrorist with the right driving license; a container ship could be rigged up as a destructive weapon as surely as a civilian passenger plane; a dock worker could sink a civilian vessel – indeed, fears that al-Qaeda had bought a cargo ship and was aiming it at US ports floated in the press from 2001 onwards. In response, US officials decided that all transport workers should carry a special identity card. Those who failed unspecified background checks would not be able to work as drivers or dockers. Critics worried about the card's implications for civil liberties. In 2002 President Bush broke up a strike of west coast dockers by invoking 'national security' – so fears of the misuse of the anti-terror slogan in the transport industry were keenly felt. But Lockheed entertained no such worries; it simply encouraged the government to implement the card by promising that it could do the job. It became the front-runner for the contract after management consultancy firm

BearingPoint claimed that its 'decade of experience in security and identity management solution programs' meant that it could come up with a prototype transport workers' identity card. BearingPoint spent millions, but failed to come up with a working prototype, giving Lockheed a chance to step in.

Lockheed won a further major security contract thanks to another company's failure. The Science Applications International Corp. (see Chapter 6) became one of the leading contractors in the war on terror. Many of the military contractors were called 'body shops', because they sold warm bodies to beef up the slimmed-down state; but SAIC were seen as a 'brains shop', selling intellectual power to the government. SAIC was founded in 1969, and lived by selling high-tech solutions to the US military, with particular strengths in nuclear weapons technology. SAIC's nuclear work included a bizarre set of contracts relating to nuclear scrap in the 1990s: the firm was simultaneously developing guidelines for 'safe' levels of exposure to nuclear scrap for the US government and working as a subcontractor for British Nuclear Fuels on a scheme to recycle US radioactive waste into cutlery, hospital beds, and other materials. Shock about the apparent conflict of interest, and about the dangers posed by nuclear scrap, brought both these SAIC contracts to an abrupt end, when a campaigning Washington lawyer exposed the company's contradictory roles.

SAIC won its military, civil and nuclear contracts while stacking its management with former generals, admirals, diplomats, and intelligence officers.[17] John Deutch, who had led the CIA under Clinton, served on the SAIC board, as did one-time CIA director Rear Admiral Bobby Ray Inman. SAIC won a host of contracts relating to the occupation of Iraq, but dropped the ball when it came to its most prominent homeland security contract. In 2001 SAIC won the contract to replace the FBI's inadequate, dated computer databases with a new system called 'Virtual Case File'. The FBI had many possible leads into the 9/11 conspiracy, with a number of the terrorist plotters showing up in FBI investigations prior to the suicide attacks. However, partly because of archaic computer systems, the information was not properly collated before the aeroplanes crashed into the Pentagon and the World Trade Centre. SAIC's Virtual Case File was supposed to make all FBI data from wiretaps, criminal records, financial transactions and the like available and searchable electronically. But by 2005, after SAIC had burned up $100 million of FBI money, audits and tests showed that the system was useless. The Justice Department's inspector general said that this meant agents were left at 'a severe disadvantage in performing their duties'.

David Kay, a former SAIC vice president and one-time weapons inspector in Iraq, was clear that the company carried some of the blame. He argued that the FBI had given SAIC the wrong instructions, and had not managed the contract effectively. But SAIC shared responsibility for the failure because, rather than pointing out these problems, the company had blithely continued to take the money. In Kay's words, 'SAIC was at fault because of the usual contractor reluctance to tell the customer, "You're screwed up. You don't know what you're doing. This project is going to fail because you're not managing your side of the equation." '[18] This was very bad news for the FBI, which had wasted years and millions of dollars only to be left with the same antiquated data systems. It was also an embarrassment for SAIC – but it was good news for Lockheed, which promptly won a contract to replace Virtual Case Management with a new system, called 'Sentinel', that would cost three times as much. The homeland security boom meant that the government was driven into the arms of one contractor after another, throwing ever-larger sums at the private sector for new information technology solutions to the political problem of terrorism. Contractors screwed up; but in a market dominated by a handful of multinational giants, this meant only a turn of the wheel, with the replacement of one company by another. Lockheed made its own contribution to contractor failure with its 'Secure Flight' system. It was a major supplier of this scheme, commissioned by the Transport Security Administration. Secure Flight was a direct response to 9/11, involving pre-flight screening of all passengers against terrorist watch lists. By the end of 2006, with over a £100 million spent, Secure Flight was suspended after auditors identified security vulnerabilities.[19]

These 24-carat information technology programmes are just a few examples from the gold-rush of companies seeking homeland security contracts from the government, whose ability to manage information was seriously weakened after twenty years of privatization and contracting-out. Officials had weak defences when it came to negotiating deals with security-focused corporations. But the same officials were thoroughly seduced by the promise of technological solutions to the terrorist threat, and enticed into buying 'big brother' solutions. When these solutions failed, governments shuffled the deck and picked out a new contractor.

Those companies with access to the government through traditional military–industrial links had some advantages when it came to winning contracts; and those that had spent time trying to build civil, welfare-based work had even more advantages when it came to offering techno-authoritarian promises to willing administrators. In the UK, high-tech companies followed a similar arc. Firms that had enriched themselves in the Cold War years of high military spending now chased work emerging from welfare privatization to offset any losses. Military-oriented multi-nationals started work on authoritarian welfare systems. These same companies then found that the links they had built up with government paid massive dividends when politicians began looking for answers to the terrorist threat. Contractors moved from warfare to welfare, and from there to the new, security-focused database state.

SEMA was a French firm working on warships and avionics in a joint venture with BAE called BAE SEMA. In 1995 it was revealed that SEMA was so enthusiastic about the navy that they had recruited eighteen of its senior ex-officers, including four Royal Navy commanders, a vice-admiral and a rear admiral.[20] Former First Sea Lord Sir Julian Oswald was SEMA's chairman for much of this time (the revolving door between private and public military institutions was just as busy in Europe as in the US). But the company was anxious about its future. In 1996 it ran a conference called 'the spoils of war', emphasizing that the methods it had learned as a military contractor could be applied in banking and finance. The company, anxious about 'sluggish defence markets', tried to build work in finance, telecoms and 'outsourcing'.[21] Outsourcing, in the shape of welfare privatization, became an important part of the company's income. In 1998 the New Labour government made one of its first big privatizations, when the Department of Social Security handed the Benefits Agency Medical Services to SEMA in a £205 million, three-year deal. The warship firm was now responsible for checking applicants for disability benefit. SEMA employed doctors to check whether claimants were really incapacitated, or were just faking it. The government claimed that the privatization was 'about utilising private sector expertise by producing a better deal for customers and taxpayers'. The ministerial announcement to parliament declared that 'this would be a government of ideas and ideals but not of outdated ideology. What counts is what works'. But the privatization did not produce a better deal for disabled 'customers'. A select committee report savaged the contract, its MPs declaring: 'Present performance is not acceptable', and wondering whether 'standards are coming second to profitability'. The disabled suffered long waits, cancelled appointments, and even racist attitudes from retired, burned-out and under-trained doctors. Like the US welfare privatizations, this deal had an authoritarian, punitive approach. The company was hired to drive out fraudulent claimants, and many disabled applicants complained that they had been treated as if they were dishonest, and unfairly denied benefits that they were forced to win back through long and complicated appeals.

While SEMA claimed that it was driving fraud out of the welfare system, its managers were themselves up to no good. In 2000 the company came close to going bust in the wake of a financial scandal. Insider dealing was exposed on the part of one of the directors, involving £24 million of his own shares, and investors punished the firm by driving its price down to rock bottom. The benefits contract was one of the jewels in a very tarnished crown, and this part of the business was sold on to Schlumberger, a US oil services firm. Thus were disabled Britons traded on international markets. Former CIA director John Deutch was a director of Schlumberger, as well as working for SAIC. Consequently, the SEMA sale meant that America's one-time top spy was now responsible for British disability benefits. Later still, the privatization unit was sold on to another French company, Atos Origin.

In all of this trading, the benefits privatization was the most valuable item. But after 9/11 the company found a new way to boost its profits: the identity card. The company had moved away from military markets and into welfare privatization, but the war on terror gave the company an opportunity to move back into the security business. It was able to use its experience of privatizing government, and the contacts with the political and civil service elite built up in that business, to win new post-9/11 security contracts. In the US, the diffuse, federal nature of the state meant that the war on terror spawned numerous, overlapping databases. In more centralized Britain, politicians latched onto the technical authoritarian gesture represented by the identity card. A national identity card scheme had been considered within Whitehall for some years before 9/11, but the projected £1 billion price, and the political difficulties involved in its introduction, meant that these plans remained in Home Office filing cabinets. Within four days of the 9/11 attacks, Home Secretary David Blunkett floated the scheme again. For some years, however, ministers remained tentative and apologetic about the scheme – trying, for example, to dress it up as an 'entitlement card' designed to help people get benefits, rather than a way of policing the population. Blunkett was himself a prime example of the free flow between security-minded politicians and security-oriented contractors: after leaving his job as home secretary, Blunkett became a consultant to Entrust, a US firm seeking work from the identity card scheme.

The contractors sensed an opportunity, and began encouraging the government to commit to the identity card. At the best of times, the New Labour administration found it hard to resist the call of business lobbyists, and the identity card was no exception. The Labour government and the commercial lobbyists discovered a mutually supportive relationship: the contractors offered pre-packaged solutions to warfare, welfare and security issues, while the government offered long-term contracts. In 2002, SEMA was a financial contributor to the Labour Party, and also ran all of Labour's membership databases. The company also helped out when senior Labour figures hit trouble. Philip Chalmers, the special adviser to Labour's First Minister of Scotland, Donald Dewar, lost his official job when he was arrested drunk at the wheel of his car – in a red light district, accompanied by a prostitute. The firm quickly hired the disgraced Labour aide and put him in charge of a Scottish tourist website that they were running for the government. As the government dithered about introducing the identity card, SEMA decided to put its influence to work, commissioning surveys showing popular support for the scheme, and launching a campaign to lobby MPs.

When the company reverted to French ownership, the change in management made no difference to its lobbying strategy. Now named Atos, the company hired a Labour member of the House of Lords – former cabinet minister Lord Barnett – to head its board; it contributed money to think-tanks close to the Labour Party, and continued lobbying in favour of the identity card. In this it was joined by other players: UNISYS sought to move beyond its US security database market, and started lobbying for the identity card. UNISYS put money into the Fabian society, the Labour Party's oldest think-tank, to fund work supporting the card. This move was part of a global drive on the part of UNISYS towards selling security systems. UNISYS's international work actually threw up more problems for its reputation – but these were ignored as ministers and lobbyists looked forward to a rosy future in high-tech security solutions.

One of the company's international security systems came unstuck in 2003, when Panama's electoral commission cancelled its four-year contract for the high-tech digital cards. UNISYS was sacked after a Colombian man was found in illegal possession of 500 blank cards, and the company admitted that it too had 30,000 blank cards – all of which should have been handed to the Panamanian government. While the electoral commission dismissed rumours that the blank cards were part of a voting fraud or drug crime plot, it terminated the contract over general security concerns. UNISYS responded by trying to sue the Panamanian government.

One might think that these events would have worried British legislators hoping to use UNISYS to introduce their own identity card – but the drive to adopt the new system was unimpeded. Perhaps UNISYS lobbying was too effective; or perhaps, once ministers had committed themselves to the identity card scheme, it was hard for them to turn back. The contractors offered an easily digestible answer to the new security problems: if ministers began to see flaws in their solution, they would also have to think of an entirely new strategy for dealing with terrorism. The high-tech salespeople offered a comforting, packaged policy solution which was too attractive to reject, even when this meant ignoring warning signs about potential failure.

SEMA and UNISYS were joined by another company with a defence background bidding for work on Britain's identity card. German electronics giant Siemens has a long and sometimes inglorious history of military service. Most infamously, the company used slave labourers from the concentration camps to help build electrical switches for Hitler's war machine. Siemens expanded its military assets at exactly the wrong time: in 1988 the German company bought British electronics firm Plessey, giving it a major interest in defence electronics. The fall of the Berlin wall a year later drastically reduced the market for Siemens' newly acquired high-tech warfare products, and the company felt a very painful and direct injury from the subsequent decline of the Russian threat.

Siemens Plessey began developing Vixen, an electronic warfare system, for the British army in 1987. The Ministry of Defence expected Vixen to enter service by 1991. In 1997, after a decades work, Siemens had still not delivered its weapon. Trials of Vixen in 1996 failed to achieve any of the predicted standards. Siemens must have known that it was not at all unusual for the Ministry of Defence to accept such delays for big-ticket military systems with a shrug of acceptance, and to respond to news of technical failure with an indulgent encouragement to try harder next time. So the company must have been as shocked as external commentators when the Ministry did not shrug, but cancelled Vixen. This surprisingly firm action by the customer was spurred by the end of the Soviet threat: Vixen was designed to allow the British army to intercept and analyse radio traffic, using direction-finding capabilities to provide intelligence on an enemy's location. The army saw it as a tool to catch a Russian invasion, targeting Soviet troops on the north German plain; but the arrival of the barbarians had unfortunately been cancelled. The government had already paid £50 million for Vixen, and declined to throw any more at the system. This was the last straw for the German company. Existing nervousness about its military contracts had already led the company to start what was called a 'tanks to tractors' programme, moving away from relying on sales to the world's military forces. The company was trying to win more business producing cash-dispensing machines and air-traffic control systems, and thus rely less on providing missile guidance technology. After the Vixen cancellation, Siemens gave up entirely and sold its whole defence arm to BAE.

Giving up on military contracting left a large hole in the Siemens' marketing strategy. Defence contracts are typically signed for large sums of money, for long terms, and with tolerant and understanding customers. Siemens needed to find equivalent markets. Luckily for the company, defence contracting is not the only way to extract money from the government. Siemens also had experience of large civil construction projects. Like military contracts, these infrastructure deals rely on close relationships with the government – but Siemens eventually found that it was perhaps too close to key officials. In 2006 and 2007, Siemens' chief executive, Klaus Kleinfeld, seemed stunned by the scale of the allegations of corruption against his firm. '[W]e do not tolerate illegal business practices and that is not negotiable', he claimed, but the evidence to the contrary was mounting. Two Siemens executives admitted to paying around €6 million in bribes to win a contract for power turbines from Italy's state-owned power firm. One of the executives, Horst Vigener, said that 'such practices were well known to many people at Siemens', and were common worldwide.[22] His assertion seemed to be supported by an internal report prepared for Siemens by accountants KPMG, which identified around €240 million worth of 'suspicious transactions'. Payments to middlemen and for 'marketing' went through shell companies and offshore bank accounts. Investigators suspected that possible bribes were paid by Siemens staff to win large public contracts in transport, energy, and telecommunications. Gifts of cars were associated with contracts to supply power station turbines in Serbia, while massive projects in Greece, Italy, Nigeria, Russia and elsewhere were all possibly tainted. Siemens' leadership expressed astonishment at the revelations, but clues had been clearly visible in the company's public history. In 1992, five Siemens managers were convicted of paying DM3.3 million to Munich officials to win a DM108 million sewerage contract.[23] In 1996, Siemens was barred from bidding for government contracts in Singapore for five years. The firm had been one of a group of multinationals that had paid around $20 million to the country's deputy head of public works in return for contracts.[24]

One of the problems of large civil construction contracts is that they are finite. All that effort – and in some cases all those bribes – leads to just one sale. The company had to mobilize again and again to win just one contract, one generator, one high-speed rail line, one sewer system. But the privatization drive meant that Siemens and other companies could now bid to supply services to the government. Selling services had many attractions above and beyond that of simply building things. Service contracts could be long-term or even open-ended. Siemens saw this opportunity, and made a firm move into the new government services market. In the UK this led to a particular focus on the Home Office. Siemens won two major contracts overseen by this department – at the Passport Agency and the Immigration and Nationality Directorate (IND).

Just two months before leaving office in 1997, the Conservative government announced that it had awarded Siemens a seven-year, £70 million Private Finance Initiative contract to speed up the processing of asylum claims by the Immigration Service through computerization. A year later the Labour Party, clearly impressed by their Tory predecessors' forward thinking, gave a £120 million contract to Siemens to become the 'business partner' of the Passport Agency. Needless to say, both contracts hit severe difficulties. The Passport Agency privatization process hit all groups in society, including journalists. Siemens' failures in the Immigration Service only affected 'foreigners'. Consequently, the former was very widely reported in the press, whereas the failings in the latter system received less attention. Ministers ignored warnings by unions representing Passport Agency workers and left Siemens to itself, cutting staff and adding new computer systems. As a result, the queue for passports reached half a million. An embarrassed home secretary issued a public apology, and £13 million was spent hiring extra staff to clear up the company's mess – although Siemens suffered only limited financial penalties for its failure.

Siemens would have to work hard to make the experience of immigrants and asylum seekers worse than it already was. Applicants were already forced to wait in long queues at Lunar House, the grim Home Office complex in suburban London. Backlogs of files, lost paperwork, and a demoralized workforce meant that would-be Britons were caught in a bureaucratic limbo for months on end. The Siemens contract promised to convert this mess into a 'paperless office', and sack a fifth of Home Office staff in the process. Unions warned the incoming Labour government that the scheme was flawed, and argued that the sackings should at least be delayed until the new system had bedded in. The home secretary, Jack Straw, and his minister, Mike O'Brien, ignored these complaints just as they had ignored similar warnings over Siemens' Passport Agency scheme. They must have felt that the union warnings were simply 'producer' complaints, while modern ministers should focus on the 'consumer'. A private company supplying a paperless office to run government services sounded like the purest expression of New Labour's approach. Immigration and asylum were also areas in which Labour ministers felt themselves vulnerable to populist attacks from the right. Shifting the whole business of immigration administration away from the politicians to private enterprise must have seemed like an attractive way of neutralizing the issue, and of isolating themselves from arguments about immigration. The government was also clearly focusing its privatization efforts on asylum seekers. Thanks to Straw's reforms, asylum seekers would have their applications processed by one private company. If their claim failed, they would be imprisoned by another private company before deportation; and if their case was delayed, they would live in the community on a subsistence grant in the form of food vouchers supplied by yet another private company. Asylum seekers were kept at one remove from the state by a series of commercial providers, caught in a profit-making, bureaucratic limbo. The government was experimenting on asylum seekers with privatized systems of control that would later, in the war on terror, come to be used on the general population.

The asylum seekers' limbo became even less comfortable when Siemens' system was introduced, and promptly broke down. In 1998 the paperless office had failed to materialize, and instead Siemens was offering a 'paper-based pilot scheme'.[25] Although the firm was only supposed to get paid on the completion of the system, the Home Office was making payments to Siemens in a desperate attempt to get the new procedures working. Siemens was supposed to carry the risk of failure – but when real failure arrived, the government tried to bail out the contractor. Rats were found nibbling at the files in the Home Office stores, and the backlog reached 77,000 cases. In desperation, the Home Office authorized the head of the IND to set up a taskforce with Siemens, which would be empowered to take any action that 'will not be constrained by commercial or contractual issues'.[26] Even giving the firm carte blanche in this way failed, and the government finally abandoned the system in 2001, returning to a largely paper administration. The government faced embarrassment, but asylum seekers suffered bureaucratic misery – although their travails had much less impact on the press than the sufferings of passport applicants.

A casual observer might think that Siemens would now be in real trouble. Military contracting was a dead end. Public sector contracts had ended in two disasters. The firm was surely facing a crisis. But this underestimates the reviving powers of the war on terror. After 9/11, Siemens found itself as well placed to gather the new bounty as were other firms who had moved from military to civil public contracts. Although Siemens' mistakes had severely embarrassed the government, and given a massive boost to critics of New Labour's 'Private Finance Initiative', the company still found itself a major beneficiary of the new security spending. Perhaps ministers so fervently believed in the superiority of the private sector that they overlooked the grim reality of Siemens' record; perhaps the government had allowed civil service capacity to whither so much that it had no choice but to rely on Siemens for 'capacity building' when it wanted to increase the power of the state in response to the terrorist threat; perhaps officials had become so comfortable with the company that they ignored its faults, as one might ignore the faults of an old friend.

Certainly, Siemens had done what it could to engage with the Labour leadership. In 2004 it hired Sovereign Strategy – a lobbying company run by Labour insiders, including former cabinet minister Jack Cunningham. Siemens then sponsored appearances by a number of ministers: for two years, Siemens paid for meetings on 'identity' at the Labour Party conference featuring then-Home Secretary David Blunkett and Home Office minister Tony McNulty. In 2006, the company also paid for a keynote address to Labour's Fabian Society by 'rising star' minister David Miliband.

The company's efforts certainly seem to have neutralized any residual bitterness resulting from the Passport Agency and IND fiascos. Siemens won an early bid in the identity card race, scooping up a £6 million contract to create software for the 'authentication by interview' system – a Passport Agency programme advertised as one of the building blocks for the identity card system. In 2006 Siemens Business Services reported a €549 million loss on their business, but the company was convinced that it would be saved by 'security spending' on identity cards in Britain and Europe.[27]

Postscript: Waiting for the Barbarians

In his verse 'Waiting for the Barbarians',[1] Greek poet Constantine Cavafy describes a country where all public life focuses on its enemies. Citizens wait in the forum because 'the barbarians are due'. The emperor and consuls are dressed in their finest garments to impress the barbarians when they arrive. Normal laws are suspended, and parliamentary debates cancelled during the present barbarian danger. Then the worst possible news reaches the city: '. . . the barbarians have not come. / And some who have just returned from the border say there are no barbarians any longer.' The barbarians' failure to materialize hurts more than their expected arrival – after all, '. . . what's going to happen to us without barbarians? They were, those people, a kind of solution.' A generation of Western politicians grew up during the Cold War, when the fear of the 'barbarians' of Russia and China was used as a key to international and domestic politics: all confrontations between the West and developing nations were recast as battles between freedom and communist tyranny. Anti-communism dominated home politics during the 1950s, and re-mained a significant force right up to the collapse of the Soviet bloc. Ideas to the left of the Democrats in US, or of social democracy in Europe, were often painted as illegitimate relations of the communist enemy. Some leading politicians seemed disorientated when the barbarians of the Soviet Union ceased to exist as a unified force. The Soviets had provided a 'kind of solution' to how to organize US and European government, and now they were gone.

Leaderships in the White House and Westminster have seized on the new terrorist threat as a new kind of useful barbarian, again shaping much of foreign and domestic policy into the frame provided by the 'war on terror'. Relations with the developing world are determined according to who is on side in the battle against terrorism, and who harbours the diverse terrorist enemy. Authoritarian regimes like those of Pakistan and Saudi Arabia can be part of the coalition for freedom simply by declaring themselves against terrorism. Populations or nations that find themselves in conflict with the Western consensus – like many Iraqis, Palestinians and Iranians – are lumped together with Osama bin Laden's small, violent network as part of the terrorist threat. Home politics are also bent towards an authoritarian, surveillance-happy 'homeland security', with the suspension of ordinary civil liberties and the enactment of emergency laws. The threat of the new barbarians provides a new and unhappy political 'solution'. The theme of this book has been that, while legislators and officials are drawn to this political solution by themselves, they are also encouraged along this road by a substantial business lobby with a commercial interest in militaristic and authoritarian responses to the threat of terrorism.

In March 1989 Dick Cheney gave every indication that he wanted to hang on to the Cold War even as it dissolved around him. At the ceremony where he was sworn in as the elder George Bush's secretary of defense, Cheney said, 'There are those who want to declare the Cold War ended. They perceive a significantly lessened threat and want to believe that we can reduce our level of vigilance accordingly. But I believe caution is in order.'[2] By June of that year, Cheney was predicting that the reformist Soviet leader, Mikhail Gorbachev, would 'fail' and be replaced by someone 'far more hostile'.[3] When the Soviet bloc began to fall apart, Cheney argued against a change of defence policy, because 'Europe is still divided. The Berlin Wall is still up.' Soon Cheney was no longer able to support his claim that the Russians were still the main enemy by invoking the Berlin Wall, because it had been torn down. Unfazed, Cheney began arguing that the fall of the Wall itself in fact proved that the Cold War could restart at any minute.

By March 1990, even the head of the CIA was convinced that the Russian threat had radically diminished – but Cheney was enraged when the CIA's director said that the Russians now had 'little incentive to engage in major confrontations with the United States'. Bizarrely, Cheney publicly dressed down the CIA leadership by arguing that the radical changes in Europe in fact proved that the Russians could become more warlike at any moment. Since 'nobody predicted the Berlin Wall coming down or the kind of revolution we've seen in Eastern Europe', he argued, then equally unpredictable events could lead to a new 'hostile' Soviet Union, which might suddenly become a 'military threat'. Cheney declared that reducing US suspicion of Russia was 'wrong' and 'dangerous'.[4] Cheney was desperate to hang on to his enemy, and was deeply disappointed when the barbarians decided to walk off the stage. He cobbled together a new 'Defense Planning Guidance' document with his then assistant, Paul Wolfowitz. This official paper outlines America's military plans and goals. Cheney and Wolfowitz's new version suggested, now that the Soviet Union had failed, the US must develop the capability to fight 'two regional wars' simultaneously in a new, unpredictable world. This attempt to justify maintaining massive military spending, a large army, and a Pentagon bureaucracy just about held together during the 1990s, albeit with difficulty. Without the Soviet enemy, it was increasingly difficult to maintain the political consensus behind the massive war machine.

The neoconservatives have a long history of building up the threat of the barbarians. In the 1970s George Bush Sr founded a group called 'Team B' to second-guess the CIA's estimate of Russian weapons and intentions. This group, which included Paul Wolfowitz and other prominent neoconservatives, deliberately overestimated the scale of the Soviet military and the aggressive threat of the Russian leadership in an attempt to derail *détente* between East and West. From Team B developed the Committee on the Present Danger, a lobbying group which sought to keep up political pressure for a strong, interventionist US army. The Committee fought against anti-military feelings generated by the Vietnam failure, countering them by emphasising the Soviet threat. In effect the Committee on the Present Danger, led by neoconservative figures like Richard Perle, strained to keep the Cold War going. Unfortunately, these ideologues saw their present recede decisively into the past, when the Soviet bloc fell apart during the last decade of the twentieth century.

Unsurprisingly, given this past, neoconservatives like Cheney and Wolfowitz seized on the terrorist threat as a source of new barbarians. They set out an argument that would make the Islamist terrorists into an enemy around which all Western foreign policy – and a substantial amount of domestic policy – could turn. They enthusiastically embraced the idea that the terrorist menace could replace the red menace. A new 'Committee on the Present Danger' was formed by figures like James

Woolsey to argue that the terrorist threat was not a 'law enforcement issue', but rather an 'existential war'.[5] The US leadership tried to frame all foreign policy questions in terms of the war on terror, in the same way that a previous generation of leaders had tried to squeeze all international conflicts into the frame of anti-communism. During the Cold War, the US and British leaderships were willing to back any dictator, warlord or coup that was thought to provide protection against communism. For example, millions suffered and died while the West backed the South African regime and its vile proxies in Angola and Namibia, simply because they were seen as bulwarks against the red menace. In Southeast Asia, the Cold War was very hot, taking the form of the Vietnam War. In Central and South America it meant backing death squads against anyone – whether guerrilla or nun – who looked the least bit red. During the war on terror, all conflicts have been squeezed into the framework of the battle with Osama bin Laden – even when, as in the case of Iraq, such a connection had to be fabricated. As during the Cold War, reactionary, authoritarian and bloody regimes – Libya, Egypt, Uzbekistan – were welcomed aboard as long as they were 'against terrorism'.

Dick Cheney also devoted great personal effort towards reviving the witch-hunting home politics of the Cold War. He repeatedly suggested that critics of his policy were aiding the enemy. For example, in 2006 Cheney claimed that any debate about the progress of the Iraq War 'validates the strategy of the terrorists'.[6] George Bush joined in this game, as when he claimed in 2004 that criticism of his Iraq policy 'can embolden an enemy'[7] – a theme he returned to in subsequent years. Cheney even suggested that if US electors voted for John Kerry instead of George Bush in 2004, then the terrorists would strike again. This smear strategy reached a new, unhinged level when a leading commentator on Rupert Murdoch's Fox News implied that Democrat presidential hopeful and war critic Barack Obama was some kind of 'Manchurian Candidate'-style terrorist sleeper, suggesting that he had been educated at a potentially terrorist 'madrasa', and emphasizing that he shared a name – Hussein – with the former dictator of Iraq.

Perhaps it is not so surprising that Bush and Cheney tried to update old red-baiting strategies for the age of terror, and to use the war on terror to police domestic opposition to their policies. But Cold War nostalgia was not limited to the US. British Prime Minister Gordon Brown explicitly argued that the Cold War model should be used in the new war on terror

– for example, in an article for Rupert Murdoch's daily *Sun* newspaper. Brown's apprentice in his previous post as Chancellor of the Exchequer, Ed Balls, made the same point in a radio interview. Brown wanted the Cold War analogy to sound reassuring after some of Prime Minister Blair's bellicose stands, by emphasizing the 'cultural' nature of the conflict with communism and the use of the 'soft' power of influence, as well as of the 'hard' power of war. Brown said that the Western confrontation with the Soviets had been 'a battle fought through books and ideas, even music and the arts', and a 'battle for hearts and minds',[8] as well as one of military power. The cultural war against communism included the covert funding of political organizations and magazines; the imposition of loyalty pledges; the removal of 'unsound' people from positions of influence, from Hollywood to local schools; the harassment of labour activists and campaigners – so Brown's evocation of 'soft power' offered little comfort. It underlined the fact that Brown saw himself as continuing with the policy of making into a wide-ranging 'war' a conflict with the lethal but thankfully relatively small threat of domestic terrorism.

Brown's comments about the Cold War were revealing in two ways. Firstly they showed that, though one of the main actors in the war on terror, Tony Blair, had walked off the stage, his understudy Gordon Brown intended to follow a similar script. Secondly, by invoking the Cold War Brown invited us to wonder whether the problems of the Cold War were going to be repeated in the war on terror. The theme of this book has been that President Eisenhower's warnings about the 'military–industrial complex' can be restated for the war on terror: in short, there is a new 'security–industrial complex' made up of a circle of businessmen and politicians with a vested interest in responding to the terrorist threat with ever more aggressive, broad, expensive and counterproductive overreactions on the domestic and international fronts. Eisenhower's warning came from the old Cold War years, but Brown's attempted revival of one aspect of that conflict showed that the old warning could not, unfortunately, be treated as a mere historical curiosity.

One battle over Iraq, in 2007, affords a clear sense of how closely the British and US political leaderships were intertwined with business interests in the war on terror. The battle was not fought in the streets of Baghdad, but in the courts of Washington, D.C. Rival security companies launched legal actions and political lobbying campaigns to wrestle the most significant private military deal in the Iraq theatre – the

'Reconstruction Support Services' contract – out of the hands of Aegis, the British paramilitary company run by Tim Spicer.[9] This $280 million-a-year contract was at that point one of the most complete military privatizations ever. The deal put a private company in charge of mobile armed units, called Security Escort Teams, guarding the most important political figures. The contract also demanded that the company create and run 'Reconstruction Operations Centres' in Iraq, which would be in charge of all other private security companies in the country. These centres would manage military intelligence for the contractors, which they would also provide to the US army. Clauses in the contract said that the private company must have analysts with 'NATO equivalent SE-CRET clearance', who will conduct 'analysis of foreign intelligence services, terrorist organizations, and their surrogates targeting Department of Defense personnel, resources and facilities'. The contract places the contractor in charge of the most delicate military intelligence. After gathering this intelligence, the company is supposed to use its analysis both to assist the US army in its battle with the insurgency and to help direct the other security firms – keeping them out of harms way in the dangerous Iraqi 'red zone'. Aegis itself codenamed this contract 'Project Matrix'. The company told the *Washington Post* that its teams would go into Iraqi towns and cities and report back to the US – to 'provide "ground truth" to the Army Corps' – and help guide other contractors with 'threat assessments for the people that travel the battlespace'.[10]

Aegis worked hard to keep this lucrative contract. Spicer took great pains to build relations with the US state, hiring Kristi Clemens to run Aegis's Washington office. Clemens had the right background to lobby for her new employer in the US. Clemens had previously been a spokesperson for Paul Bremer, the US viceroy in Iraq. She later became a Republican political appointee in the US Department of Homeland Security, but left that job after being accused of distorting public statements about terrorism to help get Bush re-elected. Spicer also hired Robert MacFarlane as an Aegis director. MacFarlane had worked for Ronald Reagan, helping run the Iran–Contra operation. McFarlane was central the plot, which involved selling arms to Iran in return for hostage releases, while using the profits to pay for the 'secret' US backing of the Contras in their war against Nicaragua's government. MacFarlane had been found guilty of misleading Congress in the affair, and had tried to kill himself with an overdose of Valium. He was later pardoned by

President Bush Sr. A number of veterans of the Iran–Contra affair turned up in the administration of the younger President Bush, so MacFarlane was a useful contact. The advantage to Iraqis of these legal battles and struggles for influence is less obvious.

Spicer's new links with the US security establishment did not guarantee that the company would be able to retain its grip on this slice of business. The contract was so central to the new military privatization that other leading companies tried to take over, keen for their staff to be in charge of the 'battlespace' and the delivery of 'ground truths' in Iraq. When the contract came up for renewal in 2007, this jewel in the crown of military privatization attracted multiple bids. Two of the companies rejected from the bidding – the US firm Blackwater and the Anglo-South African Erinys – immediately launched court actions, demanding to be reconsidered. One of the consequences of privatization was that the new wings of the Anglo-American intervention in Iraq now devoted valuable time and resources to fighting each other in court. Links with the political establishment – the British establishment as much as that of the American – were clearly prized by the security companies.

Two British firms were allowed to bid for this US security contract: Spicer's Aegis and the Armor Group. Aegis had hired a prominent British politician – former Conservative defence minister (and grandson of Winston Churchill), Nicholas Soames. The Armor Group's chairman was former Conservative defence secretary, Malcolm Rifkind. Rifkind had been Soames's boss in the last Conservative administration, but now the two MPs were rivals in the battle for Iraqi security cash. The fact that the military companies were so keen to employ former ministers meant that any current or future politician knew that they could look forward to a lucrative career in the new security industry. The 'revolving door' between politicians and the security business provided the basis for the new security–industrial complex. It created a financial incentive for politicians to press forward with the subcontracting of state security services. In turn, the security industry had a vested interest in persuading politicians that new military interventions or extended police powers were feasible, and even positive ventures.

This game of musical chairs between positions of political influence and the boardrooms of the security industry is now well documented. Former Conservative leader Michael Howard sits alongside former CIA director William Webster on the advisory board of Diligence, a private intelligence company set up by former MI5 and CIA agents. The traffic of personnel between the new security industry and the leadership of Britain's political parties affected both the Labour government and opposition. Prime Minister Gordon Brown made several ministerial appointments from outside his own party, announcing that he wanted a government 'of all the talents'. One such talent was the former First Sea Lord, Admiral Sir Alan West. While Sir Alan had never been talented enough actually to be elected, he did have his admirers. After resigning from the navy, Sir Alan had become a paid adviser to a company called QinetiQ, which had been formed out of Britain's military laboratories, which had themselves been sold to US-led private investors. QinetiQ's workshops once housed the historical counterparts of 'Q' – the gadget man who supplies James Bond with his spy kit. The newly commercialized boffins knew which way the market was moving, and the firm set up a 'rapidly expanding security business' to deal with 'homeland security' issues.[11] The company sells surveillance systems, 'data mining' programmes to identify 'dangerous passengers', scanning machines designed to identify dangerous weapons, and other high-tech security products.

Shortly after Brown appointed the ex-QinetiQ man, the leader of the Conservative opposition, David Cameron, made Dame Pauline Neville-Jones his own senior security advisor. She had formerly been the head of Britain's Joint Intelligence Committee, but in her retirement from public life had been chairwoman of QinetiQ for three years. So the security advisers to both the prime minister and the leader of the opposition had worked for the same security-focused company. The government could approach the terrorist threat politically or technically: it could aim to reduce the terrorist danger by trying to bring enough disaffected people into the political consensus, to isolate the hard core, violent minority; but it could also look to expensive computerized security systems as a way of trying to identify terrorist groups. The strong presence of security industry veterans in the political process makes the latter strategy more likely.

The nexus of links between the political class and the new security industry can both make company employees into ministers and ministers into company employees. Lord George Robertson – previously Labour defence secretary and then head of NATO – now works for Englefield Capital, a banking firm that owns GSL, which itself operates the private prisons, immigration detention centres and secure transport that form the backbone of the private security industry. The post-ministerial career of former home secretary, David Blunkett, includes a job advising Entrust, a Texas-based security firm bidding for work on Britain's identity card. Former Labour cabinet minister Lord Barnett runs Atos Origin, a French-owned company also bidding for work on the identity card.

De La Rue, a British printing firm based in the Hampshire town of Basingstoke, provides an illustration of the very porous walls between government and business in the war on terror. De La Rue had one of the most lucrative British contracts in Iraq: it made money by making money, literally. Iraqi oil money was used to pay the British firm to print the new Iraqi dinar. The new banknotes were not only free of Saddam's image, but also free of all Iraqi influence: the dinars were printed in east London, then flown to Iraq in twenty-four specially chartered Boeing 747 jets, with all expenses charged to Iraq's own treasury. When De La Rue won the Iraq windfall from Paul Bremer, his deputy was British diplomat Sir Jeremy Greenstock. When Sir Jeremy retired from his Iraqi role, he joined the board of De La Rue.

But the company was not satisfied with winning one of the bigger prizes in the new war on terror; it saw further opportunities in homeland security. De La Rue is bidding to help print Britain's proposed identity cards: with every citizen legally obliged to carry the card, this work has massive financial potential. In 2007 De La Rue paid for a conference on identity cards called 'Who goes there?'[12] Liam Byrne, the Home Office minister in charge of the identity card, gave a speech at the conference declaring the card 'a twenty-first-century public good' that would stop 'unregulated and unaccountable power and the risk of new inequalities'. Byrne claimed that the card was being introduced to help 'ordinary working families', rather than the 'elite' – although the elite company executives and shareholders who would cash in on the scheme – particularly those from De La Rue – were far better represented at the conference than were 'ordinary working families'. The conference was also addressed by the company's 'security adviser', David Landsman. As well as working for De La Rue, Landsman was also one of the Foreign Office's most senior security officials. He was working for the company on 'secondment', and was still officially an employee of the government. De La Rue's board also contained a senior official from the British Cabinet Office: Gill Rider was at the same time a board member of De La Rue, and the head of human resources for the entire British civil service.

Boundaries between private enterprise and the state that had been carefully built up in the nineteenth century had now broken down. It was impossible to tell who was driving British security policy – permanent officials or the directors of private companies.

This collapse of the divide between government and private companies was at least as advanced in the US. Working with private security contractors was written into the DNA of the Bush administration. Vice President Cheney's former role as chief of Halliburton – the firm that would not only run the supply lines into Iraq, but also help build Gauntánamo Bay – demonstrated the close interrelation between the security industry and political leadership. Even after the unprecedented advance of the contractors into Iraq, the US administration could still surprise the world with further commercialization of the war on terror. In May 2007, an official from the office of the Director of National Intelligence, Terri Everett, addressed a joint industry–government conference in Colorado. The Director of National Intelligence was a newly created official, reporting directly to the President, who oversaw the entire US intelligence community. Everett's presentation, called 'Procuring the Future', was supported by a set of PowerPoint slides that included a pie chart showing that 70 per cent of 'intelligence community' spending went to contractors. On current budgets, this meant that contractors had bitten off $34 billion of intelligence spending from the 2007 intelligence pie.[13] Everett made the consequences of this clear in one slide, which simply read 'We Can't Spy . . . If We Can't Buy!' Everett spelled out some other differences in the new, commercially run war on terror. She emphasized that intelligence was what her slides described as a 'Public-Private Sector Partnership (Business Relationship)', and argued that the intelligence services should now do more to break down the walls between state and private sector, including committing themselves to 'collaborate on government-to-industry, industry-to-government contracting exchange programs'.[14]

Companies hired influential people in their pursuit of these intelligence contracts. As head of the CIA, George Tenet assured George Bush that Saddam's weapons of mass destruction would turn up. 'Don't worry, it's a slam-dunk', Tenet promised the president. In fact, the ball completely missed the basket. Tenet stepped down from the CIA in some disgrace, and stepped happily onto the board of a number of security companies. Tenet became a director of British security company QinetiQ

– the company that also employed British anti-terrorism minister Sir Alan West. Tenet also took a job with a company called the Analysis Corporation. This private intelligence firm analyses terrorist threats for the State Department, and monitors classified networks for evidence of terror threats. Tenet's failed predictions about Iraq evidently made him the perfect candidate for supplying new analyses to the US security services. Tenet's new company also prepared the 'terror watch lists' – a register intended to prevent potential bombers and hijackers from boarding civilian planes, which was heavily criticized for inaccuracy and unfairness. While Tenet left the CIA for the private sector, the new Director of National Intelligence, John Michael McConnell, came in from the private sector. The country's new top spy worked for a number of companies, including Booz Allen Hamilton – a management consultancy with lucrative contracts in both Iraq and homeland security. In particular, the company held a $62 million contract to help found the Orwellian 'Total Information Awareness' system, which was aborted amid civil liberties fears in 2003.[15]

The US and British states have taken on new powers to fight the war on terror, and then promptly delegated these powers to a new and growing corporate sector. The security industry supplies troops on the battlefield, while also fighting a propaganda war through PR companies working on sensitive government contracts; private airlines ferry prisoners between secret US prisons; contractors carry out interrogations in Guantánamo and Abu Ghraib; 'intelligence corporations' carry out security analysis for governments; private companies supply identity cards, security databases and surveillance systems to monitor 'homeland' populations; private companies also run the prisons and 'control orders' that can be used against those arrested in the new conflict. A new, powerful commercial lobby has come into being that has a financial interest in more battlefields, more propaganda, more secret prisons, more interrogations, more surveillance, more security databases, more prisons, and more systems of control. Private companies did not invent the 'war on terror', but they are central to making it happen. The US and British response to 9/11 and subsequent attacks has been to try and remodel most foreign policy, and much domestic policy, under the rubric of a 'war' in which the US and its British junior partner must prevail by a firm stand. A variety of complex international conflicts are reduced to fit this simple binary opposition, with force applied against nations and groups that are crudely identified with

Osama bin Laden. At home civil liberties are pushed aside, as if Britain or the US were really fighting for their national survival, rather than facing a violent but limited terrorist fringe. US and British politicians dreamed up this approach by themselves, but there is no doubt that the existence of the private security industry encourages them down this path. Both governments have also used private contractors to shift their own military and intelligence into new, more aggressive strategies, in the same way that management consultants are used to change the culture of corporations or public sector bodies. The effects of individual private contracts in the war on terror have often been grim. The overall result of this privatization is to propel Britain and the US further along the road of interventions abroad and authoritarian measures at home.

Six years into the war on terror, there are signs of battle weariness. In January 2007, British director of public prosecutions, Ken McDonald, broke ranks with the political establishment and delivered a general warning against the dangers of a 'fear-driven and inappropriate' response to terrorism. In a striking expression of traditional legal liberalism, Sir Ken said that 'there is no such thing as a "war on terror"'. Arguing against extraordinary laws, and the suspension of normal rules, he argued that those murdered by the London Underground bombers in July 2005 'were not victims of war. And the men who killed them were not, as in their vanity they claimed on their ludicrous videos, "soldiers". They were deluded, narcissistic, inadequate. They were criminals. They were fantasists . . . The fight against terrorism on the streets of Britain', he insisted, 'is not a war. It is the prevention of crime, the enforcement of our laws and the winning of justice for those damaged by their infringement.' McDonald's statement showed that disquiet about shoe-horning the threat of terror and the priority of 'homeland security' into some overarching war reached into some of the highest echelons of society.

Discontent on the international front was even greater. Tony Blair was finally forced to announce the timetable for his own resignation when his stance over Lebanon seemed too reminiscent of the Iraq adventure. Blair's refusal to call for a ceasefire as Israel shelled Lebanon in 2006 suggested that Blair saw too many international battles as part of the war on terror that demanded vigorous resistance, rather than judging individual conflicts on their merits. If Lebanon delivered the final blow to Blair, the Iraq issue drains away political strength from George Bush with every week the conflict continues.

But discontent over individual parts of the war on terror has not yet been enough to substantially shift British or US policy. One of the many reasons that the transatlantic leadership continues to reach for militaristic and authoritarian solutions to current crises is that there is now a substantial commercial lobby beckoning them in this direction. The first step towards unravelling the influence of the security–industrial complex is the recognition that it exists. I hope this book goes a little way towards making that possible.

Notes

INTRODUCTION: 1984 PLC

1. S. Hughes and A. Barnett, 'Bush Ally set to profit from the war on terror', 11 May 2003.
2. They were Samuel Berger, H. Lee Buchanan, and Togo D. West.
3. Particularly after a groundbreaking investigation at the *Observer* by Antony Barnett, Greg Palast and Ben Laurence.
4. Claire Newell and Robert Winnett, 'Labour's lobby scandal', *Sunday Times*, 18 March 2007.
5. US Department of Defense, 'National military strategy of the United States of America: A strategy for today; a vision for tomorrow', 2004.

1 ECONOMIC MIGRANTS

1. H. Young 'The ill-gotten gains from law and disorder' *Guardian* (London), 5 November 1985.
2. See especially C. Parenti, *Lockdown America* (London: Verso, 1999).
3. Adam Smith Institute, 'Justice Policy' (November 1984). The same report also recommended more home-based punishment, using curfews or an electronic bracelet. The latter are now being used in New Mexico, and send signals to a central monitoring unit if the wearers take them off or move more than 200 yards from home.
4. D. Rose, 'Big money turns the key', *Guardian*, 11 January 1989.
5. Although Strutt was reportedly filmmaker Richard Curtis's girlfriend for a time. See C. Newbon, 'Five weddings and an inspired movie', *Mail on Sunday*, 16 November 2003
6. See Rose, 'Big money'.
7. Contract Prisons, a consortium involving US operator Pricor and UK developer Rosehaugh, was ultimately unsuccessful in its jail bids.
8. R. P. Jones 'State now admits private prison abuse', *Milwaukee Journal Sentinel*, 11 November 1998.
9. H. Mills, 'Fury as Group 4 poaches senior jail managers', *Observer*, 28 December 1997; A. Travis 'Jail service and five firms bid for Strangeways', *Guardian*, 12 April 1993.

10. N. Ross, 'Detective Firm Says It Uses Right-Wing Group's Data', *Washington Post*, 27 January 1977.
11. Hamel operated from Virginia. Wackenhut was fined for operating without licenses in the operation.
12. Mr Mark Healy (Prison Officers' Association) at the Trades Union Congress, Thursday, 17 September 1998.
13. R. Ford, 'Labour gives pledge to end prison privatization', *The Times*, 8 March 1995.
14. Antony Barnett, 'Private prison contract "was political decision"', *Observer*, 31 October 1999.
15. R. Ford 'Private jails fined £1.6 million', *The Times*, 3 September 1999.
16. L. Freeman, 'Howard aims to strike fear among criminals', Press Association. 1 July 1993.
17. House of Commons, Hansard Debates, March 1993.
18. N. Morris, '£283m for youth custody wasted', *Independent*, 12 October 2004.
19. M. White, 'Blair adopts moral values line on crime', *Guardian*, 20 February 1993.
20. T. Kavanagh 'Blair's panic memo', *Sun*, 17 July 2000.
21. The boy was called Adam Rickwood. M. Frith and I. Herbert, 'Death of boy, 14, reignites concerns over suicides in custody', *Independent*, 10 August 2004.
22. 'New Management Team Installed At HMYOI Ashfield', Hermes Database, Home Office, 23 May 2002.
23. A. Travis, 'Young offenders to be removed from worst jail', *Guardian*, 5 February 2003.
24. A. Clendenning, 'Justice Department slams Jena juvenile prison in new report', Associated Press, 23 February 2000.
25. J. McNair, 'Wackenhut Corrections: A Prisoner of Its Own Problems', *Miami Herald*, 15 April 2000.
26. 'Appeals court raps attorney but upholds inmate awards', *Corrections Professional*, 27 July 2001.
27. R. Gee, 'Caldwell jailers accused of sex with an inmate', *Austin American-Statesman*, 28 January 2000.
28. J. Bennetto, '"Racist" prison chief is urged to quit', *Independent*, 27 March 1998.
29. J. Gonzales 'State-hired expert rebuts claim of rampant abuse, inhumanity in prisons', *Houston Chronicle*, 7 February 1999.
30. J. Karpinski, 'One Woman's Army' (Boston: Hyperion, 2005).
31. *Group 4 Securicor International Magazine*, 50, October 2004.
32. B. Roberts '£3M Paedo spy farce: sex offender tracker system doesn't work near tall buildings, trees', *Daily Mirror*, 10 August 2005.
33. A. Alderson, 'Injured police may sue Group 4', *Sunday Times*, 18 April 1993.
34. P. Eastham, 'Jail firm faces sack', *Daily Mail*, 10 April 1993.
35. D. Rose, 'Drink binge of Group 4 prisoner who died', *Observer*, 9 May 1993.
36. 'Private jail security "like a film comedy"', *Evening Standard*, 15 April 1993.
37. T. Rayment, 'Group 4 faces criticism as prisoner dies', *Sunday Times*, 9 May 1993.
38. See, for example, K. Baker, 'We must not allow our tolerance to be abused', *Evening Standard*, 2 April 1992.
39. G. King, 'Kurd dies after fire at detention centre', *The Times*, 9 October 1989. The suicidal asylum seeker was called Siho Iyiguven.
40. S. Goodwin, 'Home Office unmoved by hunger strikers', *Independent*, 1 April 1994.
41. '"Leftwingers" blamed for immigration riot', *Times*, 7 June 1994.
42. A. Travis 'Group 4 sets up immigrant control squads', *Guardian*, 10 May 1995.

43. G. Cordon, ' "Moment of madness" blamed for riot', Press Association, 21 August 1997.
44. D. Taylor, ' "I do not understand why your country has done this to me" ', *Guardian*, 18 August 1999.
45. J. Chapman, 'Unveiled: £100m "last stop" for refugees awaiting deportation is last word in luxury: the asylum centre that looks like a top hotel', *The Express*, 18 January 2002. M. Clarke 'The giant detention centre that will be home to illegal immigrants destined for deportation: Last taste of Britain. Asylum rejects have no way out but can live in luxury', *Daily Mail*, 18 January 2002.
46. T. Wagner, 'Fires break out at Europe's largest detention center for asylum seekers', Associated Press. 14 February 2002
47. 'Riot-hit detention centre was "astonishingly flimsy" ', *Building*, 19 November 2004.
48. P. Foot, 'Freedom up in flames', *Guardian*, 19 February 2002.
49. S. Morris and R. Allison, 'Yarl's Wood: tinderbox that sent asylum plans up in flames', *Guardian*, 16 August 2003.
50. N. Sommerlad, 'Scandal of Yarl's Wood', *Daily Mirror*, 8 December 2003.
51. Committee of Independent Experts, 'First report on allegations regarding fraud, mismanagement and nepotism in the European Commission', 15 March 1999.
52. 'Escort staff accused of prisoner abuse', *Herald*, 17 July 2004. See also the *Sun*, 16 July 2004.
53. P. Rees, 'At home with the terror suspects in a state of limbo', *Sunday Times*, 4 February 2007.
54. J. Kirkup, 'Escaped Iraqi terror suspect was "lost" by private tagging firm', *Scotsman*, 18 October 2006.

2 BASE MOTIVES

1. See, for example, R. Atkins, 'Crash Fails To Put Privatization Programme Off The Rails', *Financial Times*, 20 June 1988.
2. 'Old soldiers "disgusted" as Japanese win property deal', *Glasgow Herald*, 4 September 1996.
3. House of Commons, 16 July 1996.
4. House of Commons, 14 October 1996.
5. National Audit Office, 'Ministry of Defence: The Sale of Married Quarters Estate', 1999.
6. D. Simpson, 'Tories attack dock privatization', *Guardian*, 29 November 1985.
7. National Audit Office, 'Ministry of Defence: The Construction of Nuclear Submarine Facilities at Devonport', 2002.
8. When I asked Halliburton how they responded to this extraordinary charge, they refused to comment.
9. *Observer*, 24 October 1999.

3 PROJECTING POWER

1. 'Public–Private Partnerships: Background Papers for the U.S.-U.K. Conference on Military Installation Assets, Operations, and Services', 14–16 April 2000, RAND MR-1309-A, 2001.

2. A. Osborne, 'Labour MP sounds alarm at £950m MoD contract', *Daily Telegraph*, 15 May 2002.
3. James Fisher Shipping website, 2003.
4. WBR Defence Partnership's 2nd Annual Conference on PFI/PPP in defence.
5. Defence Partnerships 2003 programme, organized by Worldwide Business research.
6. Simon Kershaw PowerPoint slides.
7. Ibid.
8. 'Boeing Leasing Deal Originally Conceived to Save Boeing's Faltering Operations post 9/11', Project on Government Oversight press release, 2 September 2003.
9. J. Chaffin and S. Kirchgaessner, 'Perle lobbied for Boeing's tanker bid', *Financial Times*, 5 December 2003.
10. See 'RAF tanker deal will be biggest test yet for PFI', *Engineer*, 17 August 2001.
11. Made up of military contractors EADS, Thales, Rolls-Royce, and Cobham.

4 NATION-BUILDING THE DYNCORP WAY

1. F. Fukuyama, 'Nation-Building 101', *Atlantic Monthly*, January/February 2004.
2. J. Dobbin et al, 'America's Role in Nation-Building: From Germany to Iraq', Rand Corporation, 2003.
3. 'Transcript of the First Televised Debate Between Clinton and Dole', *New York Times*, 7 October 1996.
4. Transcript of CNN from 3 October 2000.
5. 'Haitian police blamed in 15 deaths', Agence France-Presse, 22 January 1997.
6. As in DEA official Steven Casteel's Congressional testimony, 20 May 2003.
7. Fuerzas Armadas Revolucionarias de Colombia.
8. Autodefensas Unidas de Colombia.
9. US intelligence listed Colombian president Uribe among 'important Colombian narco-traffickers' in 1991. National Security Archive, 2 August 2004.
10. 'Rebels Claim Copter', *Washington Post*, 24 January 1992.
11. *El Espectador* (Bogota), 17 July 2001.
12. J. McDermott, 'US crews involved in Colombian battle', *Scotsman*, 23 February 2001.
13. See for example C. Marquis, 'Inquiry on Peru Looks at a C.I.A. Contract', *New York Times*, 28 April 2001.
14. M. Prothero, 'Claim of FARC-Al Qaida link rescinded', UPI, 9 August 2002.
15. R. Scarborough, 'Second soldier says "no" to U.N.', *Washington Times*, 10 November 1995.
16. D. Rather, 'Dyncorp president states the Lord must have had a reason for him not to go on Balkan trip', CBS News transcript from 3 April 1996.
17. 'Harassment firing', Santa Ana City News Service, 13 August 1997.
18. J. McDonald, 'Sheriff admitted touching female employee, records show', *Orange County Register*, 26 July 1999.
19. M. McPhee, 'Officer gets $1 million in Aurora suit; She was forced to work 20 feet from her abuser', *Denver Post*, 20 January 2000.
20. Interview reported in 'Hopes betrayed: trafficking of women and girls to post-conflict Bosnia and Herzegovina for forced prostitution', *Human Rights Watch*, November 2002.
21. K. O'Meara, 'DynCorp Disgrace', *Insight on the News*, 4 February 2002.
22. Ibid.

23. C. Lynch, 'Misconduct, Corruption by U.S. Police Mar Bosnia Mission', *Washington Post*, 29 May 2001.
24. HC 577 Private Military Companies: Options for Regulation 2001-02, Foreign and Commonwealth Office, February 2002 (ISBN 0 10 291415 X).
25. R. Boucher, 'State Department Briefing', *Federal News Service*, 11 April 2003.
26. M. Moss and D. Rohde, 'Misjudgments Marred U.S. Plans for Iraqi Police', *New York Times*, 21 May 2006.
27. 'Heralded Iraq Police Academy a "Disaster"', *Washington Post*, 28 September 2006.
28. Special Inspector General for Iraq, January 2007 quarterly report to Congress.
29. 'U.S. Officials Say Iraq's Forces Founder Under Rebel Assaults', *New York Times*, 30 November 2004.
30. B. Bender, 'US officer spells out Iraq police training woes', *Boston Globe*, 13 December 2006.
31. J. Glanz and D. Rohde, 'US report finds dismal training of Afghan police', *New York Times*, 4 December 2006.
32. D. Walsh and L. Gah 'Afghanistan: Special deals and raw recruits employed to halt the Taliban in embattled Helmand', *Guardian*, 4 January 2007.

5 SOLDIERS OF FORTUNE

1. J. E. Thomson, *Mercenaries, Pirates and Sovereigns: State Building and Extra-territorial Violence in Early Modern Europe* (New Jersey: Princeton University Press, 1994).
2. As described in Aubrey's *Brief Lives*. See J. Aubrey "Brief lives chiefly of contemporaries", (Oxford: Clarendon Press, 1898).
3. T. Blair, "Prime Minister warns of continuing global terror threat", 5 March 2004.
4. Ejército de Liberación Nacional.
5. Particularly by Michael Gillard in *The Times, Guardian, Express and Scotland on Sunday*.
6. M. Gillard, I. Gomez & M. Jones, 'BP hands "tarred in pipeline dirty war"', *Guardian*, 17 October 1998.
7. 'Energy: Board keeps eye on Colombian unrest', *Lloyd's List*, 12 February 1997.
8. P. Ruffini, 'Mercenaries planned psychological action against PNG rebels', *Asia Pulse*, 7 April 1997.
9. M. O'Callaghan, 'Sandline sought Bougainville mine share', *Australian*, 4 April 1997.
10. P. van Niekerk and M. Gillard, 'Steel associate's mercenary links', *Observer*, 10 September 1995.
11. P. Lashmar, 'Mercenaries win £20m for failed mission', *Independent*, 18 October 1998.
12. M. L. O'Callaghan, 'Skate to fight "blood money"', *Australian*, 26 February 1999.
13. P. van Niekerk, 'Africa's diamond dogs of war', *Observer*, 13 August 1995.
14. Sandline describe Grunberg as someone who 'has acted as a consultant' for the firm. His regular announcements for Sandline show that he was at least a very regular consultant. For Diamondworks, see D. Baines 'S. Africa mercenaries to protect Diamond Fields in Sierra Leone', *Vancouver Sun*, 13 December 1996.
15. 'Private Military Companies: Options for Regulation', HC 577 (ISBN 010291415X).

6. PROPAGANDA WAR

1. 'Hearing of the Congressional Human Rights Caucus Committee. Subject: reports of Iraqi atrocities in Kuwait. Chaired by Representative Tom Lantos' (Federal News Service, 10 October 1990).
2. Transcript of a segment aired on the 19 January 1992 edition of '60 Minutes'.
3. See especially Chapter 10 of J. Stauber & S. Rampton, *Toxic Sludge Is Good for You: Lies, Damn Lies and the Public Relations Industry* (Maine: Common Courage Press, 1995); ABC News, '20/20' 17 January 1992, 'The Plan to Sell the War'.
4. See for example S. Cutlip, The Unseen Power: Public Relations – A History' (Hilsdale, NJ: Erlbaum, 1994).
5. 'Missed Signals In the Middle East', *Washington Post*, 17 March 1991.
6. S. Mufson, 'The privatization of Craig Fuller', *Washington Post*, 2 August 1992.
7. 'H&K lands $4m Afghan PR contract', *Jack O'Dwyer's Newsletter*, 17 May 2006.
8. A. Gordon, 'PR vet assists US embassy with Kabul election efforts', *PR Week* (US), 11 October 2004.
9. 'Pentagon spokeswoman Victoria Clarke resigns', AFP, 16 June 2003.
10. 'Meyer leaves Rumsfeld for H&K', *Jack O'Dwyer's Newsletter,* 12 May 2004.
11. See for example J. Kampfner, 'The truth about Jessica', *Guardian*, 15 May 2003.
12. He posted them on his website: http://www.outragedmoderates.org/
13. 'Defense Secretary Donald Rumsfeld interview with the *New York Times* interviewer: Tom Shanker as released by the Defense Department', Federal News Service, 12 October 2001.
14. G. Lee, 'The Selling of Kuwait Moves Into New Phase', *Washington Post*, 17 March 1991.
15. J. Randal, 'Anti-Saddam Iraqis Seek United Front', *Washington Post*, 18 June 1992.
16. Document obtained by author under the Freedom of Information Act.
17. J. Hoagland, 'How CIA's Secret War On Saddam Collapsed', *Washington Post*, 26 June 1997.
18. Peter Jennings, 'Showdown with Saddam', ABC News, 7 February 1998. See also J. Bamford 'The Man Who Sold the War: Meet John Rendon, Bush's general in the propaganda war', *Rolling Stone*, 17 November 2005.
19. G. Lardner, 'How Lobbyists Briefed a Rebel Leader: Memos Prepared for Savimbi', *Washington Post*, 8 October 1990.
20. See J. Landay and T. Wells, 'Exiles' deceptions printed before war', *Miami Herald*, 16 March 2004. See also *Private Eye*, March 2004, and M. Shipman, 'US paid millions to plant anti-Saddam stories in Welsh and international media', *Western Mail*, 13 April 2004.
21. M. Colvin and N. Rufford, 'Saddam's arsenal revealed', *Sunday Times*, 17 March 2002.
22. The other stories were: D. Whitworth, 'Powell rejects call for war on Iraq', *The Times*, 22 December 2001; A. Gumbel, 'Campaign against terrorism: Defector claims he saw Saddam's bioweapon plants', *Independent*, 21 December 2001; T. Moore, 'Anthrax fears', *Daily Express*, 21 December 2001; B. Fenton, 'Defector tells of Saddam's nuclear arms', 21 December 2001.
23. C. Hitchens, 'Does Blair know what he's getting into?', *Guardian*, 20 March 2002; 'Saddam is the next US target', *Evening Standard*, 5 March 2002.

24. T. Harnden, 'Saddam "armed bin Laden and funded al-Qa'eda allies"', *Daily Telegraph*, 18 March 2002; R. Beeston, 'Saddam's terror training camp teaches hijacking', *The Times*, 9 November 2001.
25. D. Rose, 'Focus Special: The Terrorism Crisis: The Iraqi connection', *Observer*, 11 November 2001.
26. B. Bigelow, 'SAIC to settle bill-pad lawsuit brought by government', *San Diego Union-Tribune*, 28 April 2005; 'Science Applications International Corporation to pay $484,500 to settle false claims act allegations', States News Service, 24 March 2004.
27. G. Packer, *Assassin's Gate*, (New York: Farrar, 2005), p. 210.
28. S. Nagus and D. Rasan, 'Television helps break mystique of holy warrior: Twice-daily broadcast of guerrillas being paraded in Iraq has raised questions about prisoners' rights', *Financial Times*, 24 March 2005.
29. C. Murphy and K. Saffar, 'Actors in the Insurgency Are Reluctant TV Stars: Terror Suspects Grilled, Mocked on Hit Iraqi Show', *Washington Post*, 5 April 2005.
30. See for example W. Marx, 'Me, a gun, $3m and the good news from Baghdad', *Sunday Times* (London), 29 January 2006.
31. M. Mazzetti, 'Pentagon Audit Clears Propaganda Effort', *New York Times*, 20 October 2006.

7. MYSTERY TRAIN

1. S. Rayment, '"Trophy" video exposes private security contractors shooting up Iraqi drivers', *Sunday Telegraph*, 27 November 2005.
2. R. Merle, 'Census Counts 100,000 Contractors in Iraq; Civilian Number, Duties Are Issues', *Washington Post*, 5 December 2006.
3. D. Avant, 'What Are Those Contractors Doing in Iraq?' *Washington Post*, 9 May 2004.
4. The highest estimate came from the Private Security Contractors Association of Iraq.
5. R. Whittle, 'Security is biggest expense so far in Iraq reconstruction', *Dallas Morning News*, 18 March 2005.
6. 10 October 2005.
7. D. Pallister, '25% of UK Iraq aid budget goes to security firms', *Guardian*, 2 April 2007.
8. The meeting was interrupted by a lone protestor who stood up and denounced the panel for supporting the war and occupation. I expected Brigadier Westropp to leap across the table and deal with the protestor, but instead the security expert merely looked embarrassed and a little confused.
9. A. Browne, 'Iraqis not ready for democracy, says Blair's envoy', *The Times*, 3 June 2003.
10. P. Slevin and M. Allen, 'Companies Selected to Bid on Iraq Reconstruction', *Washington Post*, 11 March 2003.
11. 'Statement of Stuart W. Bowen, jr. Special Inspector General for Iraq Reconstruction before the United States Senate Committee on Foreign Relations hearing to examine Iraq stabilization and reconstruction', Wednesday, 8 February 2006.
12. SIGIR Quarterly report to Congress, October 2006.
13. 'Statement of Stuart W. Bowen, jr. Special Inspector General for Iraq Reconstruction before the United States House of Representatives Committee on Government Reform Subcommittee on National Security, Emerging Threats, and International Relations hearing on Iraq: preceptions, realities and cost to complete', Tuesday, 18 October 2005.

14. J. Vest, 'A Coalition memo reveals that even true believers see the seeds of civil war in the occupation of Iraq', *Village Voice*, 20 April 2004.

15. 'We moved our [tactical psyop team] TPT vehicle forward and started to run around seeing what they needed us to do to facilitate their mission', states a US military officer involved in the operation. 'There was a large media circus at this location (I guess the Palestine Hotel was a media center at the time), almost as many reporters as there were Iraqis, as the hotel was right adjacent to the Al-Firdos Square. The Marine Corps colonel in the area saw the Saddam statue as a target of opportunity and decided that the statue must come down.' The psychological team used loudspeakers to encourage Iraqi civilians to assist, packed the scene with Iraqi children, and stepped in to readjust the props when one of the soldiers draped an American flag over the statue. 'God bless them, but we were thinking from psy-op school that this was just bad news', the officer reported. 'We didn't want to look like an occupation force, and some of the Iraqis were saying, "No, we want an Iraqi flag!" So I said "No problem, somebody get me an Iraqi flag."' *Los Angeles Times*, 3 July 2004.

16. E. G., 'Coalition starts handing over protection of public buildings to Iraqis', Agence France Presse, 9 August 2003.

17. 'Iraqi: Death Squads Not Linked to Gov't', Associated Press, 12 April 2006, 11:43 a.m. GMT; D. Jamail and A. Al-Fadhily, 'Iraq: shadowy "protection force" linked to death squads', Inter Press Service; E. Knickmeyer, '"Out of Control" Guard Unit Established by US Suspected in Death Squad-Style Executions', *Washington Post*, 14 May 2006.

18. Bearpark left Olive to become the director of the British private military companies' trade group, the British Association of Private Security Companies.

19. Global's Gurkhas occasionally presented security challenges. In 2004 the firm's managers found that five of their men had links with Maoist insurgents in their native Nepal. When the firm tried to sack them, one of the Gurkhas attacked his manager, a former Coldstream Guard, fracturing his skull with an iron bar. Generally, however, they caused fewer headaches than Iraqi staff. O. Poole, 'On patrol with Baghdad's hired guns', *Daily Telegraph*, 4 May 2004.

20. By De La Rue, one of the main non-US reconstruction contract winners.

21. Sabah Nouri, a prominent member of the INC, was the minister arrested in April 2004.

22. W. Knickmeyer and N. Nouri, 'Baghdad Airport Closed in Debt Dispute', *Washington Post*, 10 September 2005.

23. He found that Faisal Daghistani, son of Tamara Daghistani, one of Chalabi's closest aides, was a founder director of Erinys Iraq. Erinys Iraq also received funds from another firm, Nour USA, which had been founded by one of Chalabi's business associates, Abul Huda Farouki. Ahmed Chalabi's nephew, Salem Chalabi, was Erinys Iraq's legal representative. Chalabi denied that he had any financial link with Erinys. Nour USA were also awarded a $327 million contract to equip Iraq's army. Rival firms claimed this was awarded improperly. The Pentagon apparently agreed, terminating the contract in March 2003.

24. B. Sizemore, 'Last year, a Blackwater contractor shot and killed an Iraqi official's bodyguard', *Virginian-Pilot*, 25 July 2007.

25. O. Poole, *op. cit.*

26. B. Sizemore and J. Kimberlin, 'Blackwater: on the front lines', *Virginian-Pilot*, 25 July 2006.

27. B. Yoeman, 'Soldiers of Good Fortune', *Mother Jones*, May/June 2003.

28. Badolato was not a Blackwater employee, but he has a long history of work in the military-industrial complex. He worked as a senior Department of Energy official under Presidents Reagan and Bush Sr. At the time of writing, he is the head of Homeland Security for the Shaw Group, a Louisiana-based engineering firm that itself won a $100 million contract to rebuild the al-Kasik air base in Iraq. The Shaw Group attracted controversy when in 2005 it won massive contracts for Hurricane Katrina reconstruction from US emergency agency FEMA. The Shaw Group retained Joseph Allbaugh, the former head of FEMA, as a lobbyist.

29. E. Badolato, 'Learning to Think like an Arab Muslim: a Short Guide to Under-standing the Arab Mentality', *Blackwater Tactical Weekly*, 3 May 2004. Thanks to Richard Seymour's website, 'Lenin's Tomb', for pointing me to this article.

30. M. Corkery, 'Battling for voters, one mile at a time', *Providence Journal*, 14 August 2002.

31. A. Forliti, 'Three Republicans vying for chance to face Kennedy', Associated Press, 1 September 2002.

32. M. Corkery, 'Newport man out to strike it rich in Iraq', *Providence Journal*, 25 January 2004.

33. BBC Radio 4, 'File on Four', 25 May 2004.

34. 'US Eastern Virginia District Court case summaries', *Virginia Lawyers Weekly*, 11 September 2006.

35. Y. Dreazen, 'Employees of contractor barred from Iraq resurrect business', Associated Press, 20 June 2006.

36. 'Detainee: contractors abused by US troops', *Charlotte Observer*, 11 June 2005.

37. S. Fainaru, 'Four Hired Guns in an Armored Truck, Bullets Flying, and a Pickup and a Taxi Brought to a Halt', *Washington Post*, 15 April 2007.

38. Alcohol featured in other wild shootings by contractors. A former British Royal Marine working for the Armor Group in Iraq shot himself dead after a day spent drinking whisky. He was attempting to demonstrate that his pistol was unloaded, after being told by his comrades to put the weapon down. See 'Gun-death riddle of bodyguard in Iraq', *Western Daily Press*, 20 February 2007.

39. R. Merle, 'Americans Accused of Bribery, Rigging Rebuilding Contracts', *Washington Post*, 8 February 2007.

8. SPIES FOR HIRE

1. See especially W. Blum, *CIA: A Forgotten History* (London: Zed Books, 1986).

2. D. Alper et al, 'How the CIA does business', *Newsweek*, 19 May 1975.

3. M. Struck, 'Rent-a-cop', *Washington Post*, 9 November 1982.

4. M. Struck, '1,800 U.S. Workers May Lose Their Jobs To Private Industry', *Washington Post*, 28 September 1983.

5. M. Causey, 'CIA Plans to Replace 200 GSA Workers', *Washington Post*, 23 March.

6. J. Omang, 'Virginia-Based Firm Accused Of Falsifying Clearance Checks', *Washington Post*, 3 October 1986.

7. Reagan's Republicans had launched their privatization plans in imitation of Britain's Thatcher government; but in the UK, steps to introduce enterprise into the security services were even more effectively hobbled. MI5 was even able to resist an attempt to privatize its office chairs and desks: when the Conservative Party tried to sell off the

government's official furniture provider, the Crown Suppliers, MI5 agents persuaded ministers to exempt the intelligence services' furniture from the deal. See D. Hencke, 'Security blocks sell-off', *Guardian*, 21 July 1988. Eventually the entire privatization of Crown Suppliers collapsed.

8. J. Terrell with R. Martz, *Disposable Patriot* (Washington: National Press, 1992).
9. "The Iran-Contra hearings in Washington", *The Times*, 9 July 1987.
10. See, for example, on the Contras, 'In America, counter-insurgency has been privatized', *Guardian Weekly*, 14 July 1985; M. Tolchine, 'Critics say U.S. "privatized" foreign policy on Iran', *New York Times*, 20 January 1987.
11. See *Disposable Patriot*, and also W. King, 'Private role increasing in foreign war actions', *New York Times*, 12 October 1986.
12. 'Contra backer sentenced', *Pittsburgh Post-Gazette*, 17 April 1994.
13. See for example J. Reeves, 'On parole and back home, former mercenary Frank Camper' *Birmingham News (Alabama)*, 12 June 1995.
14. *Disposable Patriot*, p. 210.
15. Ibid., p. 166.
16. C. Farnsworth, ' "the company" as big business', *New York Times*, 4 January 1987.
17. See for example P. Maass, 'The Way of the Commandos', *New York Times*, 1 May 2005.
18. P. Glibbery and J. Davies, See for example T. Coone, 'Soldiers fail to find their fortune', *Financial Times*, 11 October 1985.
19. M. White, 'North confirms UK link with Contras', *Guardian Weekly*, 19 July 1987.
20. M. Gillard 'Former MOD minister helps out arms company chief', *Observer*, 13 November 1994.
21. See Chapter 1.
22. The hearings ran alongside the Church Committee investigations into official covert action, and were inspired by a similar post-Vietnam, post-Watergate sensibility.
23. F. Bleakley, 'Wall Street's private eye', *New York Times*, 4 March 1985.
24. B. Penrose, 'Police chief is set to join private security firm', *Sunday Times*, 14 June 1987.
25. N. Rufford, 'Spies defect from MI6 for shadowy careers in the City', *Sunday Times*, 15 November 1998.
26. See for example M. Chittenden and N. Rufford, 'MI6 "firm" spied on green groups', *Sunday Times*, 17 June 2001. *Statewatch Bulletin*, 11: 2 (March–April 2001).
27. See www.burojansen.nl/ and www.spinwatch.org.
28. They were Edward Rogers and Lanny Griffiths. See for example J. Borger, 'Bush cronies advise on buying up Iraq', *Guardian*, 1 October 2003.
29. The company stated that 'Joe M. Allbaugh is the CEO of The Allbaugh Company, LLC, a Washington, D.C.-based corporate strategy and counsel firm. A native of Oklahoma, Joe served as the Director of the Federal Emergency Management Agency (FEMA) under President George Bush until March 2003. Prior to moving to Washington, D.C., he was Chief of Staff to then-Governor Bush of Texas and was the National Campaign Manager for the Bush–Cheney 2000 presidential campaign.'
30. Diligence LLC's website made no mention of Burt's role at Hollinger. See also, for example, 'Michael Howard lands new job with Lord Black's crony', *Evening Standard*, 19 June 2006.
31. N. Buckley et al, 'MegaFon diplomacy: a disputed stake pits an oligarch against a Putin ally', *Financial Times*, 24 April 2006.

32. S. Bentley, 'The "Centre" of the Storm: My Week as a CI Grunt', *Competitive Intelligence Magazine*, October 1998.
33. 'P&G ADMITS SPIES SNOOPED ON UNILEVER', *Independent*, 1 September 2001.
34. J. Meek, 'Gitmo taunter teaches tactics', *New York Daily News*, 16 March 2005.
35. J. Coman, 'CIA plans new secret police to fight Iraq terrorism', *Sunday Telegraph*, 4 January 2004.
36. See http://www.unitedplacements.com.
37. J. Stanton and W. Madsen, 'Torture, Incorporated: Oliver North Joins the Party', *Counterpunch*, 14 June 2004.
38. Larger companies also stepped into the intelligence job market. The Carlyle Group – the multinational financial company that hired former British prime minister John Major and former US president George Bush Sr – was involved through its part-ownership of a job clearance firm called USIS. Arms firm Lockheed also moved into supplying intelligence staff for Iraq and elsewhere.
39. P. Dodds, 'Guantánamo translator describes how female interrogators used sexual tactics to weaken Muslim detainees', Associated Press, 27 January 2005.
40. P. Coorey, 'Top brass blamed for abuse', *Courier Mail* (Queensland, Australia), 13 May 2004.
41. Or 'glow sticks'.
42. See for example R. Watson, 'US report tells of sadism and wanton abuses of prisoners', *The Times*, 3 May 2004.
43. The firm was originally called California Analysis Center, Inc., but are now known only as CACI International.
44. Frequently asked questions at www.caci.com.
45. D. Dishneau, 'Abu Ghraib warden says he got dog-interrogation recommendation from Guantánamo Bay', Associated Press, 27 July 2005.
46. M. Benjamin and M. Scherer, ' "Big Steve" and Abu Ghraib', Salon.com, 31 March 2006.
47. M. Barakat, 'CACI employees participated in Abu Ghraib abuse: Army report', Associated Press, 25 August 2004.
48. D. Washburn, 'Many Iraq interpreters unskilled, soldiers say; Contractor Titan's hiring faulted', *San Diego Union-Tribune*, 21 May 2004; B. Bigelow, 'S.D. firm has had the most deaths in Iraq', *San Diego Union-Tribune*, 25 March 2005.
49. S. Hettena, 'San Diego firm finds translators for Guantánamo interrogations', Associated Press, 27 June 2002.
50. M. Weissenstein, 'Prosecutors say Army translator from Brooklyn had links to Iraqi insurgency', Associated Press, 7 November 2005.
51. M. Sherman, 'Mich. translator in Iraq pleads guilty to offering bribe', Associated Press, 4 August 2006.
52. P. Beaumont, 'Abu Ghraib guard jailed for 10 years: As prison abuse ringleader is sentenced, defence contractors are given multi-million Pentagon deals', *Observer*, 16 January 2005.
53. 'Diary of Terror', *Mail on Sunday*, 11 December 2005; D. Gadher and S. Grey, 'London suspect in CIA torture claim', *Sunday Times*, 11 December 2005.
54. Gathered expertly in S. Grey, *Ghost Plane* (London: Hurst & Co., 2006).
55. T. Paterson, 'German Ministers "Knew about CIA torture cells" ', *Independent*, 25 October 2006.
56. S. Grey, 'Our dirty little torture secret', *Sunday Times*, 22 October 2006.
57. J. Mayer, 'The CIA's travel agent', *New Yorker*, 30 October 2003.

58. 'We know that such cruelty is contrary to Islam, says Blair', *The Times*, 19 September 2001.
59. A. Lines, 'War on terror: America's warning – we'll be mean, nasty, dirty and dangerous', *Daily Mirror*, 17 September 2001.
60. G. Miller, 'Spy Agencies Outsourcing to Fill Key Jobs', *Los Angeles Times*, 17 September 2006.
61. Senate Select Committee on Intelligence, 'Report on the U.S. intelligence community's prewar intelligence assessments on Iraq', 7 July 2004; 'The Commission on the Intelligence Capabilities of the United States Regarding Weapons of Mass Destruction: Report to the President', 1 March 2005.

9. DATABASE STATE

1. A new version of Total Information Awareness, called ADVISE ('Analysis, Dissemination, Visualization, Insight and Semantic Enhancement') came to light in 2007. See A. Hudson, 'Homeland security revives supersnoop', *Washington Times*, 8 March 2007.
2. 'DynCorp Captures $27 Million Health Services Contact', PR Newswire, 16 May 1997.
3. SIPRI military expenditure estimates – see www.sipir.org. 'Arms without Borders: Why a globalised trade needs global controls', Oxfam, 2006. 'Arms spending high, says Oxfam', *Birmingham Evening Mail*, 22 September 2006.
4. S. Green, 'Plenty of computer blame', *Modesto Bee*, 19 March 1998; E. Mendel, 'No "deadbeat dads" system very costly', Copley News Service, 15 September 2002.
5. 'Two companies paid $4.5 million to collect $162,000 from deadbeat parents', Associated Press, 29 December 1998.
6. S. Green, 'Computer firm brags about its abysmal failure', *Modesto Bee*, 6 November 1997.
7. M. Wines, 'Ex-UNISYS Official Admits Paying Bribes to Get Pentagon Contracts', *New York Times*, 10 March 1989.
8. 'UNISYS to Pay Record Fine in Defense Fraud', *Washington Post*, 7 September 1991.
9. G. Milhollin 'Building Saddam Hussein's Bomb', *New York Times*, 8 March 1992.
10. S. Pearlstein and B. Fromton, 'Firms Find Buyers Lacking For Their Defense Divisions; UNISYS Ends Drive to Sell McLean-Based Unit', *Washington Post*, 23 November 1991.
11. F. Fukuyama, 'The End of History?', *National Interest*, Summer 1989.
12. D. R . Francis, 'World Arms Outlays: Down, Down, Down', *Christian Science Monitor*, 23 April 1993.
13. J. Simon, 'More surprises in state's computer snafu – $782,000 settlement to contractor irks legislators', *Seattle Times*, 18 January 1990.
14. 'Flaws in state's computer system blamed for delaying welfare benefits', Associated Press, 2 September 1998.
15. E. Lipton, 'Audit Finds Mismanagement Drained Technology Project', *New York Times*, 2 April 2006.
16. P. R. Keefe, 'A Shortsighted Eye in the Sky', *New York Times*, 5 February 2005.
17. A very effective portrait of SAIC is provided by D. Barlett and J. Steele, 'Washington's $8 billion Shadow', *Vanity Fair*, March 2007.

18. D. Eggen and G. Witte, 'The FBI's Upgrade That Wasn't', *Washington Post*, 18 August 2006.
19. L. Millter, 'Background checks and IDs: Little to show for multimillion-dollar anti-terror effort', Associated Press, 25 October 2006.
20. D. Hencke, 'Arms firms tap MOD's top brass', *Guardian*, 25 January 1995.
21. C. Ayres, 'Corporate profile: SEMA', *The Times*, 23 November 1998.
22. 'Siemens corruption trial begins', *Spiegel Online*, 14 March 2007.
23. P. Norman, 'Hidden hand of corruption', *Financial Times*, 5 June 1996.
24. T. Burt, P. Montagnon, and J. Simkins, 'Singapore bars five companies linked to bribe case', *Financial Times*, 14 February 1996.
25. H. Bassirian, 'Pay-outs to Siemens contradict PFI spirit', *Computer Weekly*, 20 August 1998.
26. T. Poston, 'IT deal bypassed to clear asylum chaos', *Computer Weekly*, 8 April 1999.
27. 'SBS hopes for state orders', *Handelsblatt*, 6 December 2006.

POSTSCRIPT: WAITING FOR THE BARBARIANS

1. What are we waiting for, assembled in the forum?

The barbarians are due here today.

Why isn't anything happening in the senate?
Why do the senators sit there without legislating?

Because the barbarians are coming today.
What laws can the senators make now?
Once the barbarians are here, they'll do the legislating.

Why did our emperor get up so early,
and why is he sitting at the city's main gate
on his throne, in state, wearing the crown?

Because the barbarians are coming today
and the emperor is waiting to receive their leader.
He has even prepared a scroll to give him,
replete with titles, with imposing names.

Why have our two consuls and praetors come out today
wearing their embroidered, their scarlet togas?
Why have they put on bracelets with so many amethysts,
and rings sparkling with magnificent emeralds?
Why are they carrying elegant canes
beautifully worked in silver and gold?

Because the barbarians are coming today
and things like that dazzle the barbarians.
Why don't our distinguished orators come forward as usual
to make their speeches, say what they have to say?

Because the barbarians are coming today
and they're bored by rhetoric and public speaking.

Why this sudden restlessness, this confusion?
(How serious people's faces have become.)
Why are the streets and squares emptying so rapidly,
everyone going home so lost in thought?

Because night has fallen and the barbarians have not come.
And some who have just returned from the border say
there are no barbarians any longer.

And now, what's going to happen to us without barbarians?
They were, those people, a kind of solution.

Constantine P. Cavafy (1904)

2. Federal News Service, 21 March 1989.
3. G. Sperling, Jr, 'Meet the new Richard Cheney', *Christian Science Monitor*, 27 June 1989.
4. P. Arnold, 'Cheney splits with CIA on threat', *Washington Times*, 5 March 1990.
5. See, for example, the founding statements of the Committee on the Present Danger by Daniel Pletka and Laurie Mylroie.
6. M. Abramovitz, 'War's Critics Abetting Terrorists, Cheney Says', *Washington Post*, 11 September 2006.
7. 'An Un-American Way to Campaign', *New York Times*, 25 September 2004.
8. G. Brown, 'Gordon Brown writes for the Sun', *Sun*, 8 September 2006.
9. See Chapter 7.
10. S. Fainaru and A. Klein, 'In Iraq, a Private Realm Of Intelligence-Gathering', *Washington Post*, 1 July 2007.
11. QinetiQ press release, 6 December 2004.
12. At the establishment think-tank Chatham House, 19 June 2007.
13. The estimate comes from T. Shorrock, 'The corporate takeover of U.S. intelligence', Salon.com, 1 June 2007.
14. Everett PowerPoint slides courtesy of the Federation of American Scientists.
15. See Chapter 9.

Index